The American History Series

SERIES EDITORS

John Hope Franklin, *Duke University*

A. S. Eisenstadt, *Brooklyn College*

Elizabeth Hayes Turner
University of North Texas

Women and Gender in the New South

1865–1945

Harlan Davidson, Inc.
Wheeling, Illinois 60090-6000

Library of Congress Cataloging-in-Publication Data

Turner, Elizabeth Hayes.
Women and gender in the new South : 1865–1945 / Elizabeth Hayes Turner.
p. cm. — (American History Series)
Includes bibliographical references and index.
ISBN 978-0-88295-265-9
1. Women—Southern States—History. 2. African American women—Southern States—History. I. Title.
HQ1438.S63T87 2009
305.40975'0904—dc22

2008040019

Cover photo: Lillian Smith (left) author of *Strange Fruit* and *Killers of the Dream* and Eleanor Roosevelt (right) are honored for their work in race relations by Mary McLeod Bethune, former director of the Division of Negro Affairs at the National Youth Administration (NYA) and founder and president of the National Council of Negro Women, February 1945, Washington, D.C. Used by permission, Star Collection, DC Public Library; © Washington Post.
Manufactured in the United States of America
11 10 09 1 2 3 4 5 VP

To Mildred Langston Hayes and to Kathryn Langston Francis who, long before I was ready, urged the writing of this book.

FOREWORD

Every generation writes its own history for the reason that it sees the past in the foreshortened perspective of its own experience. This has surely been true of the writing of American history. The practical aim of our historiography is to give us a more informed sense of where we are going by helping us understand the road we took in getting where we are. As the nature and dimensions of American life are changing, so too are the themes of our historical writing. Today's scholars are hard at work reconsidering every major aspect of the nation's past: its politics, diplomacy, economy, society, recreation, mores and values, as well as status, ethnic, race, sexual, and family relations. The list of series titles that appear on the inside covers of this book will show at once that our historians are ever broadening the range of their studies.

The aim of this series is to offer our readers a survey of what today's historians are saying about the central themes and aspects of the American past. To do this, we have invited to write for the series only scholars who have made notable contributions to the respective fields in which they are working. Drawing on primary and secondary materials, each volume presents a factual and narrative account of its particular subject, one that affords readers a basis for perceiving its larger dimensions and importance. Conscious that readers respond to the closeness and immediacy of a subject, each of our authors seeks to restore the past as an actual present, to revive it as a living reality. The individuals and groups who figure in the pages of our books appear as real people who once were looking for survival and fulfillment. Aware that historical subjects are often matters of controversy, our authors present their own findings and conclusions. Each volume closes with an extensive critical essay on the writings of the major authorities on its particular theme.

The books in this series are primarily designed for use in both basic and advanced courses in American history, on the undergraduate and graduate levels. Such a series has a particular value these days, when the format of American history courses is being altered to accommodate a greater diversity of reading materials. The series offers a number of distinct advantages. It extends the dimensions of regular course work. It makes clear that the study of our past is, more than the student might otherwise understand, at once complex, profound, and absorbing. It presents that past as a subject of continuing interest and fresh investigation.

For these reasons the series strongly invites an interest that far exceeds the walls of academe. The work of experts in their respective fields, it puts at the disposal of all readers the rich findings of historical inquiry, an invitation to join, in major fields of research, those who are pondering anew the central themes and aspects of our past.

And, going beyond the confines of the classroom, it reminds the general reader no less than the university student that in each successive generation of the ever-changing American adventure, from its very start until our own day, men and women and children were facing their daily problems and attempting, as we are now, to live their lives and to make their way.

John Hope Franklin
A. S. Eisenstadt

CONTENTS

ACKNOWLEDGMENTS

I am deeply grateful to a body of scholars, most of them southern and women's historians, for the information they mined and the ideas, theories, and revelations they shared—especially in excellent studies generated during the last thirty-five years. Their work has allowed me to evaluate and analyze the New South from the perspective of gender, and my tribute to them can be found in the Bibliographical Essay.

This book began as a course proposal while pursuing a Fulbright Lectureship to the University of Genoa in the spring of 2003. Valeria Gennaro Lerda, director of the Fulbright Program at the University of Genoa and founder of the Center for Euro-Atlantic Studies, has become not only a colleague but also a dear friend. It was she who encouraged the creation of the course, "Women and Gender in the New South." Professor Lerda allowed her twenty-two students to take it, and it is to them that I owe a great debt, for they asked scintillating questions and kept me working to find answers. Roberto Maccarini, colleague and friend at the University of Genoa, listened to my thoughts over an espresso after every class and generously shared his own ideas on American history. When I returned to the University of North Texas, I taught the same course again, both at the undergraduate and graduate level, each time with a bit more confidence as more material made its way into my notes and as students in these classes asked thoughtful questions and pushed for good answers. They provided a great deal of inspiration, as did my colleague in North Carolina, Sally G. McMillen. Friend and collaborator Gregg Cantrell offered wisdom and advice while we co-edited another, book, *Lone Star Pasts: Memory and History in Texas*. Over the summers the research and writing continued until a manuscript appeared. At that point, graduate students came to the rescue: Rhonda Ragsdale searched for photographs thanks to a grant from the Department of History at the University of North Texas; Simone De Santiago Ramos, and Kevin Eades helped with editing the earliest rough drafts; while Jessica Brannon-Wranosky, Lisa Fox, and Jerry Coats read later drafts of the manuscript. I thank them all for their willing participation in this project.

Reviews of individual chapters and the preface came from historians Cita Cook and Richard Lowe, who with their experience and knowledge of Civil War history helped immensely. Editors A. S. Eisenstadt and John Hope Franklin approved the manuscript in its early stages, and John Hope generously read a later copy with full editing comments and humorous asides. Archivists Dawn Letson and Ann Barton at Texas Woman's University lent their expertise in sifting through photographs. Professors Stephanie Cole and Anastatia Sims spent many hours reading, marking, and giving the manuscript a critical once over. I am grateful beyond words for their sage advice and expert editing. Lucy Herz added her copyediting expertise to the manuscript, making it a much more readable book. Andrew Davidson has been a patient mentor, thorough editor, and a good friend throughout this whole process, and without his support this book would not exist.

I owe my deepest thanks to Al Turner, the other historian in the family, whose understanding and acceptance of the time it takes to research and write makes the long hours seem less so. I owe a special debt of gratitude to my late father-in-law, Wallace B. Turner, and my sister-in-law, Martha Turner Keber, also historians, who shared their love of the profession and the South with us at every turn.

Finally, the book is dedicated to my mother, Mildred, and my aunt, Kathryn, because this work really began with them.

EHT

PREFACE

This is a history of southern women since the Civil War that has been longer in the making than one lifetime. I come from a long line of southerners on my mother's side, whose roots reach to colonial days and the creation of nationhood when one of our ancestors served in the Virginia Assembly. Growing up, colonial history was never much the topic of conversation between my mother and my aunt, however. The two sisters, the older one born in 1899 and the younger one, my mother, in 1902, spoke of the war. There was only one war.

They regaled my brothers and me with stories, real history, of the farm owned by my great-great-grandmother in Louisa County, Virginia. Ann Anderson, my great-grandmother, had been a teenager during the Civil War. Her father had died years before it started, leaving her with a widowed mother and a sister. In the hushed voice of a raconteur my mother told of the night that a band of rebels came to the door of the farmhouse and asked to be led through the woods and around enemy lines. Ann was the only one who knew the way, so she saddled her horse and in the black of night led the men safely around the lines, not returning until dawn. Here my mother would pause and describe a night so dark that young Ann could not see her hand before her face, and she would hold up her own hand inches from my nose for emphasis. It was through the countless telling of stories such as this that I learned a smattering of southern historical pride and prejudice. We're not sure which northern troops came and "liberated" the farm toward the end of the war, but in my mother's telling of it, Union officers billeted at the house. When they departed, they tied the unwilling slaves to mules and carried them off. Before they left, however, the men dumped all of the bedding, molasses, and usable items into a great pile in the yard and burned them, leaving nothing for the women to live on. Then, to add a note of real tragedy to the memory, as if it were not sad enough, a mother hen and her chicks came out from under the porch, whereupon one of the officers took his sword and cut the heads off of every one of those chicks. This made refugees out of my mother's grandmother and great-grandmother.

After the war Ann met her husband, a surgeon for the Confederate Army. She made the best of postwar reality, living with defeat and raising their children, my grandmother among them. They moved to Fayetteville, Tennessee, where great-grandfather Joseph Dinwiddie opened a dentistry practice. My mother and aunt were born in Fayetteville, and they remembered Ann Anderson Dinwiddie as Granny.

Needless to say I never met my Confederate ancestors and hearing tales of southern adventures only mildly piqued my interest. Growing up in Los Angeles in the 1950s and 1960s, I had other things on my mind—horses, then American Bandstand, and finally boys with their 1957 Chevies. I was aware of the civil rights movement but was confused by the attitudes of white southerners. My parents did not display racial hatred or intolerance, and perhaps because my mother and aunt had lived in California since the 1920s, they were out of touch with the true nature of race relations in the post–World War II South. Yet, they assured me that there were good decent white folks in the South. You just didn't hear about them in the news—this after seeing on television the relentless drubbing of peaceful marchers at the hands of Bull Conner with his fire hoses. In my college days, my mother and aunt both in separate but undoubtedly coordinated interviews, advised me to study southern history, even to write my honors thesis on southern women during the Civil War. Nothing could persuade me to take up that topic, and I went as far away as I could from my southern heritage. My senior honors thesis detailed the economic lives of the Jews of France and Germany from the ninth to the fourteenth centuries.

Fate has a way of meeting us even when we turn in the opposite direction. I never dreamed that I would some day make the South my home. Nor did I expect to take up the very subject I had rejected in college. By living first in North Carolina and then in Texas, I came to understand that one's past and the study of the past do not necessarily have to succumb to the same interpretation. This came home to me when my mother, in the course of clearing out her house and giving away her treasures, handed me a package that had come, she said, from my great-grandmother Ann Anderson Dinwiddie. I opened it to find a huge Confederate battle flag, hand sewn. This led my mother to tell another story. Living in Chattanooga with her grown daughter and son-in-law, most likely around 1910, Granny had stolen away to her bedroom to make this flag. Soldiers from the northern Grand Army of the Republic, in reconciliation with whatever remained of the Confederates, were to march down the street just below her bedroom window. Secreting herself away until the day of the reunion, she made her appearance just as the Union veterans paraded past. Then she unfurled the flag before their eyes, and they saw the symbol and the face of an unreconstructed rebel woman. I held in my hands the physical evidence of her values, that of a southerner who had lived through the war and carried those memories clear into the twentieth century. Moreover, it was and is a family heirloom, made by the patient fingers of one related to me, of one whose brave and risky deed in the dead of night I cannot help but admire. It was and still is a difficult object to revere, knowing that it symbolizes a history fraught with the painful legacy of slavery, segregation, and violence. I believe that slaveholding southerners were wrong to defend that peculiar institution in a bloody and tragic war. I do not display this flag; indeed it remains in its package. But I bring it out every now and then and think about the lives that my relatives and millions of other southerners lived and of the legacy of the event that changed them and the nation forever. Now I study southern women's history, not through the eyes of my ancestors but with an aim to understand and explain as best I can what moved southern women—black and white—from the ravages of one war to the opportunities of another.

Women's history has evolved in the past forty years. Second-wave feminism, beginning in the 1960s, raised the consciousness of scholars toward the absence of women in their accounts of the past. Looking through American history textbooks written in the 1950s revealed the need for a comprehensive change in the method used to analyze the past and women's roles in it. When scholars tackled this objective, they began simply by recounting the deeds of the most visible and famous women who appeared as leaders in an array of categories. This "compensatory" history, necessary to identify outstanding women from the past, evolved into a more complex study of women in organizations and movements. The discovery of sources that had been ignored or little used by previous historians enlightened scholars as to the numbers of women involved, for example, in the Populist and the Progressive movements. Called "contribution" history, historians took into account women's public roles as leaders, writers, organizers, and marchers, especially in female-oriented political movements such as the woman suffrage movement or labor revolts organized by women workers. Contribution history, however, did not elucidate the private lives of women who seldom ventured beyond their homes. A need to understand ordinary women coincided with the advent of social history, an encompassing area of study that borrowed heavily from the discipline of sociology to explain trends and change over time, and it proved useful for the understanding of women's private roles. The dichotomy between public and private histories, and a flirtation with the concept of a woman's separate sphere, sisterhood, and women's culture evolving out of the private domain as well as single-sex institutions and organizations absorbed the attention of women's historians in the 1970s and 1980s. Subsequent students of history began to question the notion of separate spheres and noticed that much depended on class and race in the creation of a separate women's culture. In addition, for most women their private and public lives invariably included men, and, given the economic discrepancies between the sexes that was universally accepted by society, their status varied depending more often on men than on their own resources.

Questions as to why women remained in a subordinate position to men of their same station throughout history led to deeper analyses of class, race, and gender differences. For upper- and middle-class women, respectability, femininity, and pretensions toward superior status marked their lives, whereas working-class women—or slave women—found these standards unattainable or difficult to achieve. Moreover, scholars wondered, why did such prescriptions for womanhood exist? Male and female attitudes toward gender roles and masculine or feminine behavior captivated scholarly attention and led to the development of gender analysis. Concluding that gender prescriptions are the result of social construction based only in part on biological differences between the sexes, historians drew once again on another social science to elucidate their studies, this time the discipline of anthropology. Pundits often say that biology is destiny, but studies show that different societies in past eras created varying expectations for men and women beyond simple biology. Nonetheless, studying the cultural prescriptions regarding men and women and their roles or places of superiority or subordination in differing societies explains much about the history of women.

Perhaps one of the most important ideas stemming from gender analysis is the concept of gender-role expectations in relation to power. Or, said another way, gender analysis is a way of seeing the world through the socialized notions of what it meant to be male or female and the power relationships that evolved historically from those ideas. In western societies gender expectations took on polarities: for example, if men were strong, women were weak; if men were intellectual, women were emotional; if men were warriors, women were nurturers. These assumptions, created through various forms of media as well as intellectual circles and educational institutions, perpetuated power relationships in which most women were regarded as inferior and in need of male protection. The notion that women were the bearers of future generations strengthened the male concept of protectiveness toward them and elevated women's status during the nineteenth century, but reproduction came under male control—through anti-miscegenation laws and the use of violence—in order to legitimize genetic continuity. Nowhere was the application of power and protection stronger than in the American South, where the ideal of Southern Ladyhood could only be realized if white women maintained racial purity. Thus class and race collided at almost every level with gender in southern society and history.

Power and its application to relationships between men and women in households and in such diverse public arenas as the law, education, religion, and medicine, left little to the realm of women's activism. In every age and in every culture, there have been women who challenged the prevailing gender prescriptions and struck a nerve resulting in waves either of social and political change or of repression. There have been others who worked within their gender-prescribed world and still brought significant contributions. This would seem to bring the study of women and gender back full circle to seeing, as historian Mary Ritter Beard wrote in 1946, "woman as force in history." This book draws on concepts of women as agents of social change, on notions of gender prescriptions, and on change over time to explain much of the history of women in the South since the Civil War.

At first, southern women in the post–Civil War period did not gain the attention of women's historians, in part because few southern women were seen as being worthy of study. The trend in the 1960s and early 1970s favored seeking feminist actors in historical context, and at first there appeared few southern women who claimed allegiance to feminist goals. Rather the region's conservatism, the strength of male patriarchy, and the strict codes of racial separation that remained largely unchallenged seemed to obscure southern women of note. Then two pioneering books from the 1970s changed the scene: Anne Firor Scott's *The Southern Lady: From Pedestal to Politics, 1830–1930*; and Jacquelyn Dowd Hall's *Revolt against Chivalry: Jessie Daniel Ames and the Women's Campaign against Lynching*. Scott's book challenged assumptions about southern women's lack of public activism, supporting instead a cogent analysis of women's public roles from the Civil War through the Progressive era. Hall's work brought to light a courageous woman at the head of an organization that addressed a deep wound in southern society, a festering sore that poisoned race relations and denied black men and black and white women the freedom to move about without fear. That women openly challenged violent racial mores in the early twentieth century foreshadows the subsequent civil rights movement, in which women continued to work toward racial justice. Studies of southern women since the 1970s have accelerated, and despite the extremely conservative nature of the region, historians have found women activists in areas of labor, education, politics, culture, and especially race relations. They have also uncovered histories of women in organizations that defended Lost Cause values (that reconciled white southerners to their defeat in the Civil War) and perpetuated southern notions of white supremacy, such as the United Daughters of the Confederacy. Other historians concentrated on exploring the lives of farming women, textile workers, educators, and professionals. Still others sought to understand the impact of such momentous national changes as the Great Depression and World War II on the lives of southern women. Gender studies revealed much about the harmful combination of images used by white men against black men, whom they depicted as rapists of white women in order to suspend mobility for African Americans and suppress black political power. This form of gender analysis, peculiar to the South, extended to arenas of labor, politics, economic, and cultural history.

A synthesis such as this offered by the American History Series naturally draws on a multiplicity of sources and concepts. This book seeks to bring together in one volume older and more recent historical information regarding southern women while at the same time attempting to understand how women from different backgrounds weathered and helped shape the shifting political and cultural changes in the region. Since 1982 when I first began studying the subject of southern women after the Civil War, the field has expanded to include women's and men's experiences in southern history. The complexities of gender history are compounded when race and class relations are added, making the study of women and gender in the post–Civil War South a dynamic and fluid endeavor. Every day new material is uncovered and articulated about the lives of women and men, black and white, and their relationship to race, class, and power, especially the power of men who labeled the region in which they all lived "white man's country." Yet we can find evidence that women also acted to influence events, that freedpeople even while repressed had opportunities, and that gender held a shaping influence over many of the postwar political and economic processes. Today southerners continue to find the legacy of race, class, and gender challenging, and these themes are central to this overview of women and gender in the New South.

INTRODUCTION

Women and Families in the Civil War Era

No history of the postwar South can begin without some understanding of the impact of the Civil War on the future of the region and the entire nation. The Civil War transformed the antebellum southern way of life from a slave- to a free-labor system, from a large-plantation economy to one based on small farms, and from a predominantly agricultural area to a region committed to industry with a constellation of growing towns. For men and women the Civil War had different meanings and different effects. The war called forth three out of every four men of military age and left 258,000 of them dead: this from a total southern population of 9 million. The war did nothing less than free 4 million slaves—an astounding event given the size of the slave population and the amount of resistance mustered. It made paupers out of some who had come into the war with means, and it made others rich. It pushed the small farmer into near penury and drove thousands from their homes. The war divided families and the nation, changing forever the way southerners viewed their society, politics, and place in the social order.

The Civil War officially began April 12, 1861, when Confederate armies fired on the Union-held Fort Sumter in the middle of Charleston harbor. It ended April 9, 1865, with the surrender of the Confederate Army at Appomattox, Virginia. The surrender came approximately four years after the bloody war had started, and the war ended almost ten miles from the place where Union and Confederate armies first met face to face at the Battle of Bull Run or First Manassas. Historians recognize that men and armies fought either to establish a separate nation or to preserve the United States, to continue to hold slaves, or, ultimately, to destroy slavery. Regardless of the purposes of the war, scholars have always recognized that in the South there were two active fronts: the battlefields and the home front.

In the light of gender studies, the home front has taken on even greater importance. African American women, children, and men, white women, children, the elderly, and occasionally men who were relieved of duty or bought their way out of military service, constituted the home front population. This group, like the nation at large, divided along class, race, gender, age, and geographical lines, complicating the story of survival and endurance. At the beginning of the war, white southern women of means were among the Confederacy's most ardent supporters, cheering on troops and rallying forth men to the army by their taunts of cowards who did not come to the defense of the homeland. Women fought the war at home by making socks, uniforms, quilts, bandages, and flags for departing soldiers. As they continued their sewing throughout the war, often in church groups, they outfitted poor soldiers as well as those from their own class. They raised money through typical domestic tasks and entertainments: cake sales, concerts, fundraising parties, and bazaars where they sold their "fancy work." They tended the wounded as volunteer nurses in hospitals, hid renegade soldiers, and offered food and comfort to Confederate troops in soldiers' "wayside homes."

The majority of southern women maintained their domestic roles as caretakers of the home and remained on the home front, but 400 women on both sides of the conflict disguised themselves as men, took up arms, and fought alongside their brethren. There were daring women, such as the Confederate Belle Boyd, who dressed as a man, spied for the Confederacy, spent time in the Old Capitol Prison in Washington, D.C., and lived to write her memoirs after the war.

A great many white women were challenged to sustain their income and household while the men were at war. Some earned money outside the home. Emma Holmes of Charleston, who before the war considered herself above such things, took on work as a governess during the war years to bring in extra income. Working for wages in government offices, especially the Confederate Treasury Department, opened new opportunities for income mostly among educated women. Others accepted positions as matrons in Confederate hospitals, despite the stigma that such work was unwomanly. In Chimborazo Hospital in Richmond, for example, Phoebe Yates Pember's duties as matron included supervising volunteer nurses, directing paid or slave laundresses and ward cleaners, ordering food, following the directives of the army surgeons, and successfully guarding the hospital supply of liquor used for anesthetics. The Confederacy sponsored 153 general hospitals, 20 of which were in Richmond. Chimborazo Hospital consisted of 150 buildings, and 8,000 beds, where 75,000 men were treated from 1862 to 1865. It employed 50 surgeons and 46 matrons; women found that hospital work demanded stamina and a lack of squeamishness, but these hospitals provided jobs.

White women of all classes sought work for wages in textile mills. By 1863, 700 women worked in factories in Richmond and Manchester, Virginia, making cloth for the armies. Additionally, 3,000 women worked as seamstresses making tents and uniforms for the government. In Augusta, Georgia, nearly 700 white women worked in the Augusta Manufacturing Company. The owners of this clothing factory paid subsistence wages but insisted that they were offering "philanthropy" to women whose husbands could not provide for them. States also hired poor women to sew clothing for the army in the "put out," or home, system, but the work was by the piece and there were long periods of unemployment due to shortages of cloth. Here the government took over the role of the patriarch by hiring women at subsistence wages, yet it was never enough.

Mostly single working-class women found jobs in munitions factories. Nearly 300 women and girls worked in a manufactory on Brown's Island in Richmond where they made percussion caps, friction primers, and small-arms cartridges. They supplied the Army of Northern Virginia with nearly 150 million of these items during the course of the war, earning an average of $1.70 a day in 1863. By November 1864, workers were making as much as $7 per day, cartridge makers up to $14 a day; they were the best-paid female government laborers in the Confederacy, but their work was extremely dangerous. Indeed, in the spring of 1863 the Brown's Island cartridge laboratory blew up, killing forty-three girls and women. Throughout the Confederacy six such explosions took place in munitions factories, three of them at the Brown's Island factory, harming mostly women.

In the rural areas of the South, women of slaveholding families managed plantations, often without male kin but sometimes with the help of an overseer. There, planter women faced problems of holding the farm or plantation together and provisioning workers, family, and the soldiers who came to take what they needed. While men in service tried to send home instructions on everything from hiring overseers to bookkeeping, the letters were slow to arrive or, with the exigencies of the war, never did. Planter women, for the most part, were on their own, and those who knew how to use a shotgun did so. But the obvious role reversal of women managing households, farms, or small businesses without husbands or other male relatives was just one of many adjustments required by the war. The irony is that while men went to war to save the Old South and its gender prescriptions, the war changed women's roles dramatically. This shift challenged the ideal and ideology of domesticity that called for women to hold moral superiority through piety, homemaking, submissiveness to males, and benevolence to subordinates. These roles had served to put elite women on a pedestal in southern society. Unable to remain on a pedestal as the war progressed, women learned that there was far more substance to their roles—and that they were far more capable as decision makers and workers—than the images of elite womanhood had suggested.

The disruptions of the war made slave managing difficult for all slave owners, male or female, but for planter women, managing slaves posed their most vexing task. However much planter women may have been a part of the slave-owning system, they did not command the same authority as men, nor were they able to wield threats of physical discipline over a large slave population except through overseers or other male relatives. Slaves, especially on large plantations, knew this and used it to stage work slowdowns, disobey orders, run away, or, as in the case of a Winchester, Virginia, family, bring black Union soldiers into the kitchen for companionship. Plantation slaves helped other slave refugees, providing them food and lodging as they made their escape. Complaints to the Confederate Congress over the lack of white men to supervise unruly slaves were read, debated, and analyzed, but manpower for the military was the nation's first priority no matter how much slave resistance existed on the plantations. Toward the end of the war, fear often gripped planter women who had no assurances that their slaves would not harm them. The slave system was failing, and women were among the first to observe this and voice their laments. Gertrude Thomas of Georgia confided to her diary that she was not certain that "*Slavery is right.*" Other planter women began to rethink the peculiar institution in light of their own inconveniences. "If we lost everything I believe I'd prefer the servants leaving us … they would be a trouble and a care. Poor things, I am truly sorry for them," wrote one woman honestly. Not all women expressed doubts about the morality of slavery, and many of them stuck to their proslavery opinions. A great many others, however, saw the dissolution process as a harbinger of the future and began a reassessment. Undoubtedly the difficulty of managing slaves, suffering the loss of husbands, sons, and brothers, and enduring deprivations while trying to keep a plantation running left elite women harried and anxious.

Nonslaveholding women on small farms with husbands or sons at war often lived with no menfolk to do the plowing, planting, and harvesting or to help with the hog slaughtering, smoking, curing, fence mending, wood chopping, branding, and horse shoeing. Finding laborers to take on these tasks and the money to pay them became increasingly difficult. A North Carolina woman wrote Governor Zebulon B. Vance: "There are many others besides myself who have neither brother husband nor Father at home to cut our wheat & no slave labor to depend on in this part of the country." She went on to raise the specter of starvation. "Without something done to save the present crop we are a ruined & subjugated people without substainence [sustenance]." Yeoman women, poor white women, and free black women worked long hours to survive the war, yet in some ways their plight was tempered by their years of hard work in the household or on the farm. Yeoman women were adept in many areas, as they had been taught to do for themselves. Their skills included all household tasks as well as a knowledge of local plants and herbs for medicines, coffee, tea, and dyestuffs. Depending on the region, most were familiar with tanning hides into leather, spinning flax into linen, and weaving cotton or wool into cloth. Like women from all levels of society, they worried about their men at the front, struggled to make a crop, and did their best to raise children alone.

It was slave families, however, that suffered the greatest privations, especially when the Confederate army conscripted male slaves into forced labor, and planters pressed the remaining men, women, and children into overwork. African American women shouldered the burdens of the home front in worsening economic circumstances, and, like white women, they often did this without the comfort of their husbands, brothers, or sons. In South Carolina, slave owners took hundreds of male bondmen and put them to work creating defenses for the lowcountry, sending slave families into severe crisis. Men, who had taken a role in rice cultivation, were put to work in salt manufacturing or in impressment labor, leaving women to complete the rigorous tasks of rice tending, ditch repairs, threshing, and winnowing. Male slaves in the upcountry, who had done the heavy work of plowing fields and harvesting cotton, when impressed into Confederate service left behind wives, children, and the elderly to do this work. Slave women were sometimes hired out to serve as laundresses and cooks in Confederate hospitals, causing more family disruption.

Then the federal blockade of southern ports led to a shortage of provisions such as shoes and cloth, normally purchased by owners for their laborers. The first to suffer privations were slaves; owners cut expenses by simply allotting less cloth for dresses and coats and by buying fewer shoes for either men or women. Women slaves found themselves working in the rice fields wearing rags on their feet and complaining bitterly to their overseers and owners. Winter dampness and chill and subsequent bouts of pneumonia carried away many an underdressed slave. Even if bondwomen worked a full day, they often had to spend their nights carding, spinning, dyeing, and weaving wool or cotton on looms that had not seen service in decades. In some cases they were forced to weave cloth and make clothing for the soldiers until past midnight. Old and time-consuming skills were brought out as slave women made soap, candles, and shoes. These women struggled to provide for their own families given how little they received from their owners. Slave rations could not be maintained at prewar levels on many plantations, and planters "put their negroes on half allowance," forcing them to forage, fish, steal, or starve. Rice planters in the lowcountry, in a move toward economy, took away molasses, bacon, and corn and put their slaves on a diet solely of rice; they found that over time this diet killed slaves rather than sustaining them.

Some women slaves figured out ways to ameliorate their situations. With fewer white males to enforce labor, they realized they could slow their pace of work, which decreased production for their owners. Others fled to the advancing federal armies. Escaping to Union lines created other hardships for slave families, as the trek often ended in disease or death, and the federals at first were unwelcoming to the refugees. Women with families had the most difficult time escaping, burdened as they were with the care and protection of children. Separation, deprivations, and anxiety all took their toll on slave women. The one remaining hope for those able to endure the trials was the prospect of freedom.

Invading armies tested the strength of white women left to defend home and children. Cornelia McDonald of Winchester, Virginia, who had nine children, remembered when the war came to her doorstep. She wrote,

> I could see from the front door the hill side covered with Federal troops, a long line of blue forms lying down just behind its crest, on the top of which just in their front a battery spouted flame at the lines which were slowly advancing to the top. Suddenly I saw a long even line of grey caps above the crest of the hill, then appeared the grey forms that wore them, with the battle flag floating over their heads.

In fact, during the course of the war, citizens of Winchester saw five battles nearby and endured eight occupations—half Union, half Confederate.

The Union occupations of Winchester began in 1862, came in waves, and led to the appropriation of McDonald's house for officers, her yard for foot soldiers, and her fence for kindling. Things only got worse after that, as soldiers came and went from the house, stole what they could, and humiliated her in the process. For McDonald, when life could not seem more grim, her babe in arms died, leaving her so saddened that she could only dread the future before her. Forced out of her home, she left Winchester for Lexington, Virginia, where McDonald learned of the death of her husband. By then she was destitute, without enough food to supply her family; she finally sent her older boys to work, offered art classes, and accepted charity from those who could spare "victuals" at the end of the war. Women like McDonald who had expected to live out the war at home were ill prepared to take on the role of refugees, yet many of them were forced to flee and at great sacrifice find succor in other parts of the South.

Those women who remained in occupied territory found themselves living in a discomforting environment. When Union soldiers bivouacked in towns or occupied farm houses, women were often forced to feed and house the men, or worse they were subjected to harassment, even rape. Union soldiers searched their homes for arms, stole their meager food supplies, destroyed their stock, ripped their clothing to shreds, "ran off" with their slaves, and sometimes burned their houses to the ground. Never in their wildest dreams did southern women expect to encounter the brutality and inhumanity of modern war. Nor did they anticipate a Union strategy designed to starve and make homeless noncombatants who had difficulty enough staying alive. Many saw themselves in captivity as opposed to the freedom they had experienced before the war. These southern women considered so evil the strategy of bringing the war into their homes, subjecting them and their children to deprivation as a tactic to conquer men, that for many it led to their undying hatred of Yankees.

The invasion of domestic space by occupying soldiers—an act of war—constituted male intrusion into female controlled homes, and it infused the outside political, military world of men into the private domestic realm cherished by families but preserved by women. Some women "fought" daily within their own space and on their own "front," while their husbands, sons, or brothers battled in other theaters of war. Thus included in the annals of war, white women shouldered a burden that they never expected to bear. Even as they wept and fumed, they began to engage in political debate, sometimes with divided family ties. Eliza Andrews of Georgia defended the southern cause in long discursive battles with her Union-supporting father, even as her two brothers fought for the Confederacy. The literary critic Anne Goodwyn Jones described the white southern woman as "the soul of the South," and as such she contributed not only to the patriarchal order but also to the political and military defense of their nation.

As the war continued, morale declined. The separation of families at all levels in the South led to complaints to the Confederate government of hardship. Everyone griped about the lack of goods. Shortages began to appear early in the war, and with the federal blockade in place by 1861, goods coming into southern ports nearly ceased. By 1863 in many parts of the South such staples as meat disappeared, and diets consisted of corn, greens, molasses, and field peas. Coffee, tea, and manufactured cloth were hard to find except among the very wealthy. By 1863 even planter families faced a dearth of salt, a necessary mineral for meat curing, animal health, and medicines, especially quinine to palliate malaria. Inflation soared as resources grew scarce. In Richmond by 1864 prices had risen 900 percent. A pound of bacon in 1863 rose to $10, when an ordinary soldier's pay was $11 a month. Confederate money became nearly worthless; by 1865 its value was one penny on the dollar. After Congress passed the impressment acts in 1863, allowing Union officers to scour the countryside for provisions, they often took what they needed from farms, including bacon, molasses, flour, cornmeal, and coffee. Confederate troops also foraged and harassed southern home-front families, leaving women, children, and the elderly at the mercy of their own armies as well as those of the enemy.

This created real economic hardships for those who remained at home. Profiteers, who had these commodities but wanted higher prices, withheld their goods from the markets. State and local governments, as well as wealthier individuals, tried to offer relief to the poor, but the problem of destitution caused by the dislocations of war was never adequately addressed. In the latter years of the conflict, white women and some men began stealing to sell goods on the black market. More often theft was a matter of necessity, not profit, and, according to historian Victoria Bynum, women attacked "the two groups most obnoxious to poor people . . . merchants and Confederate agents." In Orange County, North Carolina, three poor women with large families looted a mill and stole the flour slated for government use. In Granville County, ten women and three men took 100 pounds of cotton—an act they justified, no doubt, by the disparities of resources. By 1863 women, hungry and desperate, organized a bread riot in Richmond, Virginia, fueling the sense of chaos and disintegration within the Confederacy. They smashed windows with axes, broke into stores, and carried away flour, bacon, and other commodities. Jefferson Davis, president of the Confederacy, responded by throwing fifty-cent gold pieces to the rioters before threatening the crowd with gunfire. Forty-three women and twenty-five men were arrested, and the city newspapers labeled the women viragos, prostitutes, and amazons. Rather than admit that scarcity of food caused the problem, the city hurled attacks at women who had transgressed gender proscriptions.

From every corner of the Confederacy it became apparent that as the war dragged on, it was taking its toll on the home economy. Shortages of food were severe, but the inability to transport foodstuffs became the Achilles heel of the Confederacy. The war pulled thousands of men from the fields; thus planting and crop production declined. The availability of draft animals—mules and horses—diminished as well, and transportation networks by rail, river boat, and road were disrupted. The blockade effectively cut off supplies from the North and abroad, while slaves, whose labor had kept food on the table, fled to Union lines when they got the chance, and refugees forced to abandon their farms ceased to plant. The early enthusiasm for the war expressed by white women of means had turned, by war's end, to cries for help at home. "Everything seems trembling around us," wrote wealthy Charlestonian Ann Morris Vanderhorst in December 1863, "the fifty negroes are gone[,] our house at Kiawah demolished — flocks stolen & the Yankee running wild over the land—the house in town in danger of being torn up by Yankee shells. . . . How I toss on my pillow from night to morning. . . . Grant's overwhelming force preparing to crush us. Famine threatened and our people driven about like straws before the wind. . . . " The pleas of women left to manage by themselves began to tax the morale of men fighting for the South's "way of life." That way of life—agricultural, slaveholding, independent, and self-sufficient—was now threatened by the very act of trying to secure it. Margaret Easterling of South Carolina wrote to Jefferson Davis to complain over the fact that two of her sons were in the army, while she needed at least one of them at home. "I need not tell you of my devotion to my country, of what sacrifices I have made, and of the many more I am willing to make. . . . But I want my oldest boy at home." Historian Drew Faust argues that the hardship of all who stayed on the home front led to several outcomes. Women felt the loss of the protection they had come to expect under the southern patriarchal system. When a woman gave birth without her husband present or when fathers and husbands left their families unprotected to defend southern cities, white southern women began to question the validity of their own subordinate position in marriage and in society. Giving women no voice in politics had led to little consideration of their need for support. Some Confederate women discovered for themselves a new identity borne of hardship and want. Finding strength from within, they eventually used it to cope with the aftermath of war—with the loss of loved ones, the emancipation of slaves, the disabled veterans of the war, and their straitened economic circumstances. But just before war's end women began to complain in letters to their husbands, to their senators, or to anyone who would listen. Some asked their menfolk to leave the cause, and more and more Confederate soldiers, especially yeomen farmers, deserted the army to plow their fields, harvest their crops, and tend to their families. Thus, Faust argues, demoralization of men in the army, in part created by the discontent of their families, contributed to the defeat of the Confederacy.

War's End

When surrender came in April 1865, a range of emotions—disbelief, relief, anger, and fear—washed over women and men. Some questioned God for the South's failure: Was this punishment for holding persons in slavery? Were they being chastised like the Israelites for their faithlessness? Would repentance bring them solace if not victory? The answers were elusive, but for some the questions led to self-doubts as well as self-analysis.

Thoughts of bitterness over defeat led southern women of different classes to vent their feelings at various targets. Yeoman farmer women resented the Yankees for their deprivations, but some blamed the Confederate government for dragging their families into a war to protect slavery and plantation culture. These women, whose families owned small farms, were more likely to resent freed slaves as economic competitors. Elite women, for the most part, did not vilify the Confederate government or the cause for independence from the United States; rather it was this class of women that helped to form and keep alive a notion that the southern effort had been noble, even if doomed, a notion reified as the Lost Cause. To do so, they formed the Ladies' Memorial Associations and later the United Daughters of the Confederacy. These women developed oppositional points of view with regard to manhood; they had reason to hate the vulgar, uncivilized "Damn Yankees," who destroyed their privileged lives. Yet, while eulogizing their brave Confederate soldiers, they quietly resented the fact that southern men had been unable to protect them and their privileged position as ladies. They had difficulty coming to terms with defeat, male post-traumatic stress disorder, and their own wartime experience with its changed responsibilities.

With respect to attitudes toward African Americans, white southern women blamed Yankees for bringing into their towns and villages black soldiers, whom they feared. In turn they accused northern soldiers of influencing slaves to abandon their white owners. One slave mistress exclaimed with distress, "Our slaves were most generally the repositories of our family secrets. They were our confidant[e]s in all our trials. They joyed with us and they sorrowed with us." Or at least she believed they did. In dealing with emancipation, some white women feared violence from their former slaves, while others regretted the loss of unpaid workers. They had difficulty believing that their slaves, some of them treated as pets, would prefer freedom to security. Thinking that nothing good could come of slave independence, they projected a tragic future for their former bondpeople, especially the women.

Female slaves, on the other hand, rejoiced at the victory of Union troops, honored black soldiers as heroes of the nation, and praised Jesus for bringing them emancipation. No amount of sorrow on the faces of whites could reverse what the Union had accomplished through the long and bloody war, their Freedom War. They saw emancipation as their own biblical exodus, not unlike when Moses led the Hebrews across the Red Sea to freedom. That analogy teems with irony, however, for freedpeople wandered in a wilderness of economic and social hardship far longer than forty years before enjoying the Promised Land of full equality.

When slaves learned that emancipation had arrived, many of them took to the roads and headed for freedom, as though it were a destination. Felix Haywood from Texas remembered it this way, "We was free. Just like that we was free. . . . Right off colored folks started on the move. They seemed to want to get closer to freedom, so they'd know what it was—like it was a place or a city." Even before war's end, thousands of slaves had run away to the Union lines as they made their way through the Southeast. Federal troops represented "the new order of things," as expressed by Annie Harper of South Carolina. At first Union soldiers were uncertain how to handle the waves of slave refugees and camp followers. But between 1862 and 1864, 16,000 slaves ran to the Union lines and sought protection from federal troops. Congress saw the advantage of allowing "contrabands," as escaped blacks were called, to come under Union protection, making sure that slaves were not returned to their owners and putting them to work for the Union cause. After 1864 southern black males were allowed to enlist in the U.S. Army, in which they received training, wages, and a boost to their sense of patriotism and manhood. Black women found themselves working as cooks, laundresses, and seamstresses, even as they cared for their own children or relatives. Some survived through prostitution, others by selling baked goods or their own handiwork; still others were given work as field laborers on land confiscated by Union troops.

Eventually, with the departure of the Union armies, freedpeople had to fend for themselves or with the help of the Bureau of Refugees, Freedmen and Abandoned Lands, known as the Freedmen's Bureau, a federal agency that managed relief efforts, supervised labor contracts, and established schools and hospitals for freedpeople. Many former slaves made their way to towns and cities where they hoped to find work. Other freedwomen, who did not escape to Union lines, went in search of their children, spouses, and relatives. The transitional period just after the war was full of danger, especially in states like Texas, where freedpeople became targets of vengeance by roving whites. Susan Merritt of Rusk County recalled that, "Lots of Negroes were killed after freedom . . . bushwhacked, shot down while they were trying to get away. You could see lots of Negroes hanging from trees in Sabine bottom right after freedom. They would catch them swimming across Sabine River and shoot them. There sho' is going to be lots of soul cry against them in Judgment."

Despite the difficulties, many African American women actively abandoned their former lives in search of freedom. They also saw a reconstruction of gender roles. More often than not, former slave women left the plantation and exerted their independence. This was critical because they had always been subordinate in slavery to whites and often to black men. The image of the faithful black mammy, who stayed on with her owners, as in *Gone with the Wind,* was more fiction than reality. Age had a lot to do with it; extremely elderly slaves had little hope of surviving in freedom and often chose to stay with their owners not so much out of loyalty as out of necessity. Some freedmen and women returned to their former owners, but they came to work for wages or to ask for a loan, or eventually to farm as sharecroppers. Some slave women took things they felt entitled to after the sweat of their labor had brought profits to their owners. In shifting to a wage economy, they had to negotiate their relationship with former owners, and whites found it difficult to refrain from treating freedpeople as slaves rather then accepting them as wage laborers or farmers under contract. Labor negotiations were only part of it, however. Other adjustments—profound in their impact on the region—had to be made as well.

CHAPTER ONE

Women, Gender, and Race in Reconstructing the South

Reconstructing the South

Southerners in the aftermath of the Civil War faced difficult dislocations in their lives. Whites saw their hopes for a separate nation die; surviving troops returned home to an uncertain future; African Americans, while rejoicing in freedom, faced the unknown. The world recognized the Civil War as America's defining moment, yet in that moment of disengagement—a moment that lasted into the summer of 1865—chaos reigned. Uncertainty was a constant companion; it stemmed in part from the enormous losses: lives ended, farms and plantations ruined, houses sacked, railroads twisted into unusable pretzels, cities burned and bombed, a nation defeated. There were no assurances within the new order. White southerners who supported the Confederacy faced psychological and financial loss. Land values diminished, investment in slaves disappeared, and sometimes entire homesteads were lost. But African Americans endured the greatest changes—from slavery to freedom.

In defeat, the South went from being a separate nation to a defiant yet *conquered* region. The two most important political and social questions facing the Union at the close of the Civil War were: how to bring the former Confederate states back into the Union and how to ensure civil rights and liberties for the newly freed slaves. Everyone wondered how the nation would reorganize southern state governments and readmit them to the Union. Further, how could the nation administer the civil and economic transition to self-sufficiency for former slaves? At war's end, white southerners had different concerns. They questioned how to bring white leaders back into office and how to mitigate notions of political equality rising among their former bondpeople. All southerners worried about the transition of former slaves into freedom. Whites moved to control and subordinate the former slaves while freedpeople—under the most tenuous of circumstances and with loosely defined political rights—sought economic and legal advancement under the protection of the Union.

The political part of the problem—that is readmitting southern states into the Union—took nearly two years finally to resolve. In the meantime, southern states would have to accept the Thirteenth Amendment that emancipated slaves. In 1865 and 1866, however, southerners proceeded to govern their states and instituted Black Codes to limit the freedom of former slaves. Although freedpeople were now allowed to marry, own rural property, sue and be sued in court, and testify in court against whites in six states, Black Codes in some states prohibited African Americans from owning land in towns, restricted their gun ownership, bound farm laborers to a year-long contract, and allowed local sheriffs to arrest black men on vagrancy charges if seen not working. Once convicted of loitering, black prisoners were made to work in gangs, their labor auctioned to private contractors. This system resembled slavery in many ways, and it was a deliberate attempt to control black labor.

Equally ominous for freedpeople was the apprenticeship system, the ability of southern courts to take away black children who were not living in families with male protectors. Single mothers were the most likely to be harassed by whites to release their children to more "stable" families under apprenticeship. For example, the Mississippi legislature passed the 1865 Apprenticeship Act, allowing the courts to place African American children under the guardianship of whites until they reached their majority if they were orphans or came from indigent households. These children were promised training and education, and even a suit of clothes, under apprenticeship codes, but it was galling for parents to see their children taken away and put back into the hands of their former owners. Thousands of such children were "bound out" by the courts in North Carolina and Maryland to white guardians without the consent of relatives. Their conditions resembled slavery in every respect except that the child's freedom was granted at majority. As historian Laura Edwards has shown, women were among the first to enlist the aid of the Freedmen's Bureau, Union soldiers, and even the courts to retrieve children who were so bound out.

While freedpeople struggled with oppressive laws aimed at curtailing their civil and personal freedoms, many whites, on the other hand, found the condition of black freedom intolerable. White-on-black race riots erupted in 1866—one in Memphis, in which 46 blacks and 2 whites died; another in New Orleans, which resulted in 150 casualties. The rioting demonstrated to northern Republicans that southern whites were defiant, violent, and disrespectful of the rights of African Americans. White violence toward blacks across the South brought enmity from Union officers. Adele Petigru Allston of South Carolina made the point when she wrote in July 1865, "I wish the divisions of our land could be healed and that our southern people could act and think with moderation. I hear that they have been so excessive in the upper districts, in flogging the negroes and not keeping faith as to alienate the authorities who were well disposed to them and that [Union] General [George L.] Beal who was friendly to the whites has gone over to the negroes entirely."

When Congress saw that southern whites had not understood the meaning of freedom for African Americans and had not sufficiently repudiated rebellion, it enacted the Military Reconstruction Act in 1867. This divided the South into five military districts; eventually Congress further demanded that southern states ratify two more amendments: the Fourteenth Amendment, guaranteeing citizenship and protection under the law to freedpeople, and the Fifteenth Amendment, which claimed that the right to vote could not be denied anyone on account of race, color, or previous condition of servitude. Women were not included in the Fifteenth Amendment, much to the disappointment of woman suffragists such as Elizabeth Cady Stanton and Susan B. Anthony, who had lobbied for women's right to vote. Fearful that the amendment would not be ratified if women were given the franchise—then considered a masculine prerogative—Republicans in Congress believed that the nation would not accept two reforms at once and thus heeded the words of Frederick Douglass that this was "the Negro's hour." By giving black men the right to vote, Republicans took the opportunity to build a stronger party network in the South and maintain their hold on power in Washington, D.C.

Beginning in 1867, the Union army occupied the eleven former Confederate states, oversaw elections there, and allowed for the continuation of the Freedmen's Bureau to set up schools and mediate between white planters and black workers. For the most part, southern Republicans in the state assemblies wrote their state constitutions because many former Confederate Democrats were denied office holding under the Fourteenth Amendment. For a time, former Confederates remained disfranchised while voting rights were extended to black men as well as northerners (Carpetbaggers) and Union supporters (Scalawags). These conditions lasted in a few southern states until 1877; ex-Confederates considered them a blow to their manhood, while black voters and white Republicans were elevated by the political changes.

Reconstruction governments included approximately 2,000 black office holders at all levels of government. State legislators instituted land taxes, universal manhood suffrage, public education, welfare institutions such as orphanages, asylums, and systems of poor relief, divorce laws (except in South Carolina), and married women's property rights, while sweeping away the more onerous Black Codes. They endorsed black office holding and party politicking, encouraging education for African Americans.

African American Families after the War

Voting rights for black men became one of the principal ways in which African American males could assert their manhood—a form of "gender reconstruction." By entering into the body politic through voting, actively pursuing party politics through Union Leagues, serving on juries, and electing office holders from among their own race, black men acquired a new confidence and a new definition of masculinity for themselves in freedom.

For men and women, marriage was one of the most important changes toward gender reconstruction, changes that freedom brought to former slaves. More than for sentimental ties alone, marriage was essential to the black household for protection of civil liberties. As a civil contract, marriage carried with it legal rights awarded by the state. So important were these rights that it led Corporal Murray of Company A of the U.S. Colored Troops in Virginia to say, "The Marriage Covenant is at the foundation of all our rights. In slavery we could not have *legalised* [sic] marriage: *now* we have it . . . and we shall be established as a people." Legalizing marriages for freedpeople, previously seen as simply formalizing unions and obligating men and women to assume conjugal responsibilities, actually expanded their civil rights. Black men found in the marriage covenant the right to head-of-household status, the right to the status of fatherhood, and thus the legal right to protect dependents within that household. Under slavery, in the absence of state-protected marriage contracts, white male owners used their power of possession to denigrate black manhood, even to the point of raping slave women despite their marriages to black men, which were recognized in custom but not in law. For women, legal marriage resulted in protection of their children from court-ordered removal, since unmarried mothers had no formal right to their children. Illegitimate children, in fact, became wards of the state, subject to apprenticeship to a qualified "master." Black heads of household and their wives, though recently freed, used the legal system to defy the Black Codes that led to apprenticeship and establish rights to their children and other family dependents. Kate Durham of North Carolina sued for the return of her children who had been apprenticed before the war. She claimed that since she was now married to London Brame, and because he assumed head-of-household status, she was entitled to her children. The court did not mind that Brame was not the children's father; it was his marriage to Durham that mattered because it posited a future of male supervision and support. Courts, according to historian Nancy Bercaw, stood on the "front lines of freedom."

During Military Reconstruction (1867–77) a black married couple was entitled to protection under the laws of the state. In those years, African American heads of families had little difficulty keeping their children, who were now less likely to be threatened with apprenticing to former owners. Children, especially older ones, became part of the family economic unit, and by working chores or paid jobs were able to contribute to the comfort and welfare of the family. Married women were presumed to be protected within marriage and the household, whereas single women were still considered legally vulnerable. Therefore, many men and women embraced traditional marriage gender roles. While a man became the head of the household, a woman took on the role of housewife and mother, caring for her children and the elderly, who in slavery had been cared for in groups. Freedwomen now had less time and interest in field work, which they did only on occasion to help the family.

Although slavery had kept the majority of southern blacks in economic dependency, and the road to prosperity after the war was long and hard, class divisions, already in place before the war, became more pronounced in freedom. Many middle-class African Americans, especially in Virginia, South Carolina, and Louisiana, had been free before the war. Others were the children of white men and slave women, whose unions produced families of remarkable resilience; their histories differed from those of the majority of blacks in the South. Many free black children had been sent north to complete their education and returned to the South just when emancipation and Reconstruction opened for them economic and political opportunities unseen before the war. Norris Wright Cuney, the child of a white male plantation owner in Texas and a female slave, found politics to his liking. He became a leading Republican in the South and was finally appointed collector of customs for the Port of Galveston in 1889 by President Benjamin Harrison. It was the highest-ranking patronage post given to an African American in the South before 1900. Cuney's wife Adelina was also the daughter of a white plantation owner and a slave; together they constituted "aristocrats of color," sending their own children to northeastern schools and devoting their lives to community service.

Adelina Cuney did not need to work outside the home, but many middle-class black women did, most commonly as teachers. Just after the war, they taught in schools that had been organized by northern volunteers—mainly women—as part of the American Missionary Association's efforts to educate freedpeople. Frances Rollin, the daughter of free blacks in Charleston, decided to teach the children of Hilton Head Island for the Freedmen's Bureau, established March 3, 1865, and later for the American Missionary Association. She earned $15 a month and worked with another middle-class free black woman, Charlotte Forten, of Philadelphia.

When Reconstruction governments instituted public education, many teachers already in the classroom held their jobs and continued in paid employment. Across the South black women and some men, on their own initiative, took over the schools that agents of the Freedmen's Bureau left after Reconstruction ended. African American educators continued teaching children and adults eager to learn to read and write until the schools were finally incorporated into the states' reconstituted public school systems, often as late as the 1880s. Again, these educators often retained their positions, and middle-class women embodied an amazing contrast to the idea held by many whites that blacks, due to their inferior nature, would never succeed in freedom.

White Families after the War

Many slaveholding women admitted in their letters and diaries that they were relieved to lay down the burden of owning slaves. Caring for and controlling slaves were jobs that planter women found extremely difficult. At the same time, they were shocked to learn that some of their slaves had little affection for them and even left, upon emancipation, without saying goodbye. Those house servants who did stay on with their owners aided the latter in the transition. In one such interesting arrangement, in the family of Emma Holmes of Camden, South Carolina, former owners became students of their former slaves. In an upside-down world, middle-class Emma and her sisters learned to cook, wash and iron clothes, and clean house under the tutelage of their servants. Emma lamented in her diary, "I was very tired yesterday after my various pieces of manual labor." Her new chores took skill, practice, and stamina. Cooking was especially tricky because it required knowledge of ingredients and their properties, and it demanded improvisation when particular spices or herbs were unattainable. Stirring ingredients together and then adding heat (a skill in itself when cooking with a woodstove) as for stewing or baking called forth a chemical process that led either to a palatable meal or a disaster. Food preparation demanded contact with animals, as in milking, feeding, and slaughtering. Washing and ironing alone was an enormous job. It usually took two strenuous days of work each week, and women groaned at the piles of linens, towels, and clothing facing them. Emma Holmes welcomed her instruction as necessary for the future, yet she confided to her diary, "But I don't like cooking or washing."

Eventually most domestic servants left their old owners to pursue lives of independence, although they often took jobs in service elsewhere. They left behind white women, who were just beginning to understand the tough road ahead of them, with heavy household chores. One white woman in South Carolina lamented, "Now we can only deal with hard realities of the present. We have truly said goodbye to being ladies of leisure, my time is fully occupied, often not having time to sleep. Rise at 5 o'clock, dress, come down to see after breakfast, then a multitude of small cares. . . . I don't like to live among the pots and kettles." Now many genteel women took up chopping wood, stoking cook stoves, cooking, washing, ironing, tending to children, gardening, and cleaning house. They chafed under hard labor and learned to live with less. Women had felt themselves entitled to the role of Southern Lady; now they had to adjust to a life of hard work and little leisure. There was very little money for servants' wages. Even if women could afford to hire servants, they believed that keeping them was more difficult than training and regulating slaves. White women found the old (even if only imagined) intimacy between servant and mistress gone in the new wage-earning system; thus former slave owners were quick to condemn the emancipated slaves who had abandoned them as ungrateful and disloyal. White women's ideas of servant/mistress relations and obligations buckled under the institution of free labor, and they found themselves longing for the return of their privileged status.

In addition to housekeeping, many white women had to find paid work, usually as teachers, shopkeepers, seamstresses, or landladies who took in paying boarders. Others used their domestic skills to save or earn money from their homes. Mary Chesnut, whose husband James had been a senator from South Carolina and then a brigadier general during the war, went to live at their home, Mulberry, near Camden, where she recycled her old dresses into new fashions and earned pin money by selling eggs and butter. Finding it impossible to repay their debts, Mary Chesnut wrote three novels and her famous memoir, *Diary from Dixie,* none of which were published during her lifetime. Gertrude Thomas of Georgia, whose diary over many years provides much insight into the thoughts of middle-class white women, found that she needed to take a job as a teacher to help pay the bills. Her husband Jeff objected because it made him appear to be a poor provider, which he was. She entered the classroom full of enthusiasm but soon learned how difficult it was to work all day, manage students, and tend to the family at night. She grew to dread the job and determined to quit in 1880, but her husband informed her that they needed her salary.

Just after the war single young women worried about finding husbands, while married women were concerned over the return of theirs. Southern men often came home from war depressed or suffering from physical or mental damage. They found that their wives and daughters were not the same people who they had left behind. In truth, white women had also suffered the pains of defeat, the loss of loved ones, and the shattering of their lives, yet they had to cope with male failure and contend with defeated attitudes and fatalistic outlooks. It no doubt took a toll on those whose own humiliations, fears, and discomforts were very recent and raw. Elite men had embodied power and authority in public life as well as in the home, and their wives and all other dependents, including their children, had subjugated themselves within the patriarchal order. The quid pro quo in this arrangement was the promise of protection for family dependents. White women had found that the patriarchal system indeed had not protected them during the war from occupation or harassment by Union soldiers. Some women forgave the system, welcoming a return to their old subordinate status, but others realized that by themselves they had coped. Such women felt that responsibility had changed them. Now they would have to secure their place within the new order, launch their economic recovery, locate their voices, gather their strength, and, for many, discover avenues for public activism. The defeat of southern men and the strengthening of many southern women meant that there would be a reconstruction of white male-female relations in response to their respective war experiences. Whether in resignation or relief, most women accepted the return of white southern manhood to its exalted place in exchange for their return to the status of Southern Lady. In the end they accepted a kind of "gender rehabilitation" by taking southern patriarchy back into their lives. Other women welcomed the return of their menfolk but understood that women had changed as a result of the war and, if they chose, would take on more public roles in such places as churches, relief organizations, and clubs.

Yeoman-class women found that they had to take up many tasks: reunite their families, bolster their menfolk, deal with war tragedies, and maintain an active economic role in the home and the fields. Even if they owned their own land, after the war they had less to live on and fewer options, but their roles had changed little otherwise. Until the 1880s, farming was their only way of life, and it grew more difficult as cotton and tobacco, with their cycles of boom and bust, became driving forces.

One of the hardships for yeoman women was that they were not afforded the status of Southern Lady. They were seen as lower class, and bias persisted toward them from elites and from some African Americans. As time passed, more white women had to work in the fields to produce cash crops and to stay ahead of and pay off their debts, which meant less time for domestic chores and household production. Even by working in the fields and in the home, the relentless downward spiral of the economy led some to lose their land and others to keep it but choose to work elsewhere. One solution to the dilemma of the declining farm economy was to find work in the textile and tobacco mills after 1880, where such yeoman women were labeled working-class and out of reach of middle-class respectability.

Farming among African Americans

White planters had experience with African Americans functioning as slaves, working the cotton fields in gangs, living in slave cabins, and being supervised by their overseers or owners. They tried to continue this system through the 1860s, but African Americans, who had little enough experience with independence, were certain they did not want to go back to the old ways. White owners, however, still needed labor, and freedpeople needed to work. The majority of white landowners insisted that black workers sign contracts, stay until they had worked a year, and accept their pay only at the end of the harvest. After several years of contract labor that satisfied neither landowners nor freedpeople, both parties sorted out their labor needs in a cash-poor economy. Former slaves had strong attachments to the land of their birth; the woods, streams, fields, and roads were familiar to them and represented the home of their ancestors. In most cases, freedpeople wanted to stay where they were raised, but they resisted all arrangements that felt like slavery. They rejected living in slave cabins and working in gangs on land owned by whites. Freedpeople wanted their own homes without white interference, their own land, mobility, and their own social networks. The compromise over land and labor that followed evolved into the system of sharecropping, which was in place by 1880. Economist Gavin Wright noted that, "Sharecropping was a balance between the freedman's desire for autonomy and the employer's interest in extracting work. . . ."

Because freedpeople sought independence, white landowners divided up their plantation lands into smaller units—of twenty to forty acres each—and built houses for freedpeople, often providing them with fertilizer, seeds, plows, mules, and some furnishings in exchange for one-half of the crop. If farmers brought their own tools and animals, they could have the use of the land in return for a share of their crop to the land owner—usually a third of their corn and a fourth of their cotton. This system allowed black families semi-independence, living away from the daily oversight of white landowners. But there were pernicious aspects to the sharecropping system that came when families used credit to buy food, clothing, and other supplies at the local store. A furnishing merchant or landlord (who might well be the same person) often owned the store, and because sharecroppers could not pay with cash, they mortgaged their future crop. This arrangement, called the crop-lien system, could harm a family's chances of improving economically, even keeping it in debt for years. When that happened, sharecroppers found themselves in debt peonage, which meant that as long as they owed money, state laws prevented them from leaving the land, on which they would have to work until the debt was paid. This exploitative system gave much power to whites and little to blacks. It was rife with fraud because many sharecroppers were illiterate and could not check the books kept by the store owners; even asking to see the books was considered an affront to a white man. The system gave African Americans little or no negotiating power, and it could lead to poverty, keeping talented workers from achieving the economic independence they desired.

Women's Invisible Household Economy

The work of freedwomen, however, could make a difference in this potential downward spiral. Once established on their allotted land, freedwomen often chose not to work in the fields every day as most had been forced to do in slavery. Instead, they picked cotton at harvest time or worked steadily through the year on tobacco crops, which could be grown on small household plots. Women in the lowcountry of South Carolina gradually withdrew their full-time labor so that by 1868 only 34 percent of them worked a full day for white rice planters. The women made it clear that they would control their labor as they chose and would not repair irrigation systems or work beyond their limits. Freedmen's Bureau officials, who stayed in the South until 1868, accused women of loafing, some refusing to work for whites and resisting field work. Many northern officials held to traditional views of black women laborers—as either field-hands or servants—rather than as mothers and homemakers, whose domestic duties were as vital as field work. Instead, freedwomen resisted working for whites if it meant performing both field work and domestic labor, and they sought to care for their own children or elderly parents in their homes. Having choices, however limited, was one of the benefits of freedom, and freedwomen exercised their right to decide how and when they would work.

Despite the poverty experienced by many former slave families as a result of the sharecropping system, poorly paid domestic service, or annual contracts with whites, an amazing thing happened. By 1880, 20 percent of blacks came to own their own land, and by 1900, 25 percent were landowners. It was not a large percentage, but it was an important indicator that some freedpeople had been able to escape debt and acquire equity in land. Black families had the most difficult time getting ahead in the commercial nexus, and yet they found the money to build schools and churches and, in some cases, to buy land. How did they do it?

Most freedpeople saw sharecropping arrangements and tenancy (renting land rather than paying with crops) as a starting point; their goal was to own land and live independently. When freedpeople started farming after the war, they had the opportunity to control their own household production in such a way as to save money toward the purchase of land. The household economy—explained below—sustained the families of freedpeople (as well as those of white yeoman farmers) and complemented the sale of cash crops. The salient difference between household production and cash-crop farming—both of which freedpeople managed to do—was the control they exercised over household production. Freedpeople could decide for themselves how best to allot their labor. The sale of cash crops on the other hand put them at the mercy of conditions outside their control: the weather, the price of crops, and discrimination from buyers.

The household economy depended mostly on women and children. Because women withdrew their daily labor from the fields, they had time to do domestic tasks, giving their children the freedom to attend school. The productivity of black families in freedom probably decreased as far as crops were concerned, but their overall standard of living rose considerably in comparison to that during slavery. When freedwomen concentrated on household chores, they had the time to sell their labor or homemade products, thereby adding to the income of the household economy. Historian Sharon Holt defined the household economy to include the work of every member of the family, but it did not include work or earnings related to cash crops. The wages that men, women, and children earned by hiring out their labor were considered part of the household economy. Men and boys worked as hired hands in addition to their own farming and hunting. Some girls and women worked as cooks and domestic servants or took in washing to bring in extra money. Sewing, quilting, mending, cooking, making cheese, butter, and baskets, selling eggs and poultry, slaughtering hogs, and tending vegetable gardens yielded products to sell at market or in the neighborhood. In this way, families could save money or bring extra revenue into the household economy.

Household tasks do not generally appear in accounting ledgers, so women's work seemed invisible to earlier historians. But this work made the difference between destitution and a sustainable life for many people. It allowed freedpeople to build churches and schools with their own money. To support missionary schools, they paid tuition, purchased lots, built school buildings, housed and fed teachers, and procured school essentials such as books, stoves, maps, and slates. Freedmen's Bureau agents discovered in 1865, a few months after emancipation, that African Americans had already organized 500 schools; by January 1866, 150,000 black students were learning at home or attending their own schools. Within the system of household economy, freedpeople planned to buy land, first by taking out chattel mortgages—short-term loans on the things they owned rather than on their crops. To build up chattel, they started to breed chickens, which provided meat, eggs, and feathers that could be sold or traded. Then they bought pigs, and if all went well, a cow, which allowed them not only to make dairy products for the benefit of the family but also to gain collateral for a mortgage on an acre of land. Thus women's work and household production were valuable to sustain or enhance life in a marginal economy.

Not all families were industrious—or lucky—enough to make household production work in their favor. The record is clear that farms often failed to bring in the needed revenue, and many families remained in or were reduced to poverty. Any number of factors could blindside their goals: the death of a spouse, accidents, loss of animals, poor land, and prejudice on the part of landowners, furnishing merchants, or bankers who made loans. Still, not all sharecroppers ended up in the cycle of debt and poverty, and some owned their own land thanks to the "invisible" household economy bolstering them.

African American Women and Paid Work

When African American women contemplated the choice of working for their former owners or for themselves, most chose the latter. The absence of labor-saving technologies for housework still led wealthier families to desire paid domestic labor, so while the conditions may not have been very attractive, many African American women realized they simply had to work for whites as domestic servants. White employers often expected supreme deference from employees and long hours of work for little pay, and they made it clear that maids and cooks would have to leave their children elsewhere. Nonetheless, black women found various means to control certain aspects of their work. Most chose to live in their own neighborhoods and in their own homes, not those of their employers. This way they avoided sexual harassment and assault and were able to limit their tasks to the time allotted rather than to be on call at all hours. They concentrated on breaking down domestic service into tasks—such as cleaning one day and ironing the next—thus limiting energy spent on overall household chores and giving them the time to accommodate to their own families' needs. Freedwomen knew that boundaries were necessary if they were to remain laborers under the new system.

By 1880 in Atlanta, 98 percent of black wage-earning women between the ages of ten and sixty-five (or older) worked as domestic laborers, but, if they could, they preferred to work out of their own homes as laundresses. For many black women across the South, the rise in textile factories and ready availability of cloth led not to jobs in the new factories but to more clothing to wash and iron. Washing was so arduous that middle-class white women who could afford it sent out the laundry to be done by black washerwomen. Laundresses worked hard, often six days a week; they turned their yards into washing assembly lines, hauled water to the kettles, stoked fires under steaming cauldrons of wash water, and scrubbed, rinsed, and wrung out the clothes and linens. They strung clotheslines across the yard or inside the house for drying. They chopped wood, stoked the stove, and heated the heavy irons for the miles of ironing that followed. Despite the back-breaking labor, African American women chose this over working in a white woman's kitchen for the independence it gave them. Historian Tera Hunter noted that "laundry work was the optimal choice for a black woman who wanted to create a life of her own. The washerwoman was the archetypal domestic laborer in Atlanta." Trying to establish a fair wage for their work proved difficult. In 1881, Atlanta laundresses formed a union called the Washing Society, in which they aspired to earn one dollar for every twelve pounds of washing. On July 19 they called a strike. Opponents labeled them the "Washing Amazons," but the strikers organized thousands of laundresses, hotel workers, cooks, nurses, and maids and then strategically threatened to strike during the International Cotton Exposition that met in October 1881. Their threats were taken seriously. By challenging a low-wage economy, these women tarnished the image of the New South as a racially harmonious region, an image projected by white boosters who tried to convince northerners that all was well with black workers in the South.

White Farming Families and Women's Work

For white women, the ideal expectation was that they would work in the home rather than the field or for other white families. Thus, while farming continued to be a family effort, women and children carried their weight within the household economy. Gender prescriptions often dictated that women, especially mothers, do the work of the home without much help from men or boys. Mothers could count on the help of younger boys to carry water and bring wood to the stove, but older boys and husbands did not take up household chores such as cleaning or cooking. "I had the kind of brothers that were really men. They didn't do anything around the house. Their work was strictly on the farm," explained Mary Harrington of Danville, Virginia. But at times mothers and girls found themselves working beside men and boys in the cotton and tobacco fields: ideal gender prescriptions flew out the window in the face of economic necessity.

Farming was a family enterprise that lasted a lifetime. Older children taught the younger ones to distinguish corn, cotton, or tobacco shoots from weeds, and by the time children were five or six they knew how to handle a hoe and could begin the tedious process of weeding an entire row. Mothers, though often burdened with small children or babies, would take their little ones to the field and either carry them on their backs, tote them on their cotton bag, or lay them on a quilt beside the row. William Owens of Texas remembers that his mother, a widow, did the plowing herself and "when I was big enough to crawl, my mother tied me to a stake to keep me from going off into the woods. . . . My toys were the dirt, and a stick to dig the dirt. . . . Before my first year had passed I had eaten the peck of dirt everyone . . . is entitled to."

Although many wives and mothers preferred working in the fields to housework, the chores at home made their work doubly hard. Just at the time that the cotton crop was "laid by," meaning it was maturing to await harvest, usually in July and August, the work of the garden picked up. "This season o' year men folks get a little breathin' spell, with the crops laid by, but it's a woman's hardest time, standin' over the hot stove. . . ." Preserving food was a seasonal task, but everyday chores came around no matter the season. Women were responsible for washing, ironing, sewing, and mending the family's clothes. Cleaning the house, washing dishes, milking the cows, feeding the chickens, and cooking fell to women and girls as well. Sometimes the family made older girls miss school to help with household tasks. Mollie Goodwin, a tenant farmer's daughter in North Carolina, stayed home from school on washdays to help her mother.

She remembers how much she wanted to follow her brothers to school, but she could do so only if she finished all the washing in the morning. When she did work hard enough to finish, she could go to school in the afternoon, but she was too tired to enjoy it much less to learn.

Southern women—black and white—had the highest birth rate in the nation at the turn of the century. Married women often had a baby every two to three years; just as the older child was weaned, a new one came into the world. The mean number of children per mother was 6.3 in the 1930s. Annie Viola Fries, of High Point, North Carolina, remarked how hard her mother worked bearing twelve children and tending to the ten surviving ones. By the time Annie was old enough to go to work, her mother had become ill and could manage only with the help of her older children. The burden of too many babies caused many women to suffer lifelong pain and fatigue from perineal tears, fallen uteruses, and hemorrhoids. Hiring a trained physician cost money that many did not have, so women delivered their babies with the help of midwives, and few had medical attention from physicians after the birth. The reasons for the frequent pregnancies varied, but one rationale was the traditional value of a family raising its own farm hands. Once children grew to be eight or nine, their work was valuable within the household economy. Additionally, birth-control information was not available to many poor families; thus fertility remained largely unchecked until the establishment of birth-control clinics. In 1931, women opened such a clinic in Little Rock, Arkansas, for example, and in Dallas, Texas, in 1935. State health departments made contraceptive advice and devices available to poor families, but in fact, in 1930 there were only fifteen cities in the nation that had contraceptive clinics, and most of these were not in the South!

From Family Farm to Mill and Village

The new entrepreneurs of the post–Civil War South liked to think of the cotton mill movement as a crusade. Economic historian Broadus Mitchell recalled that when mills opened, with high risk on the part of the investors, they gave employment to the "necessitous masses of poor whites." Southerners thought that the mills represented a philanthropic incentive, offering work to yeoman families whose farms had played out and whose children were suffering the pangs of deprivation. Mitchell positively glowed with warmth for the mill owners and capitalists who brought this great "moral movement to help the lower classes." Of course, the cotton mills were part of the New South industrialism, which boosters bragged would increase the productivity of the masses, advance the region, and become the symbol of the New South.

Historian C. Vann Woodward explains that from 1860 to 1880 the leading cotton mill states, North Carolina, South Carolina, and Georgia doubled and even tripled the value of their production over antebellum days. Output improved even more between 1880 and 1900, when the number of mills increased to 400. Measuring the number of spindles, workers, and bales of cotton consumed gives a picture of unparalleled economic growth. In 1890 the total number of spindles reached nearly 4 million, the workers nearly 100,000, and the number of bales used to make cloth nearly 1.5 million; the money invested was $125,000. Towns that had been sleepy hollows, coming to life only on market Saturdays, were transformed by factory fever. Investment dividends were high; in the beginning of the mill crusade, investors earned between 18 and 25 percent a year. Mill workers, on the other hand, earned on average 12 cents a day, laboring from nine to twelve hours over the humming, buzzing, and lint-spewing machinery. Wages did increase until by 1915, Alice Evitt, a North Carolina spinner, earned $1.44 a day. While textile workers gave up their youth to the mills, risked lay-offs, work speed-ups, and brown lung disease caused by inhaling fiber lint, investors and owners carried off the profits. The story, however, is not entirely one of an oppressed people forced by economic hardship to labor under intolerable conditions. There is a great deal more to say about the workers themselves, why they came to work in the mills, and their ability not only to adapt and survive but also to overcome.

In the southern Piedmont, a push-pull force accelerated the move of laborers from farm to cotton-mill factory. Self-sufficient farming families who mostly produced their own food and also devoted a portion of acreage to growing a cash crop were becoming fewer and fewer. More farmers moved toward cash crops exclusively to increase their earnings because their lenders—often merchants or landlords from whom they borrowed to tide them through to the next crop—wanted it that way. With the advent of the crop-lien system, and cotton prices plummeting due to the overproduction of cotton in the world market, hard times began in the cotton patch.

Overproduction, due in part to the rich cotton lands in Texas, lowered the price farmers could command for cotton from 11 cents per pound in 1870 to 5.8 cents per pound in 1894—a drop of 48 percent. Small farmers, tenants, and share croppers struggled to get ahead. By 1900 more than half the farmers were tenants in South Carolina, Georgia, Alabama, Louisiana, and Mississippi. In the other southern states between 30 and 50 percent had lost their land and were either tenant farmers or sharecroppers. Still, as railroads penetrated the South, bringing merchandise from the North, and as the Sears Roebuck catalog found its way into rural homes, southerners sought needed cash. Fewer farm families could survive economically without outside work.

Jobs became available through cotton-textile manufacturing in the Carolinas and Georgia, but the same market forces that drove the small farmer down through excessive interest rates put money in the bank for manufacturers who borrowed to build factories. Mill owners depended on farmers to fare poorly in the cotton nexus because those farmers who failed took up factory work, forming a pool of cheap labor to tend the machines. Owners exploited the poor economic situation while farmers sought a way to escape their misery. Mill owners offered them steady work at consistent wages. Still, the first members of farm families to take up the offer of work for wages—called public work—were women.

When recruiters for the cotton mills in the 1880s came to the countryside asking for workers, yeoman farm families in poverty considered the change to mill work. At first those who ventured out to earn wages were widows, single women, girls, and itinerant laborers. Widows with a passel of young children, caught in the grip of descending cotton prices and a family to feed and clothe, often went first to apply for a job tending the whirring machinery. The job came with a house in a village of mill workers that could be family to anyone who lived there. Daughters of farmers, considered expendable by men who did the heavy work of the fields, made their way to the mills, hoping to trade housework for a bit of independence. Thus the earliest mill villages and factories were dominated by women. As the economy went through cycles of hope and despair for farmers, more men joined the ranks of mill workers, until whole families turned to textile work. Many men found factory work and the loss of independence that it represented more difficult to tolerate, and some of them never did get used to it. They let their wives and children work in the mills, while they continued to farm or to work at odd jobs.

After the Civil War, tobacco factories also hired women and men. The early manufactories, centered in Durham, North Carolina, made plug and pipe tobacco and handmade cigarettes. In the 1880s, James B. Duke invested in inventor James Bonsack's cigarette-making machine and aggressively advertised and marketed packaged cigarettes. Duke's company took off until by 1889 a consolidated cigarette industry, the American Tobacco Company, emerged with James B. Duke as president. As the tobacco industry expanded, Durham grew from a town of 300 in 1865 to one of 5,000 by 1884, its growth fueled by the prospect of jobs in tobacco factories.

Positions in the textile mills and tobacco factories were separated by sex and race. White men were given work in the textile mills labeled heavy, skilled, or responsible; thus they took over the carding of cotton (heavy), the repair of looms (skilled) and supervisory positions over workers (responsible); they shared jobs with women in weaving the cloth, but not much else. Women mainly took on light work; they cleaned the cotton and tended spinning jennies and looms. Children as young as four ran between the machines, replacing spools, carrying water to the workers, and playing at the feet of their working mothers. African American men who lived near mill towns found jobs only in the first-floor, lint-laden opening room, where they stripped the jute covering off of bales of cotton and prepared the fiber for carding. They had almost no contact with white women at the looms upstairs. Employers felt an obligation to keep black men out of contact with white women, because of the proscription against interracial/intersex mixing. African American women did not find any sorts of jobs in most textile mills until the 1960s; rather they found work in tobacco factories in North Carolina, preparing leaves by hand–stemming or stripping them of their midrib—for chewing tobacco and cigarettes. White men also worked in the tobacco industry, but they monopolized the skilled jobs by tending to the machines that processed the tobacco while white women held "clean" jobs, running the machines that packed, sealed, and labeled the cigarettes. Black men handled the tobacco leaves, feeding them into the drying machines, packing the leaves into hogshead barrels, and blending and shredding the leaves once they had matured. They seldom had contact with white women.

In both the tobacco and textile industries, discrimination in hiring and promotion followed lines of color and gender. African Americans were assigned manual labor with few opportunities to become skilled workers. White women, with their nimble fingers and sleight weight, were thought better suited to jobs that entailed spinning, tying up loose threads, and operating light machinery. The racial and sexual division of labor led to wages scaled along the same lines, leaving African American women the lowest paid workers in both industries.

The work day in the early cotton mills began at 6:00 AM and ended at 6:00 PM, six days or seventy-two hours a week, with one hour off for lunch. In 1903 the hours were reduced to sixty-six per week. Women earned 60 percent of what men earned. Children under the age of sixteen earned one-third of adult wages, and they could begin actual work in the mill at age six or seven. Because families had always worked long hours on farms, it seemed natural to labor long hours in the mills. Conditions in mills, however, were unhealthy. In summer the rooms were unbearably hot; lint covered workers' hair and clothing, leading to the epithet "lint-heads" used by those outside the mills. Cotton dust filled workers' lungs and could lead to brown lung disease (byssinosis). Accidents—especially to hands and arms—were almost inevitable with pulleys and machinery running at a frantic pace. When injuries occurred and workers needed time off to recover, they lost days of wages. Although white men received better pay and more responsible jobs than women, when it came time to protest and strike, both women and men walked off the job.

Village life succored many a worker after long hours in the mill. In 1900, 92 percent of families working in southern mills lived in mill villages. Mill houses, churches, stores, and schools provided a respite from the heat, humidity, and constant drone of machinery in the mill. But even these places were owned by the textile company, which rented out the housing, hired the preachers, ran the stores, and subsidized schooling for the first seven grades until the 1920s. This reminded residents that only their families, labor, possessions, and friendships were their own. Community gatherings fostered a feeling of family and a sense of who one could count on for aid. Some women achieved prominence through the practice of herbal medicine and midwifery. Folk remedies and a midwife's help in deliveries were more important to mill villagers than were doctors. Village men achieved prominence through their music—banjo, fiddle, and guitar playing. They would make music on weekends, providing entertainment and recreation in the days before radio. These were the ties that most mill hands remembered with gratitude.

Gender and Race in the Coal Fields of Alabama, 1878–1908

Historians have often thought that black and white men who worked in the same areas as lumber men, dockworkers, farmers, and coal miners after 1880 were in direct competition with each other and that this could lead to conflict and violence. Indeed, the South was known for its racial violence based on economic competition or on the desire of whites to control labor and markets. But episodes of interracial cooperation in fact were in evidence in the Alabama coalfields, where black and white men worked together and belonged to the same union. Similar episodes of interracial cooperation among dockworkers in New Orleans have also been cited. The core question is why did black and white men cooperate with one another in the workplace even though they experienced segregation in all other spheres of their lives?

Coal and iron ore mining in the region of northern Alabama had been a source of raw materials for the production of steel since 1871. Mining for these two minerals and steel production made Birmingham, Alabama, the heavy industry capital of the South. The labor force was black and white from the very beginning; by 1900 black miners were in the majority. Conditions for miners created constant tensions: low wages; long hours; dangerous and unhealthy work conditions; company-controlled prices at the store and on rental housing; and the use of convict laborers brought in to work when miners threatened to strike. In short, supervisors and owners held too much power over the workers. The conflict only widened when the miners turned to unions.

The Greenback-Labor party emerged in 1878, the Knights of Labor in 1879, and the United Mine Workers in 1890. All these unions followed interracial cooperation even as Jim Crow segregation grew outside the workplace. In the world outside the mines, blacks and whites generally stayed in separate areas. Their cooperation was challenged during the strikes of the 1890s when black and white "real miners" stood shoulder to shoulder as the mine owners brought in black "scabs" or strikebreakers. After 1900 the United Mine Workers officials bowed to increasing evidence of white supremacy across the South (disfranchisement of black voters and segregation) by fixing the elections within the union to elect only white leaders. Blacks actually conceded to this tactic in an overwhelmingly Jim Crow era.

Despite this, the overall spirit of black-white cooperation continued. Historian Daniel Letwin asked how this spirit managed to survive in an era of increasing racial prejudice. He found "three broad dynamics that encouraged or enabled black and white workers to organize collectively in the face of formidable barriers." Both black and white miners as well as dockworkers found common cause in resisting the efforts of their employers to divide and weaken them along racial lines. These men shared an identity stemming from their common roots as working-class southerners. Black miners, who were union members, allowed whites to assume positions of leadership in order to avoid racial conflict. But commonalities alone do not explain the biracial cooperation among the miners. A final answer turns to issues of gender. Women played no roles in the processing of iron ore and coal. In workplaces occupied exclusively by men, such as mines and perhaps wharves, the tensions surrounding the presence of black men and white women were absent. Since the move toward segregation was driven in part by whites' fears of race mixing and desire to protect the purity of white womanhood, the absence of white women both mitigated segregation and encouraged solidarity. In addition, black and white men working side by side did not elicit a visceral negative reaction among white leaders in towns and industries.

Although men and women often worked side by side in farming and in factories, the history of women's labor in the New South has long been relegated to the periphery. When freedpeople sought a livelihood through sharecropping or tenant farming, women's contributions, especially when integrated into the commercial nexus, added significantly to household incomes. The household economy allowed even poor black families to have enough money to establish churches and schools and to buy their own land. Black women also sought work outside their homes as domestics or in tobacco factories, while yeoman white women, struggling on family farms, tried their hands at tobacco and textile work. Formerly unaccustomed to public work, white women from small farms moved to the factories and mill villages where they found an attractive salaried alternative to farming. The lure of wages in the face of declining cotton prices eventually brought men off the farms and into industry, too, a move that had consequences for women's independence and for the future of the entire family. Eventually old patterns of gender division crept into the mills, as mill owners and managers sought to replicate patriarchal and paternalistic patterns familiar to southern households. White men took the best-paying jobs, while women, child, and African American workers fell into their places in the gender and racial hierarchies. Mill-village life blunted the rigidness of these divisions somewhat, but paternalism and gender and racial codes (no black residents) reigned there as well. Only in a few sites of heavy industry and on the wharves in New Orleans did black and white men work together in a spirit of cooperation, a unity made possible by the absence of white women in the workplace.

CHAPTER TWO

Gender, Race, and the Construction of White Supremacy

In the immediate aftermath of the Civil War, white southerners had to live with defeat, come to terms with it, and somehow establish an identity apart from failure. Having lost their nation in a grueling four-year war, resulting in nearly 270,000 Confederate casualties, southern whites began to seek ways to reestablish their identity. This gave rise to a "war of ideas" and thus was born the Lost Cause, a belief that although victory was not theirs, there had been nobility in the cause itself. Confederate veterans would therefore be valued for having fought with valor to save the virtues of a vanquished Southland. Southern clergy defined this new identity in moral terms, giving it religious language for support. Southern whites had always regarded their society as one favored by God, marrying southern culture to southern churches. In the course of time, white southerners and even northerners came to accept this myth as historical reality rather than understanding it as a region's collective memory. Unlike individual memory, wherein a person's life experience is transmitted through recollections, letters, and oral histories, collective memory, held by the group, comes from a variety of sources, such as newspaper accounts, school books, plays, museums, monuments, and, today, television and film. Often descendants of the participants inherit their ancestors' collective memory as manifested in attitudes, assumptions, concerns, and fears until it becomes the common wisdom of a particular people. A culture's collective memory can and often does exert a powerful influence on regional or national identity, leading to political and cultural hegemony by those who seek to honor their society's illustrious past. The politics of memory then leads to the adoption of symbols—flags, monuments, anthems, and official histories made in support of a particular version of the past.

Collective memories of more marginalized groups, or those labeled by the powerful as "other," often become "counter memories" to those of the dominant group. For the 4 million former slaves who found emancipation in the nation's gigantic struggle, the Civil War was recalled as the "Freedom War." Freedpeople created their own emancipation celebrations and formed their own identity apart from that of white southerners. In a sense, competing collective memories ran parallel almost until the turn of the century when northerners chose to accept white southerners' version of the past over that of African Americans. As this occurred, so did an increase in racial oppression. White southern men began a campaign to discredit black men, attack them verbally and physically as beasts and rapists, and insist that white southern women were unsafe in public places and especially in the vicinity of black men. Violence followed, and from the 1890s to 1905, southern state legislators passed laws to disfranchise black voters and prevent African Americans from holding political office. Then, legislators raced to seal segregation on the South, finding their solution to the "Negro Problem" in the separation of the races. The re-creation of the South as "White Man's Country" can be seen in the rise of the Lost Cause as a tool of southern memory and in the effort of a people striving to attain a manly identity and to protect, by force if necessary, southern white womanhood.

Creating the Lost Cause

White southerners over time created the Lost Cause to include a belief that while the antebellum North had been atheistic and immoral, the South had been a haven of virtue. The Lost Cause has been likened to a civil religion, one in which believers could worship at the shrines of fallen heroes and revere the lost saints of the battlefield. "At the heart of the religion of the Lost Cause were Confederate heroes, who came to embody transcendent truths about the redemptive power of Southern society," writes historian Charles Reagan Wilson. In Richmond elaborate measures were taken to establish and maintain Robert E. Lee's reputation as a great general, even though historians then and now believed that Lee had committed his troops to suicide attacks at Gettysburg. The Southern Historical Society, founded in 1869 in New Orleans and controlled by Jubal Early, William Jones, and Fitzhugh Lee, issued the *Southern Historical Society Papers,* one of the most influential Lost Cause magazines in the South. The SHS, the Association of the Army of Northern Virginia, and the Lee Memorial and Lee Monument associations, created after Lee's death in 1870, constituted the organizational core of the Lost Cause. They convinced the entire nation that Lee had become a symbol for the nobility of the South. Thus in the name of God and southern manhood, a cause to redeem the South was born.

Race was fundamentally important to southern culture and intimately connected to the story of the Lost Cause. In defense of southern civilization, whites invented a memory of the prewar South as a place that had enjoyed harmonious race and gender relations, which, they said, had been disrupted by northern aggressors. White southerners reviled Reconstruction and what they considered the introduction of "evil" into southern life (black soldiers, black voters, black office holders, so-called forced equality between the races). It was necessary, they countered, to defend white womanhood and manhood through the rise of a protective—and redemptive—paramilitary force, the Ku Klux Klan. In their view, the KKK preserved southern values and white dominance and brought about the restoration of order to the South. These haunting collective memories adopted by most southern whites took on the importance of gospel; thus imbued with religious dimensions they gave the ideology of the Lost Cause hegemonic authority.

White southern women made a powerful contribution to the creation of the Lost Cause. In the early years of the war, they formed ladies' aid societies that raised money, sewed shirts, and nursed the wounded in town hospitals. At war's end these women took on the grisly task of finding the remains of southern soldiers slain on battlefields and of those who had died in hospitals. Re-interring them in decent burial sites such as church graveyards, town cemeteries, or, later on, Confederate cemeteries, became their "holy" mission after the war. Thus they transformed their aid societies into Ladies Memorial Associations (LMAs). As it was considered a woman's task to tend the graves of family members, so the custom extended to the Confederacy's dead.

One of the first Confederate cemeteries was in Raleigh, North Carolina, where the women met as early as 1865 to form a Ladies' Memorial Association and plan a dignified last resting place for Confederate soldiers. They began by organizing themselves into a fundraising body. Then they persuaded men in the state legislature to shepherd through a bill to help fund the cemetery. Hard work preceded the eventual removal of all of the dead to their new graves. At the site of a wartime hospital, the remains of some 800 men waited to be removed to the LMA's newly envisioned cemetery. The women marked headboards, made lists of the names before the graves were opened, and then transported the remains to new resting places where a wooden post noted the spot for each grave. In February and March of 1867, the women were forced by federal order to meet a removal deadline. Summoning another army of men with wagons, carts, shovels, and pickaxes, the ladies oversaw the hurried removal of the remaining 400 bodies. Accounts of this winter re-interment push the limits of the horrific. As one young volunteer remembered it, when removing a coffin from a wagon, he saw the lid come off and the corpse slide out. "His hair had grown all around his body to his feet and it was thick and as coarse as horse hair and he had a sword buckled to his waist." Terrified, the young volunteer ran for home. By spring, the LMA had readied the "Memorial Cemetery" in Raleigh, with winding gravel walkways and ornamental shrubs; flowers and lawns covered the gravesites. On May 10, 1867, the LMA held services for the re-interred, a solemn affair attended by nearly 600 mourners. Having established a Confederate cemetery in the state's capital, the women continued through the years to embellish the grounds with obelisks and stone markers, neatly aligned and surrounded by shade trees. Eventually LMAs across the South replicated the work of the Raleigh LMA and brought Confederate Memorial Day to the calendar. Each year for decades, white southerners honored the Confederate dead on April 26, the day the last major southern army surrendered.

In the course of remembering and memorializing, middle- and upper-class white women of the South contributed not only to Lost Cause memory but also to the reconstruction of white manhood. Women found themselves empowered as they organized, campaigned, and sought public acknowledgement for their work of honoring slain soldiers. These efforts, designed to rehabilitate a failed sense of manhood on the part of living veterans, ultimately led to a reinvigoration of male energy and control over politics, race relations, and, in some cases, over women themselves.

After Reconstruction ended and white men regained political power, grief for fallen soldiers turned into a celebration of the nobility of the South's cause and the honorable actions of its defenders. Even as industrialists were introducing factories, expanding railroads, and building shipyards, supporters of the Confederacy insisted on paying homage to the culture of the Old South. Thus a New South Creed, to spread the industrializing spirit among the classes and the masses, had to be propped up by an Old South myth with reminders of the sacrifices of southern soldiers to a noble cause. To this end, Confederate veterans from Virginia planned to raise one of the first monuments to its own Robert E. Lee, but they released the fundraising to women, who then, because they held the purse strings, gained control over the design, placement, and timing of the project. Southern women learned quickly that money meant power, and they used this knowledge to build future monuments, thus shaping the visual landscape according to the tenets of the South's dominant collective memory. By the mid-1880s, veterans came together for reunions; they organized themselves into camps and met annually, drilling, reminiscing, and perpetuating Civil War memories. Women advocates joined them by forming ladies' auxiliaries. When Jefferson Davis died in 1889, it was as if a generation had passed a significant milestone, but the Lost Cause memory did not wane, it only grew stronger.

By the 1890s, a change so apparent had come over the South that white men and women began to assert in a more formal way their own plans for the perpetuation of the Lost Cause. In 1889 Civil War survivors created the United Confederate Veterans, an organization designed to honor veterans and uphold manly pride in their military service. Within fifteen years, 80,000 men were members, one-third of all surviving veterans. Seeking to venerate a female who represented the flower of southern womanhood and to complement an array of southern war heroes, the veterans chose from among the Confederacy's first family its youngest daughter, Varina Anne Davis, known as Winnie. Born in the Confederate White House in 1864, she toddled her way into the hearts of Jefferson Davis's friends and family. The bright child of the sixties, whose happy demeanor heartened the years when Davis was imprisoned, grew to be a poised, soft-spoken young woman. After years of travel in England and boarding school in Germany, she and her mother returned to the United States just as the veterans were organizing into self-defined units. Touring with her father, the veterans began to see the young Winnie in her twenties as a symbol for the virtuous South, calling her "The Daughter of the Confederacy." When Jefferson Davis died in 1889, the mantel was stuck firmly on her. This was an iconic position that Winnie neither sought nor particularly relished. Unable to marry the love of her life—a

Yankee—due to financial difficulties and intense prejudice against northerners, she died in 1898 at the age of thirty-four. In death as in life, she remained a "Confederate icon," a powerful, if reluctant, symbol for the nobility of the Cause and a standard for the Southern Lady.

During the years of the Davis family veneration, white women across the South moved to form a national organization. Building on the work of the LMAs, Confederate veterans auxiliaries, and Confederate veterans' homes associations, in 1894 Caroline Meriwether Goodlett, president of the Nashville Ladies Auxiliary to the Confederate Soldiers' Home, and Anna Davenport Raines, secretary of the Ladies Auxiliary to the Confederate Veterans' Association in Savannah, founded the National Association of the Daughters of the Confederacy (later renamed the United Daughters of the Confederacy or UDC).

This was the era of "hereditary-patriotic" organizations: The Daughters of the American Revolution; Daughters of the War of 1812, Daughters of the Republic of Texas, and Colonial Dames, to name a few. They formed local units designed to provide social outlets for middle- and upper-class white women. In the case of the UDC, its goals were also to revere history according to Lost Cause interpretations, act benevolently towards veterans and their descendants, memorialize southern heroes, and educate the next generation in the "true" history of the South. With their versions of the past came the rehabilitation of white male honor and the continuation of women's public roles in service to the Lost Cause. Seeking a place for themselves in the arena of sacrifice, women lauded men while bringing themselves into public view. Traditional and conservative, these elite women were in fact creating new—and in the eyes of their male "protectors"—legitimate avenues for women's public activism.

The organization quickly spread to towns and cities across the South, leading in 1895 to the creation of local chapters even in far-flung Texas. By 1918, 100,000 women had joined. UDC members raised funds to create homes and asylums for the aged Confederate soldiers and for aging women of the Confederate years. Their first mission, however, was to memorialize heroes of the Confederacy; thus state and local UDC chapters took to decorating the graves of Confederate soldiers and found money to raise statues and monuments to common soldiers and sailors on the grounds of state capitols and courthouses across the South. The national UDC raised at least three grand monuments, one to Jefferson Davis in Richmond, another to soldiers at the battlefield at Shiloh, Tennessee, and finally one to the soldiers and their supporters in Arlington Cemetery in Virginia (Robert E. Lee's former home but now a national military cemetery). Today, Monument Row and the Confederate Memorial Institute or "Battle Abbey" in Richmond, Virginia, along with Lee's Chapel at Washington and Lee University, stand as visible emblems of the Lost Cause. They also represent the power of organized womanhood that strove to keep white southern collective memory in a dominant position.

Educating the New Generation

The UDC took on the task of educating the next generation in a version of the South's history, one that passed their scrutiny and followed traditional Lost Cause ideas. Hence, by their lights, the antebellum South represented the flowering of civilization with its cotton prosperity and legions of happy slaves. The North, an industrial aggressor region, had circumvented the U.S. Constitution's guarantee of states' rights and, by attacking slavery, had left southern states with no choice but to secede from the Union. A war of northern aggression ensued, in which the valiant men of the South did their best to win but were finally defeated by the larger, wealthier armies. Worse was yet to come with Reconstruction—military occupation, black voting and office holding—or, in short, black rule with the help of Scalawags and Carpetbaggers. Redemption, they opined, came with the rise of the Ku Klux Klan, which used persuasion and secrecy to regain power and home rule for white southern men. Members of the UDC took it upon themselves to edit history books and articles. Men, they thought, were better suited to the business of the present, while women—close to hearth, home, and family—were best equipped to look to the past for its usefulness in the present. They hoped to prevent white children, who had never lived with slaves, from endangering the region's collective memory with errant views critical of slavery or of the Lost Cause.

As guardians of the region's past, UDC members allied with Confederate veterans and pressured public libraries and schools to adopt only their certified histories. They found allies among clubwomen, many of whom founded public libraries in southern states. In Texas, for example, 85 percent of public libraries had come from the fundraising efforts of women, and they continued to influence library holdings. It did not take much for the UDC to convince clubwomen to select carefully those histories, biographies, novels, magazines, and volumes of literary criticism that were acceptable to southern views. As one Texas clubwoman put it, we are "true Southern ladies, all of whom are eligible to [become members of] the Daughters of the Confederacy. Its policy has ever been to place upon the library shelves the very best of Southern literature. Especial attention has been paid to juvenile books pertaining to the growth and true history of our beloved Southland." In case "true versions" of the past escaped readers, the UDC produced its own primer. As one matron expounded, "[We] urge upon you as Southern mothers the sacred duty of teaching your children the truths of history and ask you to use as a home textbook the UDC Catechism written by our beloved Mrs. Cornelia Branch Stone. Its truths will sink so deeply into their young hearts that their after lives will be firmly imbued with the belief in a cause that was just."

Cornelia Branch Stone, a prominent Galveston clubwoman and former president of the General UDC, wrote for the Texas Division a question-and-answer booklet called the "U.D.C. Catechism for Children." Its sale contributed substantially to the UDC monument fund and was widely used among southerners to train and instruct young people in the proper history of the South. Typical passages included:

Question: What causes led to the war between the States?
Answer: The disregard on the part of the States of the North, for the rights of the Southern or slave-holding States."
Question: What were these rights?
Answer: The right to regulate their own affairs and to hold slaves as property.
Question: How were the slaves treated?
Answer: With great kindness and care in nearly all cases, a cruel master being rare, and lost the respect of his neighbors if he treated his slaves badly.
Question: What was the feeling of the slaves toward their masters?
Answer: They were faithful and devoted and were always ready and willing to serve them.
Question: How did they behave during the war?
Answer: They nobly protected and cared for the wives of soldiers in the field. They were always true and loyal.

Members of the UDC became noted speakers and educated others in the virtues of the Old South. The robust Mildred Lewis Rutherford, Historian General of the UDC from 1910 to 1915, gave her lectures dressed in clothing from the 1860s. "The selling of slaves in the South did not separate mother and child as often or with as much cruelty as did the slave traffic in Africa . . . , and there was no such thing as chattel slavery in the South," she flatly announced. Reconstruction, she allowed, "was the real blow aimed at the overthrow of the civilization of the Old South. The men of the South were then put under military discipline which actually tied their hands and only the Ku Klux, the 'Chivalry of the Old South,' could break these bonds that fettered them." As cultural transmitters and preservers, white southern women funded cemeteries, censored written texts, and memorialized the heroes of the past. Theirs was an undeniably powerful role made even more so by their support of white supremacy. As apologists for the emerging racial order, the UDC and its philosophies provided white office holders and potential women voters with rhetorical assurances that the emergent Jim

Crow policies contributed to the restoration of Old South values. By publicly justifying the past violence of whites in the defense of southern civilization, they articulated an implied rationale for continued segregation, discrimination, and bloodshed.

Changes in Whites' Attitudes

Mildred Rutherford and others recalled a time when southern whites held a paternalistic view of blacks, seeing slaves as childlike, dependent, and unable to succeed in the world on their own. They rationalized that as long as they were under the care of their owners, African Americans would remain objects of benign paternalism. Lost Cause rhetoric, as displayed in the UDC catechism, praised slaves for their loyalty to white families. In the postbellum era, however, ex-slaves proved that they could maintain their independence, advance economically, and attend colleges and universities. When some blacks became middle-class doctors, lawyers, teachers, and professionals, white assumptions of paternalism changed, and they looked at blacks as economic, cultural, and sexual competitors.

With these attitudes on the part of whites came a more radical form of racism, emerging from the fear of black success. By the 1890s a new generation of African Americans not born into slavery threatened white assumptions, and whites moved to say that freedom had changed blacks. The black man was "greedy as a prairie colt," announced one city mayor. Black women were seen as promiscuous and black men as either lazy or dangerous. Although the resulting era of disfranchisement, segregation, and violence that emerged in the 1890s constituted an intricate web of economic, political, social, and ideological construction, at the heart of this Jim Crow conceit was gender.

The term *Jim Crow* probably came from a northern white minstrel in black face, named Thomas "Daddy" Rice, who in 1828 performed a "colored" dance while singing, "I jump jis' so, An' ev'y time I turn around I jump Jim Crow." The implication was that blacks were forced to perform, in the words of C. Vann Woodward, a "precarious balancing act . . . in which the wary partners matched their steps, bent, and whirled in an unending series of deadly improvisations." Jim Crow pushed blacks to maneuver the treacherous landscape of the segregated South, yet the words of the ditty also suggest that African Americans used their talent, energy, and intelligence to jump Jim Crow, to circumvent the color lines and resist them when they could.

The concept of Jim Crow was the "result of a calculated campaign by white elites to circumscribe all possibility of African American political, economic, and social power," write historians Glenda Gilmore, Jane Dailey, and Bryant Simon. It stemmed from notions of white supremacy, that members of the white race were superior intellectually and physically to members of every other race, but especially the black race. White supremacists made "whiteness" the qualification for membership in the civilized community, and white women were the cornerstone of the community since they bore children who could inherit their patrimony only if they were completely white. Underlying the concept of separation based on the superiority of the white race was the notion that black men were bestial in nature, possessed uncontrollable sexual drives, and wanted above all else social equality so as to be able to marry, cohabit with, or sexually molest white women. The protection of white women, then, became one of the justifications for the worst sort of interracial violence—lynching. There was great power in this racist ideology.

The rationale to separate the races by law continued with railroads which, by the 1890s, had implemented separate cars for whites and blacks. By 1896, in *Plessy* v. *Ferguson*, the U.S. Supreme Court upheld the policies of "separate but equal" (although equal was almost never applied), and the southern states went on a campaign to separate by law nearly every form of public activity. Schools, hotels, and restaurants were already segregated by 1896. Churches had become segregated by choice as African Americans preferred to fund and build their own houses of worship free from white control. But by the turn of the century, whites no longer allowed blacks to worship with them. All public parks, swimming pools, drinking fountains, restrooms, mortuaries, cemeteries, and trolley cars became segregated by 1915. Even Washington, D.C., which had formerly been a place where whites and blacks—especially government employees—worked and ate together daily, was segregated under the direction of Woodrow Wilson's administration. Some cities provided blacks with their own facilities such as hospitals and parks. Black citizens also either bought their own land for parks in cities or raised their own funds for hospitals, orphanages, and schools. Only in private homes (and the occasional nightclub) did whites and blacks co-mingle, but as employers and servants, not as equals. As mentioned earlier, when white women entered the work force, such as in textile mills, pencil factories, or retail shops, owners deliberately separated them from black men.

Jim Crow remained a fact of southern life until passage of the Civil Rights Act of 1964, and it involved the almost total disfranchisement of black voters, sweeping segregation in social relations, and attempts to keep blacks from succeeding economically. Jim Crow used formal codes and laws to separate the races (de jure segregation), and informal codes and customs to maintain white superiority (de facto segregation). Historians have looked not only at the creation of Jim Crow laws but also at the creation of ideas about "whiteness." With this they have examined black resistance to white oppression and discovered that gender mattered a great deal in these struggles.

The Gendered Origins of Disfranchisement

After the Union troops left the South in 1877, the southern state governments returned to office white Democrats—ex-Confederates—known as Redeemers or Bourbons. These politicians did not move immediately to disfranchise black voters. They tried to control the black vote for their own elections, but eventually white legislators came to the conclusion that disfranchisement should be used to eliminate black voters completely from the electorate to undo the work of the Fifteenth Amendment that in 1870 had enfranchised black men. Race lay at the heart of these actions, but so did gender.

Disfranchisement measures began in some states with the use of separate ballet boxes in 1882. The Australian (secret) ballot, touted as a means of ending voter manipulation because one voted in private without help from "mentors," actually served as a literacy test. Those who could not read the ballot or did not know how to mark it were effectively disfranchised. This was successful as a means of reducing the number of black (and some white) voters. After 1892, whites were no longer satisfied with manipulation at the polls, and they sought to make registration and voting as difficult as possible. Thus white politicians ran disfranchisement measures through their legislatures, where they were ultimately enacted as state constitutional "reforms." Eventually, the Redeemers effected the disfranchisement of African Americans through the use of the secret ballot, the "understanding clause" of the state constitution or a literacy test, property qualifications, poll taxes, and the white primary.

Because a few of these measures might also disenfranchise uneducated whites, some states passed a so-called grandfather clause: if one's grandfather had voted in or before the year 1867, then the applicant did not have to take the literacy test in order to qualify to vote. Of course, no blacks had voted in the South before 1867, that is, before Congressional Reconstruction. When black males did finally get the chance to vote, they considered casting a ballot or participating in local or state politics as a privilege of citizenship—as well as validation of their manhood. Black politicians who had been elected to local, state, and national office were heroes of their race. Naturally, the diminishment of black voting after the 1890s took its toll on the pride of race and manhood. This, of course, suited southern white males just fine. In their view, only they deserved the often-stated "best men" status of the South, something black men had proudly shared during Reconstruction.

Poll taxes, a payment for the right to vote, would "improve the electorate," whites argued, by eliminating uneducated and ill-informed potential voters. In states like Texas, poll taxes were used as revenue for the school system, leading white women reformers to campaign for its passage. The poll tax did not completely eliminate blacks from voting in Texas, which had no literacy test, but it was expensive. By 1910 every southern state had a poll tax. This disqualified poor whites and blacks and, after 1920, many women who had won the right to vote. A poll tax cost usually between $1.00 and $1.50. If a household could afford to buy a poll tax for only one adult, it was usually the man who voted for the rest of the family, including his wife. The poll tax, thus, had a devastating effect on poor white women as well as on black women, who in any case were discouraged from going to the polls. In some states, Georgia for example, the poll tax was cumulative: one had to pay it every year, keep the receipt and show it when voting; if not, the back taxes would be due the next time one went to register. In states like Louisiana, which incorporated a literacy test and a poll tax, disfranchisement was so successful that black voting declined in 1910 by 99 percent: from 130,344 to 1,342. Another factor in disenfranchisement were white primaries, i.e., party primaries in which only whites could vote. Since the Democratic party dominated southern politics—"the one-party South"—the primaries were the only elections of real choice, most general elections being foregone conclusions. The result was that the South became a region with the smallest electorate in the country, where a fraction of the eligible voters (by age) could participate, and where Democratic office holders were returned to the state assemblies, the Senate, and the House of Representatives year after year. There they gained seniority on powerful committees and protected the interests of white southern men over white women, black women, and black men. Thus the region became known politically as "The Solid South."

The Success of the Populist Party and its Aftermath

Disfranchisement was not the result of racism alone. It followed a near upset of Redeemers (Democrats elected to office after the end of Reconstruction) from state office at the hands of discontented farmers, who fought to improve their economic and political prospects. Beginning in the 1870s and 1880s, disgruntled farmers, mostly in the Midwest and the South, saw the price of their crops fall. In response they organized Farmers'

Alliances, which called for selling and buying supplies in cooperatives, railroad regulation, currency inflation, and more direct democracy, such as the direct election of U.S. senators and state referenda and initiatives. Most important, in the South farmers formed separate white and black alliances in a movement fueled by grassroots politicking, evangelical oratory, and family-centered camp meetings. In time a tentative form of interracial cooperation emerged, with black and white farmers recognizing their common interests and affirming this first through the Alliances and later via the Populist party. The separate Farmers' Alliances had nationally about 1.5 million white and 1 million black members by 1890. Southern women constituted an important part of the movement, and they shared their political opinions in essays and letters to the *Progressive Farmer* and the *Southern Mercury,* two Alliance/Populist newspapers. The movement swelled as a glut of cotton on the market led to drastically low prices, and state Democrats seemed interested only in holding onto the reins of government.

By 1892 Alliance members formed the Populist or People's party and hoped to win offices outright or in "fusion" tickets with Republicans. Men in the Alliances, who represented the yeomanry of the South, supported the Populist party for various reasons. Among the most important was their opposition to the Democratic party and its stranglehold on southern politics that did little or nothing for farmers. The other reason stemmed from the first: their voices had not been heard; their concerns ignored; their economic interests betrayed; and their dignity assaulted. Called hayseeds and hicks by Redeemer Democrats, Populists turned to politics, and they turned to each other regardless of race. Populist candidates counted on black votes. The Republican party found itself courted by Populists seeking to fuse and join them in contests against Democrats for seats in the statehouse. Although not entirely liberal on issues of race, Populists, like Tom Watson of Georgia, urged black and white farmers to vote for Populist candidates.

Although as a national third party Populists won few contests in the South, one victory came in the 1896 election in North Carolina. There Republicans and Populists fused to win

129 out of 169 seats in the legislature, leaving the Democrats with only 45 seats. The cooperation of black and white voters so frightened Democrats that they began a campaign for the elimination of black and many poor white voters. It was a shakeup fueled by the worst form of racist demagoguery on the part of the defeated Democrats. Racial hatred spewed forth with a gender twist as Democrats accused blacks of wanting to have sexual relations with white women, claiming that white women were no longer safe from the advances of black men. They called on white men to defend white women from rapacious black upstarts. In the meantime, the United States went to war with Spain and called up volunteer forces. African Americans offered to fight for their country, took up arms, and shipped out for training. The specter of black men in military uniform was too much for white segregationists in North Carolina. Newspaper editorialists mocked the blacks' status as soldiers, libeled them as unfit to serve in the army, insulted their manhood, and intoned against their citizenship when they returned to civilian life. Politicians followed suit and soon began a campaign to discredit black voters. At the same time they made overtures to white yeoman farmers, inviting them back to a Democratic party that would protect their women from the incursions of blacks in uniform and in politics. The need to protect the virtue of white womanhood—a classic gender argument—produced a powerful fear-based weapon against the fragile alliance between white and black voters.

Given the volume of hate recorded in newspaper accounts, in 1898 one of the state's worst race riots unfolded in Wilmington, North Carolina. White rioters used cannons and an infantry division fresh from the Spanish American War to kill ten blacks and destroy black homes and businesses. The intended lesson was that blacks should never vote again in North Carolina.

Lynching for Southern Womanhood

If African Americans tried to protest or circumvent the laws, whites were ready to use violence for social control. In hundreds of ways black citizens of the South might suffer humiliations, beatings, and intimidations, but lynching was the ultimate form of violence used against them. The greatest number of recorded lynchings occurred between 1882 and 1930. According to statistics gathered by the National Association for the Advancement of Colored People (NAACP), at least 4,761 persons died at the hands of lynch mobs. But the worst years for lynching were between 1889 and 1898, when 1,613 people were killed; 1,123 of them were black, and 94 percent of them were murdered by white mobs. By far the majority of the victims (86 percent) were lynched in the South. In the years between 1882 and 1930, Mississippi led the states with a total of 545 lynchings (500 black), followed by Georgia with 508 (474 black), and Texas with 494 (349 black). Almost fifty women were also lynched between 1892 and 1918.

A lynching in the South most often occurred when local police arrested a black man. If there was any hint of sexual misconduct in the arrest—and rumors were quick to fly—a mob formed, surrounded the jail, overwhelmed the sheriff, took the man, and supplied summary justice, either with bullets or a noose. Lynching might also include castration and other forms of mutilation, as well as burning—before or after death. After 1891, crowds of whites gathered for such events, sometimes catching a specially chartered "excursion" train to the lynching. Whites sought entertainment in witnessing the grisly spectacle—the consequence, in part, of a rapidly spreading consumer culture, writes historian Grace Elizabeth Hale. Postcards and pamphlets written by witnesses describing the scene were widely distributed. Souvenir gatherers eagerly sought the victims' fingers, ears, testicles, or bones, some of which were displayed in shops.

The most potent and poisonous rumor to spur a lynching was that a black man had raped or murdered a white woman or child. And, as if to underscore the message of the lynchings, white women and children attended such spectacles. In 1897, Rebecca Latimer Felton, an ardent suffragist from Georgia, wrote in the *Atlanta Journal*: "When there is not enough religion in the pulpits to organize a crusade against sin; nor justice in the court houses to promptly punish crime; nor manhood enough in the nation to put a sheltering arm about innocence and virtue—if it needs lynching to protect woman's dearest possession from the ravenous human beasts, then I say lynch a thousand times a week if necessary." Although Felton's beliefs on the political equality of white women were embodied in the woman suffrage movement, she still held to the shibboleth of white supremacy and the myth of the pervasive black rapist.

Historians find that in at least 77 percent of the lynching cases there were no sexual charges ever alleged or proved. In Texas, where Mexicans and Mexican Americans may have been just as likely to be lynched as African Americans, borderland tensions and conflicts over land, property, and murder were more likely to lead to mob violence. Any group labeled as degenerate by Caucasians could be vulnerable to vigilante justice. Certainly, this can be seen in the lynching of eleven Sicilians in New Orleans, Louisiana, in 1891, or in the death by mob violence of Chinese and Indians in the West. Although alleged gross criminal activity most often triggered lynchings, at times there were simply petty crimes involved, such as stealing a cow, or even no crimes at all. Nonwhites could be lynched for infractions such as arguing with a white man or attempting to register to vote. African American journalist Ida B. Wells told of a case in 1893 when two Louisiana black men were suspected of stealing hogs, and, as a warning to the black community, were taken by a mob and hanged.

Sociologists Stewart Tolnay and E. M. Beck argue that there was no lack of formal justice in the South. Criminal laws existed in every state, courts gave out stiff punishments and held executions, and policing systems functioned even in rural counties. Why, then, did people lynch? Historians point to the legacy of slavery, the cotton culture that relied on exploited black labor, the frustrated aggressions of whites, especially where economic competition with blacks existed, the weak constraints against white mob violence, and racist ideology.

Notions of white supremacy had been in existence long before 1900. By the end of the nineteenth century, however, intellectuals, many of them part of the new discipline of social science, developed race theories based on such obvious outward traits as skin color, head shape (connoting brain size), phrenology (bumps on the skull), hair texture, and height. Social scientists, such as economist William Z. Ripley and lawyer Madison Grant, with their new race theories, targeted immigrants from eastern and southern Europe as much as they did Africans and Asians. Yet pseudo-scientific theories gave southern white supremacists an intellectual premise on which to base their arguments for discrimination. If one believed sincerely that genetics controlled the destiny of human beings, and that whites, regardless of class or education, embodied the highest form of intellectual capacity, then all African Americans, even college professors, were inferior to all whites. This form of racism was accompanied by the historical memory of blacks as slaves and the reality that most blacks, because of white control of the political and economic system, were in an inferior financial position in relation to most whites. So strong was the notion among white supremacists that blacks could not succeed due to their innate inferiority that when survivors of slavery, such as Booker T. Washington, did become successful, it was impossible for whites to suspend their prejudice. In their view, all other races, defined as any non-Nordic types, were inferior, and only through determined vigilance could the white race maintain its purity. Those who supported lynching saw it as a means to warn inferiors that race mixing and interbreeding were punishable offenses.

While racial ideology may have been one of the leading intellectual justifications for mob violence, another important reason that lynching increased in the 1890s was the poor economy. In 1893 the nation suffered the worst depression in its history up to that time. This depression lasted five years and the rate of unemployment reached 20 percent. Cotton prices plummeted to 5 cents a pound in some areas in 1894 (down from 15 cents in 1887). Factories laid off workers, displacing them from mill villages and creating real hardships. Tolnay and Beck argue that lynchings increased when cotton prices plummeted. As the economy drove people from their jobs, competition with blacks for employment prompted white violence. "For poor whites, violence was a response to fear of black competition for economic and social position." With the rise of the Populist party and agrarian threats to the political status quo, the spread of radical theories on the savagery of the black race, and the price of cotton reaching its lowest point in 1895, lynching increased. When cotton prices went up again, as they did just before World War I, and continuing until the end of the war in 1918, lynchings declined somewhat. But when the cotton economy began to falter again after the war, the Ku Klux Klan reorganized (in the 1920s) and again popularized the theme of black-on-white rape, leading to an increase in mob violence and lynching.

Lynching was not just an act of violence to maintain white supremacy, it also made manifest white male superiority. White women, the alleged potential victims of sexual abuse at the hands of black men, found themselves victims of another sort, supposedly in need of white male protection, just at the time when the South was beginning to modernize. With industries, businesses, and urban entertainment outlets available to women, the southern economy turned increasingly toward including women in the workforce and in public spaces. As more women actively sought a presence in colleges and universities, club work, voluntary organizations, reform groups, and woman suffrage associations, as well as in dance halls and jazz clubs, the established order of so-called male hegemony began to crack. The fear of the black rapist could work to put white women in a position of vulnerability—and therefore under the control of white men—just as they were entering public work or public spaces.

Threats of violence affected black women as well, for they feared for their husbands, fathers, brothers, and sons who had to make their way in the world. Black women were not immune to threats of violence either, especially as many of them worked in white households where white men had daily contact with them. Miscegenation, or sex between races, whether forced or voluntary, always existed on its own, although intermarriage was against the law in every southern state by the turn of the century. Social enforcement against miscegenation only applied to black male/white female relationships. White men took advantage of or had sexual relations with black women with near impunity; yet a romantic tryst between a black man and a white woman was impossible for white southerners to tolerate without violent reprisals.

Ida B. Wells, a courageous African American reformer, clearly saw the hypocrisy of this white southern way of thinking. Born in Mississippi in 1862, she moved to Memphis, Tennessee, in 1880, where she taught school. Writing was her passion, and she began a newspaper column that quickly became nationally syndicated. In 1889, she became part owner of the *Free Speech and Headlight,* a newspaper owned by J. L. Fleming and the Rev. F. Nightingale, pastor of the Beale Street Baptist Church. He counseled his large congregation to subscribe to the paper, and it flourished, allowing Wells to leave her position as a teacher and take up journalism.

In 1892 three of Wells's friends, Thomas Moss, Calvin McDowell, and Wil Stewart, were lynched. The three men had owned People's Grocery Company in Memphis, and their small grocery was so successful that it took customers away from a competing white-owned business across the street. An altercation instigated by the white grocery-store owner led to an angry assault on People's Grocery, but the owners fought back, wounding several of the attackers. Moss, McDowell, and Stewart of People's Grocery were arrested, but a lynch mob broke into the jail, dragged them away from town, and shot all three to death. This atrocity galvanized Ida B. Wells. She daringly wrote in the *Free Speech* that lynching was not caused by black rapists; rather it was the result of economic competition. She went further to imply that some white women had love relationships with black men. For this editorial, whites destroyed the newspaper office, smashed her printing presses, and threatened her life. She fled to New York and then Chicago, where she continued her blistering written attacks on southern injustices. Wells became especially active in investigating and exposing the fraudulent reasons for lynching. "Nobody in this section believes the old threadbare lie that Negro men assault white women," she wrote. By raising the argument that some white women sought sexual liaisons with black men, she exploded several myths: that white southern women were asexual beings uninterested in sexual pleasure; that white women were considered too pure to be interested in black men; and that black men were uncontrollable sexual predators. She also addressed the beliefs that black women were too licentious to deserve protection from encounters with white men. Since they were considered depraved themselves, black women could not possibly prevent black men from raping white women. By this reasoning, justice could only work one way, with white men protecting white women against lustful blacks and upholding "civilization." Wells demurred that white women felt sexual pleasure and could and did seek out black men for sex. African American women, who were more often the victims of white rapists, were seldom vindicated through the courts. Black men, she held, were the target of an unfair campaign to impugn their humanity. To argue otherwise was simply a justification for white supremacy.

In Chicago, Wells helped develop numerous African American women's reform organizations, but she remained diligent in her antilynching crusade, writing *Southern Horrors: Lynch Law in All Its Phases* in 1892. Unable to tolerate injustice of any kind, Ida B. Wells, along with Jane Addams, successfully blocked the establishment of segregated schools in Chicago. Wells was a fearless antilynching crusader, woman suffragist, women's rights advocate, journalist, and speaker whose work served as a model for future antilynching activists.

By 1920, white southerners had done what they thought they could to solve "the race problem" of blacks infiltrating white bastions. They were encouraged in this by national standards. The

U.S. Supreme Court in 1898 upheld the validity of poll taxes in *Williams* v. *Mississippi*. It had already sanctioned de jure segregation in 1896 with *Plessy* v. *Ferguson*. The nation turned a blind eye to lynching and race riots such as those in Wilmington in 1898 and Atlanta in 1906. Pseudoscientists and northerners had all but abandoned upholding black voting rights in the South and had accepted southern views on the Lost Cause over African American emancipationist visions of the future. Americans now concerned themselves with the results of the Spanish American War. Misapplying Darwinist theories about human evolution, so-called Social Darwinists argued that whites should rule the world, and if European nations had colonies, then so should the United States. Both the cause and the result of American imperialism rested on whites' belief in the inferiority of darker races. In 1898, Spain's former colonies—the Philippines, Puerto Rico, Guam, and Guantanamo Bay (in Cuba)—came to the United States, along with its "dark-skinned peoples." The Filipino uprising, which had accompanied the U.S. acquisition of the Philippines, led to a debate over how to handle these new territorial acquisitions and their "sullen peoples." The result was that northerners came to associate the nation's imperial problems with white southerners' views on race.

Reformers pushed in every way possible against the national monolith of white supremacy and black inferiority, one of the sturdiest social, political, and economic constructs a region had ever produced. In the South it had its origins in slavery and the racial composition of the region. The outcome of the Civil War and the rise of the Lost Cause provided the historical foundation for a new order in the postwar South. White racial assumptions based on prejudice, ignorance, and the concentration of power in the hands of a few provided justification for political disfranchisement and the physical separation of the races, especially after challenges from black and white farmers. The rationale for this was the protection of white southern civilization based on the purity of its white women. The ideas of race-mixing, so feared and loathed, provided justification for lynching, the worst form of collective violence, a phenomenon that attended the region like a dark specter. From this picture of postwar upheaval, ending in the most chaotic and turbulent decade since the Civil War, a new century would unfold and with it new opportunities for women and men to change the course of the New South.

CHAPTER THREE

Prelude to Reform in the South

One question that has always intrigued historians is this: how did southern women from arguably the most conservative region of the nation participate in the Progressive reform movement without roots in an antebellum women's movement? Women in the North valued and drew on their antebellum reform activism for wisdom and encouragement in their own struggle for change at the turn of the century. Southern women, however, living in the shadow of slavery and sectional conflict, had no opportunity to protest what seemed to them as natural law. While Elizabeth Cady Stanton and Lucretia Mott were working for the abolition of slavery and calling for a women's rights convention at Seneca Falls in 1848, educated white southern women were defending slavery and eschewing the women's rights movement as radical and dangerous. African American slave women generally had no voice to protest their enslavement, as did the escaped Harriet Tubman from Maryland or the loquacious and eloquent Sojourner Truth of New York. A history of strong abolitionist and women's rights sentiments did not exist in the southern states; here southern women had to have other avenues to discover the problems that stirred them to action and led them toward reform. One answer, born of southern religiosity, provides a partial response to this question of roots. Southern women, steeped in traditions of Christianity, encountered a new life after the Civil War outside the realms of their homes and families—in churches. There, as churchwomen, they developed women's organizations and discovered real needs among the destitute in their communities. Black and white women found that they could play an active role in such semireligious organizations as the Woman's Christian Temperance Union (WCTU) or the Young Women's Christian Association (YWCA). Jewish women found similar paths to civic activism through their synagogues and community organizations. Settlement houses sprouted even in southern cities, and women found training as proto-social workers while helping immigrant and poor families adjust to life in an urban setting.

Education, whether in colleges, universities, or women's clubs, provided another route toward Progressive reform. First organized for freedpeople by northern denominations, institutions of higher learning offered advantages and a mission, especially to African American women; their training often called them to serve as teachers and community leaders. The Populists, whose newspapers rang with the voices of rural women, placed great importance on education. Their progressive notions about higher education and vocational training for women emboldened state legislatures to create women's colleges and institutes. Educated women, attuned to the issues of the day, found through the woman's club movement as well as hereditary-patriotic organizations other paths toward civic activism and social reform. Thus, not one but many roots nourished the budding movement that would take women from the private to the public forums, from religious institutions to civic associations.

Religion and New Roles for Women

Historian Anne Firor Scott once wrote that the "the public life of nearly every Southern woman leader . . . began in a church [or synagogue] society." Viewed first as homemakers, southern women used the home and household as a base, and from it entered into the first institution that welcomed their abilities, talents, and activism in a voluntary setting. In cities and towns across the South, women found that even in the most conservative religious denominations, where their voices might be stifled in mixed company, they could form their own circles and gain a measure of power. Keeping to gender prescriptions for the late nineteenth century, women found common purpose in forming their own prayer groups, auxiliaries, societies, guilds, and sodalities. Their first goal was tending the needs of the congregation. Often forming ladies' aid societies, they raised funds for the repairs of the church or synagogue—bought new carpeting, secured new roofs, and added new altars or stained-glass windows to the sanctuaries. In some cases they even earned enough money to build structures on church grounds, such as Sunday school classrooms or parlors and kitchens, thus domesticating the church, transforming churches and synagogues into homelike places that were friendly to families. They did this by using their domestic skills in needlework, baking, and in selling their "fancy goods" at bazaars and entertainments designed to entice the men to empty their pockets and give to the "Ladies' Aid." In these groups, women learned financial skills and managed their own money. Most pastors welcomed such groups, and when male boards of control sought to siphon off the women's funds or undercut their goals, ministers often sided with the women, creating a bond between the pastor and female parishioners.

The role of the pastor, preacher, minister, priest, or rabbi was reserved exclusively for men in most denominations. Occasionally, African American women preached and took up the role of pastor, but in most African American churches, men sought and maintained governance. The tasks of deacons, vestrymen, stewards, and elders were taken up by laymen, who most often handled congregational finances and personnel concerns. Women and men shared some tasks; they filled the choir lofts, and many a budding woman musician made her entrée into the secular musical world through soloist work or by directing choirs. Some women assumed the role of church pianist or organist.

Laywomen served on cemetery committees in greater numbers than men because tending and maintaining graves traditionally constituted women's work that carried over to their parishes or congregations. Before there were mortuaries to perform proper Jewish burials in the South, women of the synagogue prepared the dead for burial. Protestant women raised funds for cemeteries and proper grave maintenance in churchyards, towns, and cities. Small country churches with their own graveyards relied on women to trim away the weeds and plant trees, flowers, and shrubs. The founding and maintenance of cemeteries for fallen Confederate soldiers, as seen in the previous chapter, was an extension of this gender-prescribed woman's role that actually began in the family and extended to churches, synagogues, and patriotic societies such as the Ladies' Memorial Associations.

Women often provided the labor for Sunday school teaching, as children were considered their special province. Laymen also helped with the Sunday schools, but usually as superintendents and administrators. Oscar Farish of Galveston's Trinity Episcopal Church likened his role as Sunday school superintendent to that of a "general at the head of an army, his teachers his lieutenants, and the scholars his soldiers." Sunday school took on an unparalleled importance after the war; it was seen by southerners as an institution capable of rescuing the South from its war weariness, secular influences, the inroads of Catholicism among Protestants, and immorality. Sunday school could train children in the paths of righteousness and "mold the next generation—ultimately the entire South—into an exalted state," argues historian Sally McMillen. As children grew up in the church, reaching pre-adolescent and teenage years, church leaders feared that it was possible to lose these youngsters to secularism unless they continued with programs designed for their specific ages. Again, women became important leaders in youth work, supervising such groups as the Baptist Young People's Union, the Methodist Epworth League, and the Luther League of the American Lutheran Church, to name only a few. A Sunday school class on occasion could become the special province of a particular woman who might teach the same class for twenty-five years or longer. These classes, usually named for the woman founder, and often evolving into adult classes, empowered women teachers who over time outlasted pastors and male governing boards. Thus, women's status in churches improved with their teaching and mentoring contributions. Few pastors or laymen could manage the many tasks associated with religious education without women, who comprised the majority of church members.

Laywomen extended their religious enthusiasm to include missionary work, often in their own cities. They began Sunday schools—actually mission schools for children—in unchurched parts of their cities. The purpose of these mission Sunday schools was to teach children to read religious materials and bring them to conversion. This attracted the parents, which in turn brought pastoral attention, preaching, and eventually the founding of a new church. Thus, women were advance agents in the evangelization of the South. Laywomen's commitment to missions led them to form missionary societies, where they met to inform themselves of the activities of missionaries abroad and to send money, especially to women, in the mission field. Lottie Moon was one such missionary whose life work in China with the Southern Baptist Convention brought funds from laywomen's societies across the South.

When churchwomen organized to help missionaries in foreign lands, their work did not bring them into direct contact with the impoverished, but when they aided home missionaries who worked in towns, communities, or in rural settings, they often became aware of the difficulties of the poor, their inadequate incomes, squalid housing, insufficient food and fuel, meager clothing, and many illnesses. In some churches and synagogues, women formed benevolent societies designed to raise funds for families in desperate straits. The women of these societies often met weekly, sewing dresses, shirts, and aprons, and making dolls to raise money for their charity. They considered supplicants' appeals and recorded the contributions given to families and individuals. Most of the applicants came to church and synagogue benevolent societies not for long-term but for temporary aid to help them through a crisis such as an injury, illness, or layoff. For women such a situation could be dire if they had no male support and found themselves unable to work. On the whole, these congregational relief societies ended up helping more women than men (85 percent of the recipients of aid in Galveston were women), because in the under-institutionalized South with no unemployment insurance and with wages for women being usually two-thirds of men's salaries, women more often faced poverty. Many of those applying for aid were widows or abandoned wives with children, who, because they were mothers, were considered self-sacrificing in their efforts to clothe and feed their families and, therefore, more deserving of charity than unemployed men or even single women. Women's church and synagogue societies served as essential "safety nets," proto-welfare agencies, for the poor and unlucky. In this way, women helped women, and they did so by crossing class and race lines. By organizing benevolent societies and assuming the task of urban poor relief, white middle- and upper-class ladies took their first lessons in civic responsibility.

For African American women the institutions of home and church sustained them in the important transitional period between slavery and freedom. Homes were the first places where black women established their own domain as evidenced in the post–Civil War era when freedpeople began working for themselves. When formerly biracial congregations separated voluntarily, black women soon formed the backbone of their churches, and their presence supported choirs, cemeteries, Sunday schools, youth leagues, home and foreign missionary societies, literary societies, and charitable groups. Most African Americans belonged to the Baptist, Methodist, Presbyterian, Episcopal, African Methodist Episcopal (AME) and African Methodist Episcopal Zion (AME Zion) churches in the South.

Sarah Dudley Pettey, who graduated with distinction from Scotia Seminary in Concord, North Carolina, discovered the powerful role a black woman could play in religious and secular life. Married to AME Zion Bishop Charles Calvin Pettey in 1889, she traveled extensively with her husband in connection with his responsibilities as bishop of Texas, Alabama, and Louisiana, and later bishop of the Allegheny-Ohio Conference. Among the Petteys' official visits, they met with the Archbishop of Canterbury and the American minister to England who presented them at the royal Court of St. James. Upon returning home, Sarah Pettey served as the General Secretary of the denomination's Woman's Home and Foreign Missionary Society. The mother of five children, an accomplished organist, and a fine theological scholar, Sarah Pettey discovered her voice by writing for the *Star of Zion,* the official organ of the AME Zion Church, where she made her greatest contribution. Beginning in 1896, she wrote a column every two weeks that praised women's accomplishments, argued relentlessly for opportunities for women of talent, and applauded when her colleague Mary Small sought ordination as an elder in the church—which was granted. A firm believer in equality between the sexes and the races, Pettey railed against race and gender intolerance, but she praised women as a force for good. "Woman's part in the consummation of any project which has to do with the elevation of mankind is of paramount importance. With her influence eliminated or her work minimized failure is inevitable. This is true regardless of race or nationality. In the civilization and enlightenment of the Negro race its educated women must be the potent factors." As to intolerance toward people on account of race or gender, she had this to say. "Those persons who are disposed to criticize the advanced woman reason from the same analogy as that class of Anglo-Saxons who believe Anglo-Africans should be educated only for manual labor." In declaring women's worth and in extolling equality of rights, Pettey practiced a form of progressive education that gave her readers hope in an era of increasing race oppression.

Whereas white churches offered women members the chance to look outward to home and foreign missions and become immersed in charitable enterprises, black churches served as safe havens from Jim Crow restrictions and forums for the expressions of race and gender equality. There black women found that they could launch vocal protests against discrimination with near impunity. Church members rallied against lynching; pastors preached prolabor union sermons; and after 1909 a multitude of black churches held organizing meetings for the National Association for the Advancement of Colored People (NAACP). Addressing Jim Crow strictures and economic discrimination, black women found ways, both economic and spiritual, to serve their communities. Middle-class African American worshipers followed a genteel code of behavior and expected to be seen as prosperous, energetic, and worthy of respect by their peers and by whites.

Relief and Benevolent Institutions

In southern cities, once women from churches and synagogues saw the true nature of poverty, a number of them moved to create institutions to help those who were most affected by it. Catholic sisters and Protestant and Jewish laywomen founded hospitals, schools, kindergartens, orphanages, homes for the elderly, and rescue homes for prostitutes. Their concern for the impoverished led them to become astute businesswomen. Often they rented a structure and hired the teachers or workers for a kindergarten. Or they raised the money to buy land, hired an architect to design a "home" or facility, and built the necessary structure. Churchwomen brought in the patients, orphans, or elderly women, hired the staff to care for the inmates (a nineteenth-century term for anyone living in an institution), worked out the legalities with the lawyers, and maintained the fundraising and the care of the institution, often through a Board of Lady Managers. They did all this while still unable to vote and, if married, unable to sign contracts. In Richmond, an interdenominational group of churchwomen funded City Mission in 1877 to distribute relief and train poor women in sewing. In Galveston, between 1888 and 1893, a coalition of Protestant (mainly Episcopal and Presbyterian) and Jewish women built four benevolent institutions, two orphanages, a home for elderly women, and a kindergarten for whites, they also helped black churchwomen found a kindergarten. By doing so they found themselves involved publicly in civic welfare concerns.

As a school for young children, the kindergarten was thought to be a useful place to Americanize immigrant children and foster a genteel learning environment for poor children of all races and religions. Churches and synagogues often housed the schools, or sometimes groups of women found space for them near factories, cleaned them, and opened them free of charge for poor children. Women experienced an affinity for the work of creating kindergartens; in their prescribed roles as nurturers of the young, and often as mothers themselves, they projected their concerns for children onto the welfare of future citizens of the South. In Atlanta as early as 1884, the American Methodist Association created a free kindergarten for black children, but its funding ran out, and it did not last. In 1905, however, African American women, at the urging of NAACP founder W.E. B. Du Bois, formed the Gate City Free Kindergarten Association. By 1906 they had opened five kindergartens for black children and by 1917 had educated 3,000 children living in poor neighborhoods. In Charleston, South Carolina, in 1893 white clubwomen may have been among the first in the South to open a free kindergarten for children of factory workers. By 1910 free kindergartens popped up in cities all over the South thanks to church and synagogue sponsorships, fundraising by clubwomen, and teachers from kindergarten training schools. Most middle-class white women enrolled their own children in private kindergartens. Class bias notwithstanding, by 1917 a drive to establish kindergartens in connection with public schools emerged in the South.

Settlement houses were first introduced to the United States by Jane Addams who founded Hull House in Chicago in 1889. By 1900 there were 100 settlement houses in cities across the nation, southern cities included. Settlement houses improved the quality of life for immigrants and working families while providing training for women who later on would be called social workers. Settlement house workers went out into their communities to pay home visits to families, which put these workers in contact with thousands of children each year. Settlement house directors often served as catalysts for other social innovators. Eleanor McMain, who directed Kingsley House in New Orleans, worked to change the state's child adoption and compulsory school attendance laws. Churchwomen also formed Methodist Wesley Houses (settlement houses) in the poorest areas of cities, mostly near factories and black neighborhoods. Day nurseries and kindergartens for working-class families were often associated with settlement houses. In Dallas, by 1901 white women saw to it that four free day nurseries for children of working mothers gave the little ones baths, lunch, and supervision. In 1915 the Kindergarten Association of Dallas founded the city's Neighborhood House, a settlement house for immigrant families. Southern urban women also founded industrial schools for poor women in the years before organized charity, when such groups as United Charities or Community Chest began to fill the need. Women, especially mothers, created a structure for benevolence and charity that paralleled the predominately male structure of politics, government, business, and the professions. All of this was preparation for the next century's Progressive era of reform.

Temperance and Prohibition

Drinking was considered both a moral problem and a male problem. In the nineteenth century that was mostly true, but it also affected women and children. Having a husband who drank could be a curse for many a married woman, who was held under a system of laws called *coverture*. Designed to protect them, these laws had the potential for harming them instead. In most southern states in the late nineteenth century, when a woman married, she gave up the rights that she had possessed as a single woman; her legal status changed from *feme sole* to *feme covert,* and she experienced what scholars call civil death. This demotion for the woman was based on the legal supposition that when two people married, the two became one—and that one was the man. A married woman could not file suit or be sued separately from her husband, keep her own wages, sign contracts, inherit property except through equity court, sign contracts, or alienate (sell) the family property. She had no legal recourse if her husband drank up the family wages or decided to sell the family home or lands to pay his debts, except in certain situations where a father or a widowed mother had written an inheritance clause in a will to protect the daughter in marriage, or in certain cases where the court asked the woman if she would allow her husband to sell her inherited property. If a couple divorced, custody of the children was more often awarded to the husband. Thus an intemperate man had inordinate power over his wife and children; battering was not considered a crime, and drunken husbands often beat their wives and children. Drinking also led to crime and violence outside the home. The Woman's Christian Temperance Union's (WCTU) message to white and black women was to organize against alcohol sale and consumption in order to protect their homes, save their families, and safeguard their communities, a perspective that did not challenge the patriarchal system head on but still attempted to defend women and children.

When Frances Willard became president of the WCTU in 1879, it was fast becoming the nation's largest middle-class women's organization. Willard wanted to make it even larger and proposed to organize southern women into the union. In 1881 she began the first of several trips to the South, where she advised women—black and white—on how to organize unions (local chapters). Emerging out of evangelical Christian roots, and thus appealing to many southern women, the WCTU became the first national organization that women from the South joined. The spreading message to fight "demon alcohol" came with another message: women could take hold of their destinies and seek change for their families and for womankind. Belle Kearney, who would become a state senator in Mississippi in 1924, greatly admired Frances Willard, expressing this the first time she heard her speak.

> Miss Willard . . . was the peerless orator, the gracious Christian, the marvelous reformer who shall stand forth in history until 'there shall be no more curse' and 'the kingdoms of this world are become the kingdoms of our Lord, and of His Christ.' While she was speaking a vision arose before me of the glad day when not one woman only, but women of all lands shall have entered into the *human* heritage—as man's equal in society, church and state.

Willard's tour served as a starting point for reconciliation between southern and northern women, and, as it was an extension of women's religious activism, it did not take women out of their prescribed roles. The WCTU brought black and white together, albeit in separate statewide unions. It also heralded women's emergence into politics.

To seek temperance—encouraging people not to drink alcohol—and then prohibition, which required legislation, was to become involved in the world of politics. The WCTU's goal was to persuade state legislators to outlaw the production or sale of alcohol. By 1911, the WCTU had more than 245,000 members, and its success was measured by the fact that in 1918 just about every southern state had passed prohibition laws. Christian women who actively campaigned for prohibition under the white banner of the WCTU were aided in their cause by the disfranchisement measures taken by southern state legislatures at the turn of the century. By restricting the vote to those who could pay a poll tax or pass a literacy test, ethnic minorities were at a disadvantage in prohibition elections. African Americans, Mexican Americans, and some Europeans such as German, Czech, and Italian voters across the South most often opposed prohibition, but with voting restrictions the electorate was reduced to middle-class southern whites, many of whom were strong supporters of prohibition. Then World War I with its patriotic, anti-German, antidrinking sentiments added to the prohibition fervor. The South supported the Eighteenth Amendment, which called for national prohibition and was ratified in January 1919.

For women involved in the WCTU, prohibition was only the end game. Frances Willard and others enlarged the organization's mission to include many other issues vital to middle-class reformers—ending prostitution and political corruption, fighting the spread of venereal diseases, establishing homes for abandoned women and children, founding reform schools for youthful offenders, and improving conditions in jails and prisons, including adding matrons in women's prisons and asylums. The WCTU advocated labor reform (particularly of the convict lease system), industrial schools for girls, and city welfare work; it believed in founding kindergartens and eliminating child labor. In 1893 it condemned lynching. The most radical of all its proposals was support for woman suffrage, and some WCTU chapters never did get on the wagon for women's right to vote. Still, by working for the WCTU cause, southern women were learning the lessons of social responsibility and loving it. The WCTU addressed so many of the ills of society that to many it opened a new world. To Belle Kearney from Mississippi, the WCTU was "the golden key that unlocked the prison door of pent-up possibilities" for women in the South.

For white and black women the specter of black men drinking was fearsome but for different reasons. Whites assumed that when black men became intoxicated, they lost control of their faculties and "reverted" to their baser natures and the desire to sexually assault white women. Black women worried that if their menfolk drank and committed petty or more violent crimes, they would be subject to harsh reprisals, even lynching. These concerns led black women to form their own WCTU societies, in part to convince men to vote for prohibition, to protect the home, to defend the reputation of the race, and to advance women into leadership positions in an organization with a national bearing. The result was limited cooperation between WCTU members along race lines in several southern states. In North Carolina and in Texas white and black women in the 1880s formed separate unions of the WCTU, but they cooperated within the statewide structure. In 1897 Lucy Thurman, president of the National Department of Colored Work of the WCTU, came to Texas, where she organized fifteen unions and a state organization for African American women. The fact that white and black unions, although separate, existed under one umbrella organization represented a momentous leap in interracial cooperation (working together to solve common problems). The efforts of African American women in the WCTU also had a lasting effect on their own vision of the South and should be considered a forerunner to multiple organizations and societies devoted to the well-being of black communities.

The mission of WCTU members was to enlist black and white male voters to support prohibition amendments to the state constitution or to vote "dry" at the polling place. As long as black men remained voters, the cooperation between white and black unions lasted, but beginning in the late 1890s, disfranchisement laws took the ballot out of the hands of black men. In a myopic worldview, white women surmised that if black men could not vote, there was no point in black women soliciting their menfolk to vote "dry" in prohibition elections and thus no reason for white women to work with black WCTU women. Voting and politics, influenced by white supremacy, thus affected the lives of women in the South in myriad ways.

White women gained entrée into the political whirl when they lobbied senators and representatives to vote for prohibition. After screwing up their collective courage to speak out, they made their way in small groups to the statehouse, where they found that many elected officials kept them waiting, listened politely (or not), and sent them on their way with no promises. Women were not voters and therefore could not remove the incumbent from office if he refused to accede to their demands. These rebuffs angered many WCTU members and made them think about their own voting rights. Thus, for reasons of expediency, among other rationales, the woman suffrage movement began tentatively to make inroads in the South by the 1890s.

The Farmers' Alliances and Women's Education

Women in the South by the 1880s and 1890s found more than one avenue toward collective reform activism. Farmers' Alliances, created in 1877 and blooming into the Populist party in the 1890s, became the most important political reform movement of the late nineteenth century. Alliance-Populist ideas forced changes in Americans' attitude toward the role of government when farmers argued that runaway industrialism and unregulated economies were destroying their future as farmers. The Alliance and Populist movements also allowed women a fairly sizable role in speaking their minds and formulating ideas on a future South free of gendered restraints. As Katie Moore of North Carolina articulated in the *Progressive Farmer,* "This is the only order that allows us equal privileges to the men; we certainly should appreciate the privilege and prove to the world that we are worthy to be considered on an equal footing with them."

Moore had a point; other organizations that advanced women into the public realm either did not espouse equality, such as churches, or, as with the WCTU, voiced equality but did not admit men. The Alliances held out the promise of women's political activism alongside that of men. One-quarter of the Farmers' Alliance members were women and in some localities as much as one-half. Women voted on potential members, held office in the Alliance, wrote speeches for the Alliance newspapers, and endorsed prohibition. They also sought better education for farm families and agricultural extension programs to teach and inform their daughters in "home economics." Their influence gave voice to the demands of farm laborers by dignifying their work and their search for a better life for their children. Populist women articulated the concerns and demands of the members and, in doing so, provided a base among themselves for reform efforts in the twentieth century.

The Farmers' Alliances are not often credited with agitating for women's education, but they did. Favoring agricultural and normal programs (teacher training), they sought to benefit "the forgotten woman" by rallying for state-supported colleges for women. Among the first universities to admit women was the University of Texas in 1883 and the University of Mississippi in 1882, but the programs there were so restricted that the state legislature in 1884 chartered the Mississippi Industrial Institute and College for the Education of White Girls. It opened in 1885 and offered a curriculum primarily for the acquisition of practical education and domestic skills eventually leading to home economics. Such skills as dressmaking, cooking, drawing, and stenography were among the many course offerings. South Carolina followed suit with a Normal and Industrial College for the Education of White Girls at Winthrop chartered in 1891 that led to a four-year program for teachers. Teacher-training institutes for women seemed a good idea to most southern legislators, and between 1889 and 1908 Georgia, North Carolina, Alabama, Texas, Florida, and Oklahoma chartered state colleges for women.

At the other end of the class spectrum were the private seminaries and colleges for white women whose families had the means to send them away for a refined education before marriage. Often southern colleges for women qualified as finishing schools rather than as first-rate academic institutions. Most private universities in the South that men attended were reluctant to admit women, but Baylor University in 1886 became coeducational with different degrees for women; a woman could earn a Maid of Philosophy, Maid of Arts, and a Mistress of Polite Literature in 1890. Even with the establishment of colleges for women in the Northeast—Vassar (1861), Wellesley (1870), Smith (1871), Bryn Mawr (1885), Barnard (1889), and Radcliffe (1894)—only a few women from the South were able to attend them. Five southern women's colleges in 1917 were able to meet the standards for accreditation set by the Southern Association of Colleges—Agnes Scott, Converse College, Florida State, Goucher, and Randolph-Macon, plus the coordinate colleges, H. Sophie Newcomb and Westhampton. Coordinate colleges were female colleges associated with male colleges, but the women kept their own faculty, buildings, and administration. Sophie Newcomb, founded by Josephine Louise Newcomb in 1887, was the first such school in the South. Associated with Tulane University, it gave white women students a sound education in the liberal arts. By 1909, two-thirds of the members of the faculty at Sophie Newcomb College were women, shedding light on their accomplishments in academia and modeling leadership roles for its future graduates. For some elite and middle-class southern women of the generation born in the 1870s, the first step into public life started with higher education. For others unable to attend a college or university, it began with churches, benevolent institutions, and women's clubs.

Certainly true for black middle-class women and those who aspired to middle-class status was the importance of higher education as well as church activism. According to historian Cynthia Neverdon-Morton, "using educational institutions and churches as bases of operation, the women brought together the three institutions that were the mainstays of black life in the United States—home, church, and school." For black women to advance their goals, they needed higher education.

In every southern state, education became the critical forerunner to reform, improvement, and the ability to help others. The solution to solving problems of underemployment, inadequate health care, poor housing, and limited opportunities was education for everyone, and this would begin with and through women's education. Learning and then teaching self-reliance would have a multiplier effect in the community, and black women's energies could be used to further the goals of the race. With regard to higher education, African American males did not have the same ambiguity about educating black women that white men did about educating white women. Most black students attended co-educational colleges and universities, which contributed to historian Glenda Gilmore's assessment that the experience created for those families "more equitable domestic partnerships and an active place for women in public life." Middle-class African American women found greater freedom from negative male opinion and possibly more acceptance of their public activism. The problem for most young women was money and the time and place to obtain higher education.

In the years after the Civil War northern religious denominations and the American Missionary Association helped support education for African Americans in the South. Many denominations and northern interests participated in and maintained these institutions; among them in 1867 the Presbyterian

Church founded Scotia Seminary (for women) in Concord and Biddle Memorial University (now Johnson C. Smith University) in Charlotte, both in North Carolina. The Protestant Episcopal Church in 1867 opened St. Augustine's College in Raleigh. The American Missionary Association created Fisk University in Nashville in 1866 and Tougaloo College in 1869 to train black teachers in Mississippi. The Freedmen's Aid Society of the Methodist Episcopal Church founded Clark University in Atlanta in 1869. African American denominations also opened colleges; the AME Zion Church, for example, established Livingstone College in Salisbury, North Carolina, in 1880. Altogether some forty institutions of higher learning offered training and education to African Americans after the war, and all of them encouraged their graduates to share their training for the "uplift" of the race.

One model for teacher training that also taught industrial education (building, brick making, and domestic skills for women) began with Hampton Normal Agricultural Institute in Virginia founded in 1870. Booker T. Washington, its most outstanding graduate, went on to found his own teacher training/industrial education school, Tuskegee Institute in Alabama in 1881. By 1915, however, academic standards had fallen in these two institutions to the point that graduates were unable to qualify for teaching positions. In part this may be explained by the role of northern philanthropists who had discovered black education as a charitable outlet. They attached strings to their gifts, however: black institutions for the most part had to accept a curriculum that included industrial education for males and domestic training for women. Mary McLeod Bethune, a graduate of Scotia Seminary, took advantage of this emphasis when in 1904 she founded the Daytona Educational and Industrial Training School for Negro Girls, which eventually became Bethune-Cookman College. Recognizing that domestic training could lead to better homes for black families, Bethune, nonetheless, encouraged simultaneous teacher-training for women. Rather than ending up in domestic service, however, after graduation some young women found careers as volunteer community leaders, teachers, nurses, librarians, social workers, and businesswomen.

Among the colleges and universities that promoted a classical liberal education (mathematics, science, philosophy, and ancient and modern languages) were Howard University in Washington, D.C. (1867), Fisk University in Nashville (1866), and Atlanta University (1865). The debate that began between W.E.B. Du Bois and Booker T. Washington regarding the best means for African Americans to achieve economic and legal equity in America spilled over into education. It concerned the educational goals of African Americans to seek classical learning and legal equality or learn manual trades and accommodate to southern whites. By 1925, it was generally agreed that both types of education were necessary. Noted black intellectual Alain Locke declared that the two were mutually supportive.

Professional schools also offered training to meet the specific needs of the black community. Shaw University in Raleigh (1865) and Meharry Medical College in Nashville (1876) prepared African Americans for careers in law and medicine. It was clear that for women at Tuskegee Institute, for example, the nurses-training program was essential to help with the shortage of trained medical caregivers, and the Tuskegee Hospital benefited directly from the program. Hubbard Hospital and Meharry Medical College trained women as nurses and doctors, one of whom, Dr. Mary Susan Smith Moore, made her way to Galveston, Texas, and in 1906 opened a surgical hospital for African Americans. She named it Hubbard Sanitarium for her professor and mentor. Often urban problems inspired institutional responses, and in 1920 the School of Social Work grew from the need to address difficulties in the neighborhoods surrounding Atlanta University. By 1916, 93,000 students were enrolled in black institutions of higher education in the South. Equally important, however, was the fact that each college or university became not only a core of intellectual stimulation for students but also an important resource for community work, a point not lost on its women graduates.

College instructors instilled in their students a sense of mission, a responsibility to use education as a gift to others and to form outreach programs and community services. They also emphasized the importance of living up to the model of masculinity fostered by such leaders as Booker T. Washington, and femininity modeled by women such as Mary Church Terrell, who would become the first president of the first national association of African American women's clubs. Postgraduate conferences at the leading black schools continued educating adults and informed them of the critical issues facing African Americans. As a result educated women knew they were facing more than just self-education; they could expect to confront possible white resistance to their postgraduate reforming efforts. As a support to black pride and consciousness, and especially to women teachers, historian Woodson G. Carter with Jesse E. Moorland created the Association for the Study of Negro Life and History in 1915. After 1924 E. Franklin Frazier, a scholar of the African American experience, urged black colleges and universities to offer classes in the study of African American history, literature, music, and sociology. Thus did black high schools, colleges, and universities offer African American culture and history classes just as a new generation of students were seeking higher education—and well before the black studies movement of the 1970s.

Obtaining higher education allowed black and white women and men the training and skills necessary to take on social problems endemic to the South. White women struggled with the prescription of the Southern Lady, for it potentially limited their participation in public life after graduation. Men expected women's education to be useful in their roles as wives and mothers, as keepers of the home fires, and as culture carriers for the family. Prescribed gender roles for men included bringing home a better income, presiding over the household as head of the family, and pursuing societal or political obligations, if so inclined. Middle-class white women who worked outside the home—some became teachers and professionals—knew well the demands the workplace put on women, and they recognized that factory women were not accorded the privileged class position of Southern Lady. Teachers, using their status as "Ladies" *and* working women, became the fiercest advocates of laws protecting working-class women. The Southern Lady image allowed white women access to certain realms allotted to men, as ladies were covered by a cloak of purity and honor. Thus white women found, for example, that they could march into mayors' offices, attend county commissioner meetings, and inspect markets and dairies in the name of motherhood and family, arguing that it was their duty to protect the home and their children from impure food. In these cases, white women activists used the Southern Lady image to their advantage.

As women sought broader applications for their education and interests through voluntary and reform associations, they brought with them an image of ladyhood that historian Anastatia Sims labels "the power of femininity." Peculiar to the South was the concept of the Southern Lady, which held white women to an exacting ideal of gentility and soft spokenness. The ladyhood ideal could be useful to women who wanted to change male opinion toward reform and open more opportunities for women's expanded public presence. Black and white women, when needed, used the concept of ladyhood to promote Progressive reforms in their communities and in the state; conservative women used it to maintain elitism, support the Lost Cause, and oppose woman suffrage, which they believed would dilute the essential differences that bolstered their privileges. So the power of femininity could work both ways, but the important gains made by southern ladies included access to public places in streets, in town halls, and in state capitols as petitioners of reforms.

Black women could not always depend on being granted Southern Ladyhood status, however, and some found this debilitating. But other black educated women did not allow prejudice to impede their activist agendas. Whereas middle-class white women were assumed to be ladies, educated black women challenged white racist stereotypes of blacks' inferior moral character and intellectual acumen. They turned their education to good advantage, teaching young people in schools, tending the sick in hospitals, providing Sunday school lessons, joining clubs and civic associations, founding community organizations to combat inferior conditions, and supporting woman suffrage—all the while advocating pride in their race. African American women found that their best chance to succeed came by embracing the "politics of respectability." Education was the key. Black middle-class women challenged white supremacist assumptions by conforming to the highest standards of gentility and ladylike decorum. Finding power in numbers, white and black middle-class women in separate organizations sought solidarity, strength, and direction for their budding political and social activism in the women's club movement.

The Women's Club Movement

The women's club movement developed in the 1890s and spread out across the South like a storm. Although made up of individual clubs, the national organization served as an institution of practical higher education for middle-class women, many of whom did not attend college or university. Middle-class black women organized the National Association of Colored Women (NACW) in 1896, and adopted the motto "Lifting as We Climb," an indication of their goal to advance economically and culturally, bringing others with them. By 1916 the NACW included 300 clubs. According to Mary Church Terrell, first president of the NACW, black women carried the double burden of race and sex prejudice. From Texas to Virginia, they introduced club programs in every state and found ways not only to better their communities but also to combat the detrimental effects of racism. For white women, the club movement solidified nationally into the General Federation of Women's Clubs (GFWC) in 1890 with 495 clubs and 100,000 members. Unlike the WCTU, which at least began as an organization that encouraged membership from black and white women, the GFWC did not allow black membership—a step backwards in race relations.

Women's clubs educated their members, trained them in pubic speaking, gave them projects to fulfill in public places, and prepared them for the future with civic and reform challenges. Although some women belonged to both the WCTU and a woman's club, for the most part these two groups did not overlap, and the woman's club movement overshadowed the WCTU after 1900. Women's clubs generally began in the 1880s and 1890s as literary societies, in which women studied literature, music, or art. The members presented book reviews and prepared papers to one another as if in a university class. Once embarked on a combined course of self-improvement, self-understanding, and learning, women at the turn of the century could not ignore societal problems and often took on various social reform projects. However, they sometimes toned down their rhetoric in the face of blatant sex discrimination, preferring instead to impress men with their Southern Ladyhood, their list of accomplishments for the social good, or as part of a feminine strategy to garner male support.

By 1900 the women's club movement shifted its emphasis from literature and learning to the pressing social and political needs of towns, cities, and states. No modern topic seemed to escape their notice after 1912. Settlement houses, urban beautification, libraries, changes in municipal government, juvenile courts, reform schools, the convict lease system, labor conditions (child labor especially), prostitution, illiteracy, clean streets, pure food and drugs, educational reform, married women's property laws, age of consent for girls, and woman suffrage all eventually came under their purview. There was practically no social project, movement, or concern that organized clubwomen did not address. For many clubwomen, eager to make a difference in their communities, the Progressive movement was exactly what they needed.

Finding women's roles in the origins of the Progressive movement reaches inevitably to home and hearth first and then to church and synagogue. As mentioned, the first passage for middle-class women into public life—and reform—often unfolded in these settings. As social institutions, however, religious congregations offered limited public roles to women, yet the call to serve in the name of faith led believers to the aid of others, especially less fortunate women and children.

From these roots emerged a focus by middle-class women on the plight of their communities, but in the humanitarian sense, it concentrated on dependents and their needs. From the creation of benevolent institutions to the formation of a welfare state constitutes a huge historical leap, but in the interim the Progressive movement, often led by women, strained against the dominant forces of economic and political conservatism and set the twentieth-century South on the road to major social reforms. Because the movement largely drew on the resources of the middle classes, higher education—most readily attainable to women in this class—also provided impetus for reform. As institutions opened their doors to white and black women, and as educators taught them about the nature of society around them, their eyes widened to the results of unbridled industrial growth as well as the failings of post-Reconstruction Redeemer governments dominating southern states. Education of another kind emerged through the women's club movement in the 1890s, and what women had learned in high school and colleges they now could apply in practical ways through these groups to aid their communities and their states. Reform movements in the South—assembled under one immense rubric as Progressivism—emerged with women among its most invested activists.

Union soldiers searched southern homes for weapons and at times stole food, destroyed stock, ripped clothing to shreds, and burned houses. "Searching for Arms in a Rebel's House in Southern Maryland," *Harper's Weekly,* November 16, 1861. *Museum of the Confederacy, Richmond.*

Between 1862 and 1864, 16,000 slaves ran to the Union lines for protection. Congress determined that as "contraband" they were not to be returned to their owners. Cumberland Landing, Va. Group of "contrabands" at Foller's house. *Library of Congress, LC-B811-383 [P&P].*

Right: Voting rights for black men became a principal means of asserting their manhood in the Reconstruction era. "Significant election scene at Washington, June 3, 1867" *Harper's Weekly,* June 22, 1867. *Library of Congress, LC-USZ62-100971.*

SIGNIFICANT ELECTION SCENE AT WASHINGTON, June 3, 1867.—[Sketched by A. W. M'Callum.]

Below: Laundering was one of the most arduous of tasks; it required hauling water, stoking fires, scrubbing, wringing, and finally ironing. Freedwomen and children washing clothes on the McFadden Plantation, Circleville, Texas. *Austin Public Library N1600 pica, 05496.*

Right: The Daughter of the Confederacy, Varina Anne "Winnie" Davis, c. 1890. *Museum of the Confederacy, Richmond.*

Left: Ida B. Wells wrote about the hypocrisy of lynching in her Memphis newspaper, *Free Speech and Headlight*. In 1892 she authored *Southern Horrors: Lynch Laws in All Its Phases. Special Collections Research Center, University of Chicago Library.*

Above: Christian women actively campaigned for Prohibition under the white banner of the Woman's Christian Temperance Union. Women and Children in White at the Lufkin, Texas, W.C.T.U. Parade, 1915. *Kurth Memorial Library, Lufkin, Texas.*

Right: The Texas legislature in 1901 chartered the Girls Industrial College [in 1905 College of Industrial Arts] in Denton, Texas. Here a student combines home economics and chemistry. Analysis of Vinegar by Lillian Kiber, a chemistry student at the College of Industrial Arts now Texas Woman's University, Denton, Texas, 1912. *Woman's Collection, Texas Woman's University.*

In 1908 Lugenia Burns Hope called on friends and neighbors to form the Neighborhood Union, which became a model for Progressive era community improvement organizations. Lugenia Burns Hope (second from right, first row), and members of the Neighborhood Union, Atlanta. *Special Collections and Archives, Atlanta University Center, Robert Woodruff Library.*

In 1906 the Louisiana Legislature passed a Child Labor Act that allowed women to become factory inspectors. Jean Gordon served as one until 1911. Factory Inspectors Past and Present. From left to right: Ella Haas, State Factory Inspector, Dayton, Ohio; Mary Malone, State Factory Inspector Ten-Hour Law, Delaware. Florence Kelley, Chief State Factory Inspector of Illinois, 1893-97. Jean Gordon, State Factories Inspector, Parish of New Orleans, 1908. Madge Nave, Factory Inspector, Louisville, Ky., Martha D. Gould, Factories Inspector, Parish of New Orleans. March 1914. Lewis W. Hine, photographer. *From the Lewis Hine Collection. Library of Congress. LC –DIG-nclc-04942.*

Young girl helping her sister in the mill. New Cotton Mills, North Carolina, 1908. *Library of Congress, LC –DIG-nclc-01544.*

A spinner in the Mollahan Mills, Newberry, South Carolina, 1908. *Library of Congress. LC –DIG-nclc-01472. Both photographs by Lewis W. Hine.*

The Nineteenth Amendment gave women the right to vote but was not ratified until 1920. This map shows the states that allowed women voting rights before 1920. Most southern states did not grant women the franchise, but those that did ratify the Nineteenth Amendment were critical to its passage.

Above: Equal Suffrage League of Virginia float in 1918 Liberty Bond Parade, Richmond, VA. *Special Collections and Archives, James Branch Cabell Library, Virginia Commonwealth University, Richmond.*

Left: Zora Neale Hurston, beating the hountar, or mama drum. She was considered part of the Harlem Renaissance, but her roots were in northern Florida. *Library of Congress. LC-USZ62-108549.*

Above: Charlotte Hawkins Brown, founder and principal of Palmer Memorial Institute in Sedalia, North Carolina, is shown here (center) with members of her faculty in 1907. After ratification of the Nineteenth Amendment she urged black women to vote, and at the Woman's Inter-Racial Conference in Memphis, October 8, 1920, she admonished women to unite against lynching. *Courtesy of The North Carolina State Archives.*

Right: Jessie Daniel Ames, founder of the Association of Southern Women for the Prevention of Lynching. *Austin Public Library.*

Jeffersontown, Kentucky. Preparing cans to be heated and cooked. The Jefferson County community cannery, started by the WPA (Work Progress Administration). June 1943. Photographer: Howard R. Hollem. *Library of Congress, LC-USW3-034352-C.*

Woman washing her clothes with a hand wringer on her farm at El Indio, Texas. March 1939. Photographer: Russell Lee. *Library of Congress, LC-USF33-012098-M1.*

Woman of the High Plains "If You Die, You're Dead–That's All." Texas Panhandle, 1938. Dorothea Lange (1895–1965), [working for the Farm Security Administration] gelatin silver print, 1960s, *Copyright © The Dorothea Lange Collection, Oakland Museum of California, City of Oakland. Oakland Museum of California.*

Emma Tenayuca, fist raised, leads a demonstration on the steps of the San Antonio City Hall in 1937. *San Antonio Light Collection, University of Texas Institute of Texan Cultures, San Antonio.*

Four Prairie View [University] graduates who are officers in the Women's Army Auxiliary Corps [WAAC], holding the rank of Third Officer – the equivalent of a Second Lieutenant's commission in the army. All are members of the first class of officers commissioned at the First WAAC Training Center at Fort Des Moines. Left to right are Anne Lois Brown, Ruth L. Freeman, Geraldine Bright, and Alice Marie Jones. From 1943 Prairie View College Panther, yearbook. *Archives and Special Collections, Prairie View A&M University.*

As many as 1,000 civilian women joined the Women Airforce Service Pilots (WASP) and ferried aircraft from factories to bases. Nancy Batson Crews from Alabama joined the Women's Auxiliary Ferrying Squadron WAFS (later the WASP), here seen at Newcastle Army Air Force Base, Wilmington, Delaware. *The Woman's Collection, Texas Woman's University.*

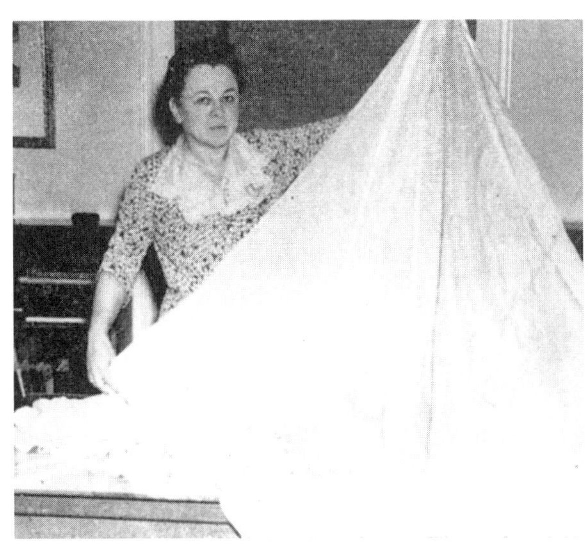

Miss Ethel Foster holds a parachute made by salvaging stockings. From Texas Federation of Women's Clubs, *Women at Work for Universal Peace, 1942-45 Year Book. The Woman's Collection, Texas Woman's University.*

CHAPTER FOUR

Southern Women and the Progressive Spirit

In the aftermath of the nineteenth century, black and white southern women found themselves at the crossroads of a new era, one that could maintain traditional values alongside innovative and exciting change. Choices widened for urban women as they faced the new century, and some realized they could not sit still while so much ferment surrounded them. Engaging in the role of "New Women" meant taking risks individually and joining with others to seek common cause. Southern women found themselves powerful at a time when their voices needed to be heard and their actions, concentrated as they were on humanitarian concerns, needed to be taken. The political importance of women and their effect on reform in the Progressive era challenges traditional political history—once considered only men's (and only voters') history. Women's energy and effectiveness, their efforts and victories led to reforming ideas and eventually to state policy. This activism, which often began in churches and moved through women's organizations into the public forum, can be seen among both black and white middle-class women, although their lives and their projects rarely intersected. Finding themselves in a rapidly changing region thanks to industrialization, urbanization, and the consolidation of power in the hands of a fairly well-entrenched white entrepreneurial elite, organized women sought solutions to problems according to their racial outlook.

Southern Progressivism

Progressivism was a national reform movement that started as early as 1895 and ended some time after World War I. At the turn of the twentieth century a diffuse progressive movement emerged mostly among the middle classes in cities across the nation. Men and women, black and white, who were born after the Civil War and had grown up during the time of the industrial revolution, came to see the nation as troubled due to the dominance of wealthy capitalists and the hardship of laboring people, child workers in factories and mines, women overworking themselves in two jobs (home and paid work), and the great unequal distribution of wealth. Government at all levels had failed to deal with these and other social abuses. Progressives wanted to take action to curb the excesses of corporate consolidation and correct the worst ills of industrialization—the exploitation of workers, children, and the environment. Nationally, those who considered themselves Progressives belonged to both parties, but in the South, the Democratic party controlled state governments. Southern Progressives, some of them coming from the Populist party, often challenged the old Democratic party regulars.

Historians have debated the nature of Progressivism in the South. Most concur that southern Progressivism was more conservative and its achievements more modest in comparison to the national movement. Southern historian C. Vann Woodward argued that Progressivism in the South was "for whites only." Other historians agreed but noted that the movement was for middle-class whites only; poor whites were often left out entirely. Previously historians debated the origins of Progressivism and its relationship to Populism, its urban-rural splits or connections, and its achievements and failings. Progressive men often focused on the struggle to level the market and political playing fields; they sought good roads, good government, and the regulation of industries, especially the railroads. Introducing white women Progressive reformers to the debate began in earnest in 1970 with Anne Firor Scott's *The Southern Lady,* which portrayed white women both as activists and as recipients. African American women and reform in the Progressive era remained virtually invisible until studies by Cynthia Neverdon-Morton and Glenda Gilmore appeared in 1989 and 1996. To say that Progressivism in the South was for (or by) whites only denies the important contributions black women made to the movement as they sought adequate funding for education, social programs for their communities, and justice for the searing pain of racism. African American women did double duty with respect to reform and race apart from white women who did not suffer racial discrimination (although some experienced discrimination due to gender and class). The study of southern women and gender as part of the history of Progressivism changes what was already a complex movement into a rich multiracial and varied social reform era. Women Progressives focused on deterring the dominance of capitalists by emphasizing human concerns and demanding state protection and regulation for the sake of families and individuals. While men and women often worked side by side on such campaigns as prison reform, child labor regulation, education, and public health, there were some reform campaigns, such as good roads, in which women seldom engaged. As often is the case, gender prescribed the areas of strongest interest for women: protection of children, families, women, and individual workers.

Women and Municipal Housekeeping

In the South, one of the great sparks of progressive reform came from the growth of large to middle-size cities in which entire industrial and commercial zones thrived. The industrial spurt of the late nineteenth century had transformed small villages into towns and towns into metropolises. The growth of southern cities outpaced urban expansion in the rest of the nation, even though the majority of the South's population (75 percent) still lived in rural areas in 1920. (The region would not see a majority urban population until the 1950s.) One example of rapid urbanization, however, can be seen in Texas, where in the first two decades of the twentieth century the three leading cities (Houston, Dallas, and San Antonio) doubled in population. Cities such as New Orleans, Atlanta, and Birmingham still outflanked other metropolises of the South in terms of size, but there were proportionately fewer folks living in urban areas in those states. Still, everywhere that factories, mills, plants, and commercial life existed, a middle-class evolved that included potential leaders for a Progressive movement. Women accounted for a sizable proportion of this leadership.

Some of the pressing problems that southern Progressives addressed included conditions in cities, and clubwomen led the campaigns for municipal housekeeping. Southern women used the argument that the modern mother had to pay attention to the city where she and her children lived; thus motherhood encouraged women to become activists. If they were to be good mothers, how could their concerns for their families stop at the household door? Their worries carried them into the streets, markets, schools, factories, courts, and prisons. By their logic, southern women felt that they had a collective duty to search out and solve urban problems. Across the South women's clubs served as a base of support to challenge male city leaders who may have been slow to challenge market forces. With or without men, women organized campaigns for reform, sought the aid of city leadership, and argued for safe drinking water, pure food and milk, clean streets, alleys, and beaches, decent parks and playgrounds, antispitting ordinances, well-baby clinics, milk stations and tuberculosis clinics for children, good schools with indoor plumbing, hot lunch programs, and annual physical examinations of children by a school nurse.

The absence in the South of government regulation of pure food and milk, and the need to enact other measures to protect public health gave women greater opportunities for public policymaking outside of formal political offices. Although governments at all levels in the South balked at many of the proposed changes, women nonetheless, most often under the aegis of women's organizations, took it upon themselves either to seek reforms or to act as if they constituted regulatory agencies. Women often stepped in where no governmental body existed. Eventually this would lead to what historian Paula Baker called "domestic politics."

By the turn of the century, scientists had discovered the role of bacteria—"the germ theory"—in disease and had identified the microbes for such deadly illnesses as diphtheria, scarlet fever, typhoid fever, infant diarrhea, and bovine tuberculosis, which could be found in milk and other foods. Armed with this information women stepped up the pressure on food and milk suppliers to produce wholesome goods, and the cause worked right into the women's activist agenda.

In Houston, women formed a local branch of the "Housewives' League" to lobby for the enforcement of sanitation in bakeries, dairies, and markets. They established a boycott system for unclean shops and dairies. In Galveston women formed the Women's Health Protective Association, which accomplished the same job, inspecting dairy herds and the milking process, publishing black lists of unclean dairies, pestering politicians, and in 1913 commissioning a sanitation survey of the city. After five years of lobbying city government for pure milk, Galveston women finally convinced city commissioners to enact stricter sanitation ordinances against the dairies, which led to the pasteurization, grading, and cooling of milk, and tuberculosis testing in dairy cattle. Dairymen took the Galveston women to court, where lawyers ridiculed the women's housekeeping standards, but in the end their campaign for clean milk prevailed. As milk and clean water were essential for children, these efforts led to lower infant mortality rates.

In Dallas, energetic reforming women led the fight for a water filtration plant and saw the need for milk stations that supplied inspected milk and gave it away to poor mothers and children. These welfare stations were proto-health clinics offering medical services to the indigent, including medicines, without charge. In southern cities, such efforts often led to city-supported children's hospitals and tuberculosis sanitariums. The links between the family and society were also forged through the National Home Economics Association, which directly influenced women's roles in municipal housekeeping. Domestic science courses at universities introduced black and white women to advanced concepts of hygiene for the home and community, and, bolstered by the support of women's clubs, led to enforcement of the pure food law by volunteer women inspectors.

Since germs and disease knew no race limits, whites began to voice their health concerns for entire cities, not just for white neighborhoods. African Americans, for years, had complained that the unfair allocation of resources led to shoddy streets and alleys and dangerous sanitary conditions in their neighborhoods. Despite obvious strides against disease made by improved sanitation, some white campaigners used racist charges, accusing black maids, washerwomen, and male servants of bringing bacteria and disease into white homes. Distrust of black health led to civic campaigns to clean up or improve black neighborhoods. The most successful city cleanup campaigns, however, occurred when black and white women's groups worked cooperatively, since both shared common concerns about neighborhood cleanliness and public health.

When Lula Spalding Kelsey founded the Salisbury [North Carolina] Colored Women's Civic League in 1913, she pushed the black community to act on its own, spurring cleanup drives. Kelsey was a businesswoman, wife of a barber, and mother of eight children. She managed a funeral home as well as an insurance business and made them prosper at a time when black-owned mortuaries and insurance companies were among the most independent enterprises—in African American neighborhoods. Kelsey brimmed with energy, faith in human nature, and a desire for a better future for her children. After Kelsey founded the Women's Civic League, she presided over it for twenty years, while tending to her growing family, her own business, and helping her husband in his barbershop. Among the goals of the civic league was improved public health, which this undertaker knew something about. The league's first encounter with white women came through a citywide cleanup day organized by white clubwomen in 1913. Earlier attempts by whites to engage the black community had failed, but when the white clubwomen introduced Lula Kelsey to the city's leaders, they realized that cooperation—not coercion—was the only way to successfully accomplish the task. The joint cleanup day depended upon the cooperation of women in the black community and led to a yearly event and an increase in interracial contact. Eventually, the Women's Civic League became a member of the city's Associated Charities, which in turn included blacks in fundraising and the referrals of charity cases. Historian Glenda Gilmore argues that this breakthrough was a crack in the wall of white supremacy and allowed a woman like Lula Kelsey to become a diplomat to the white community. A woman rather than a black male leader had a better chance of acceptance by whites after racist rhetoric had vilified and disfranchised black men before the turn of the century. Now African American women built on the opportunity to forge lasting interracial contacts with whites who needed their cooperation.

Despite some areas of interracial cooperation, the truth was that African American women faced greater needs as well as obstacles to implementing reform. There were some successes, however. More than 100 black women reformers from the Phyllis Wheatley Club in New Orleans founded a sanitarium in 1896 for black patients and nurses-in-training, the Flint-Goodridge Hospital, one of the only private facilities for African Americans in that city. In addition to addressing health-care needs in their neighborhoods, African American women found that community awareness was being raised. Often where a black college or university existed there followed the establishment of settlement houses or community clubs by members of the emerging educated middle class. In such university or college towns as Nashville, Atlanta, Washington, D.C., Tuskegee, and Hampton, Virginia, strong programs for black communities emerged.

By the turn of the twentieth century, writes historian Jacqueline Rouse, "Atlanta was the most segregated city in Georgia," yet, it had a thriving black community of 63,000 people, 4 percent of whom could be considered among the newer black elite. Members of this group were professionals and educators, some of them associated with Spelman and Morehouse colleges and Atlanta University. These colleges were in the heart of Atlanta and served as institutions for blacks who aspired to elite or middle-class status. A remarkable event occurred when Lugenia Burns Hope, wife of the renowned college educator and president of Morehouse College, John Hope, came to the city in 1898. She, in combination with the educational institutions and the city's clubwomen, formed an innovative plan for community improvement, practicing their own brand of municipal housekeeping.

Most black Atlantans worked at manual labor and lived in tumble-down housing in neighborhoods neglected by landlords and city government. Even the areas around the black colleges were in deplorable shape. The wives of the faculty and especially Lugenia Hope came up with a plan to organize and clean up the black neighborhoods of Atlanta. She called her friends and neighbors together in July 1908 and formed the Neighborhood Union, whose motto became "Thy Neighbor as Thyself." The Union decided to concentrate first on cleaning up the areas surrounding the colleges. They divided each area into subsections and conducted a survey, then assessed the work to be done. The women vowed to make "the West Side of Atlanta a better place to rear our children," according to Rouse. Union members stressed the needs of children and their goal of providing better facilities for them. Their survey showed that the streets were in bad repair and the lighting was insufficient. The area was also deficient in the number of sewer lines (water came mostly from wells not from the mains), and houses of prostitution operated near school buildings, which were also in disrepair. The list went on and on. The women began by finding ways to build playgrounds, clubs, and neighborhood centers where lecturers provided courses in intellectual development, child welfare, cultural heritage, and information to encourage the cleanliness and repair of homes. Women aimed to organize neighborhoods in every section of the city housing black residents and build settlement houses where they could do the most good by offering day nurseries, club meetings, and youth recreation.

The Union members devised an elaborate volunteer administrative structure by zones. They organized directors of districts into a Board of Directors for the Neighborhood Union, which finally incorporated in 1911. The Union proceeded to spread across Atlanta, encompassing most of the black neighborhoods in the city by 1914. The Union divided into four departments: Arts, Literary, Musical, and Moral and Educational, which introduced residents to art, literature, and music classes, clubs for youngsters, and vocational classes for such practical skills as cooking, sewing, and hat-making. The Moral and Education Department brought in speakers to inspire and motivate residents—Margaret Murray Washington, wife of Booker T. Washington, and Mary McLeod Bethune spoke about health, education, and citizenship. Union members also petitioned the mayor, the Sanitation and Health departments, and the city council about their needs. They used the courts to get decent housing and health care programs, paved streets, and more streetlights into black neighborhoods. The city government began cooperating with the Neighborhood Union in a limited way.

Although the Union founded a health clinic in 1908 and raised money to open an even newer one in 1926, schools were actually among the biggest targets for improvement. A committee of "one hundred leading women of Atlanta," after investigating the twelve segregated schools for six months, found them so crowded that the schools were running double sessions, with the teachers working two shifts and the children too confined. In 1913 the black schools could seat only 4,000 children, but 6,000 were enrolled. The committee solicited the aid of prominent white Atlanta women, some of whom visited the schools and saw the poor conditions for themselves. But getting white male city leaders to act was more difficult than getting attention from white women. In 1914, city leaders eliminated the eighth grade in black schools (the highest level) in order to save money but did not cut white children's education. In 1917, after the formation of Atlanta's NAACP, city leaders supported a move to eliminate the seventh grade from black schools in order to fund a white middle school instead. At meetings with the school board, a combination of organizations within Atlanta, including the Neighborhood Union and the NAACP, argued against this draconian measure, and the school board suspended its plan to eliminate the seventh grade. Lugenia Hope and Walter White, speakers for the black community, pleaded for more schools.

In part because of the school board's intransigence and blatant racism, Walter White left for New York to devote his life to the NAACP. Lugenia Hope stayed on in Atlanta, where her work remained important for several reasons. She and the other women took hold of the problems there and mobilized black citizens to direct their energies toward neighborhood improvement. They continually kept the pressure on the city government through court cases and petitions and through publicity demanding better services for the black community. Through the combined efforts of the NAACP, the Neighborhood Union, and an effective strategy of refusing to vote for school bonds that only favored white schools, black Atlanta residents finally won the city's attention. In 1924, the school board built Booker T. Washington High School, the first black high school in Atlanta. Hope and the others reached out to white women, thereby extending a hand across the color line, but the most empowering feature of the Neighborhood Union was its message of solidarity, community, and uplift. By the 1920s and later, their interracial efforts would result in alliances including the Commission on Interracial Cooperation. In the long run, efforts toward self-improvement and uplift allowed black Atlantans to take pride in their community and attract a growing number of intellectuals to the city. In 1933 Atlantans of both races celebrated the twenty-fifth anniversary of the founding of the Neighborhood Union.

Progressive Reform at the State Level

Progressivism in the South found reform advocates aimed at all levels of government, from municipal, to county, to state. There were so many problems to be addressed that individual reformers often had to make choices. Women's clubs, made up of thousands of members, directed their energies toward a multiplicity of reform actions. Their goals varied, but in most states they followed the advice of the national organization and pursued an agenda to create juvenile courts and asylums, enact penal reform, end convict lease, improve public education, end child labor, protect women laborers, increase public health and sanitation, eradicate hookworm, suppress prostitution, clean up the electorate, enact prohibition, and increase women's rights. Woman suffrage was among the most controversial and the most political of their pursuits, and not all women in the South were willing to go so far as to seek equal voting rights. Yet these were the statewide and national issues of most concern to women, and they garnered support from both men and women Progressives.

Reform of the Penal System

Women across the South worried about young people who succumbed to criminal activity and were then prosecuted and placed in prisons with hardened criminals. These women reformers worked within whatever juvenile justice system existed in their state (some were well established by the 1900s) and furthered their activism to develop reformatories to detain and retrain young offenders—boys and girls, black and white. Two states serve as examples. In Alabama, Margaret Murray Washington helped form the Alabama State Federation of Colored Women's Clubs (ASFCWC) in 1898. Two projects came from the energies of these capable women reformers. The Federation first created the Mt. Meigs Reformatory for Juvenile Negro Law-Breakers for delinquent boys, and it gained support from the Alabama state legislature in 1911. The Federation then sponsored without state help the Mt. Meigs Rescue Home for Girls in 1912. In North Carolina members of a white nondenominational national organization called the King's Daughters solicited the state legislature for a reformatory for white boys, who in 1886 made up 50 percent of the state's offenders. Believing that young men in prison were simply in training for a life of crime, the Daughters petitioned for a separate reformatory for juveniles. They were joined in their goal by the WCTU, the UDC, and the North Carolina Federation of Women's Clubs. Called the Stonewall Jackson Manual Training and Industrial School, in honor of the Civil War hero and his widow, the legislature finally committed funds to the school in Concord, North Carolina, in 1907. This was followed by a fight for a reformatory for white girls, the Samarcand Manor facility, which finally won state funding in 1919. African American clubwomen made a similar appeal to the North Carolina legislature and won funding for a state reformatory for boys called the Morrison Training School, which opened in 1925. But the legislature of North Carolina, in a surprisingly sexist and racist move, refused to fund a state girls' reformatory. Not to be discouraged, African American clubwomen raised funds for the Industrial Home for Delinquent Negro Girls in 1926 and continued to maintain it until the 1940s when the state finally funded a home for black girls.

Although successful on some fronts, race and gender discrimination still worked against the Progressives' efforts to bring the least powerful members of society under the protective umbrella of state government. Prison reform for adult women would have to wait until the 1920s, but clubwomen were determined to protect women prisoners from sexual abuse by male jailers and inmates. In 1927, the North Carolina legislature put up the funds, thanks to women's agitation, for a farm-reformatory colony for white adult female prisoners where they could receive schooling and training in occupations and housekeeping.

Ida B. Wells, the feisty black activist from the South living in Chicago, pointed a searchlight on the dark subject of convict lease. She intoned,

> The Convict Lease System and Lynch Law are twin infamies which flourished hand in hand in many of the southern states: Alabama, Arkansas, Florida, Georgia, Kentucky, Louisiana, Mississippi, Nebraska, North Carolina, South Carolina, and Tennessee claimed to be too poor to maintain state convicts within prison walls. Hence the prisoners were leased out to work for railway contractors, mining companies, turpentine producers, and those who owned large plantations. These companies assumed charge of the convicts, worked them as cheap exploitable and disposable labor, and paid the states a handsome revenue. Nine-tenths of these convicts were blacks.

Leasing prisoners to private companies in need of workers cut down on taxes, legislators said, because the state did not have to build secure prisons for them and made money off of their labor. It also acted as a deterrent to labor unions and kept businessmen happy. But convict lease was a blight on the South as a most awful means of racial control, for it virtually re-enslaved men convicted of petty crimes, or of offenses no worse than loitering, giving them long sentences at hard labor. The system lasted until the early twentieth century, when most states replaced it with a series of prison farms, also designed to make prisoners work for their keep, but under the eye of prison wardens rather than exploitative industrialists.

Perhaps it was the brutal conditions of convict lease that made whites cringe—even those who did not object to having blacks in prison for petty or spurious reasons. Reports from journalists, union leaders (who saw the convict lease system as competition to free laborers), and social activists drew attention to the cruelty inherent the system. Prisoners were tortured with daily beatings in which leather straps studded with wooden pegs flailed off their flesh. These and other barbarities incensed such strong reformers as Julia S. Tutwiler of Alabama. She took to fomenting opposition to convict lease through crusades and demonstrations pointing out and targeting individual politicians or specific camps where mistreatment abounded. Although Tutwiler did not live long enough to see the end of the convict lease system in Alabama (she died in 1916), she set women in that state on the road to achieving prison reform in the 1890s. Tutwiler successfully lobbied for night schools for convicts with state funding awarded in 1887. She also got the legislature to provide heat and perform sanitation inspections in jails across the state. Georgia banned convict lease in 1909, but Alabama and Florida were the last states in the South to end the system. Alabama mining companies, making profits off of near slave labor, were the most ardent opponents of reform and held many a legislator in their thrall. Alabama lawmakers insisted that if they ended the system the state's revenue would decline and schools, social services, and child welfare programs would suffer. Members of the Alabama Federation of Women's Clubs (AFWC) did not accept that excuse since other states had managed to end convict lease and keep their state-funded social programs. Finally, after the horrific murder of a convict at work, journalists with help from the AFWC launched a full-scale protest. In 1928 they shamed the legislature into passing a law that forbade the leasing of prisoners to private companies.

Educating the Children of the South

The campaign to improve education in southern states was among the most important for the numbers of children and families it affected. Virtually every southern state lacked sufficient funding to educate its citizenry for the sophisticated work and civic demands of the twentieth century. Improvement in education meant more occupational choices for southerners, a greater awareness of the world, and more opportunities for political understanding and involvement. The role of the state in educating its citizens, white and black, and the expenditures and environment for such schooling came under review by reformers.

Southerners saw how little their state governments spent on public education. In 1900 nearly 15 percent of whites and 50 percent of blacks in the South were illiterate. Children in North Carolina went to school for only seventy-one days a year—not even three months—receiving the least amount of schooling in the South. By 1920, the school year in the Old North State had increased to 134 days, or one-third of a year. Dual (segregated) educational systems were more expensive to maintain, but allotments for education were dismal anyway thanks to the Democrats' lack of interest in social services.

At the regional level, men began the reforming process by convening conferences designed to draw attention to the appalling educational deficit in the South. The Conference for Education in the South (1898) and its executive body, the Southern Educational Board (SEB) founded in 1901, teamed up with the General Education Board (GEB) formed in 1902 under the auspices of the philanthropic John D. Rockefeller family. The GEB appropriated $53 million for education with special attention to schools in the South. Together the SEB, the GEB, and myriad educators persuaded the populace and the legislatures to increase the total expenditures for state schools; funding southwide nearly tripled between 1900 and 1910 (from $21.4 million to $57.2 million). As a result, illiteracy dropped by half between 1900 and 1920 to 5.9 percent for whites and 25.8 percent for blacks. In comparison, the national illiteracy percentage in 1920 was 2 percent for whites and 23 percent for blacks. Part of the reason for increased literacy can be attributed to compulsory school attendance laws, which every state had implemented by 1920. The number of days southern children went to school varied by state in 1920, but overall the time had increased to an average of 127 days or just over four months a year. The average number of days children attended schools in the United States was 161, or just over five months. Even though the South had made significant progress, clearly young southerners continued to suffer educational disadvantages when compared to their counterparts in other regions of the nation.

Mothers were among the South's most interested partners in the push for school reform. As an extension of their maternal love for their children and their desire to see them succeed, mothers made school reform their "sacred duty." There was also some improvement for women who taught school. The states increased teacher salaries and added more training opportunities for them. Southern states built more high schools, while the state and volunteers improved the condition of existing school buildings and classrooms. Legislatures paid for these essentials by raising taxes and convincing taxpayers to support public education for the good of the state and its future. In some states onerous voting requirements were linked to public school funding. In North Carolina, illiterate whites supported a literacy requirement for voting when the legislature promised that public schools would be improved so that every white man would be able to read. In Texas white clubwomen helped campaign for the poll tax because the tax was slated for school funding and thus could be touted as a "progressive" measure.

Women teachers and mothers could not help but be involved with the improvements because they were the most likely to experience the effects of inadequate funding. In North Carolina, women who had formerly been active in club work founded the Woman's Association for the Betterment of Public School Houses in 1902 and voluntarily worked hand in glove with the SEB to improve the physical condition of schools. Historian William Link notes that the women who became part of the "school crusades" contributed their time and talents to making schools (as they had churches) more homelike, more inviting, and more feminine. This complemented the trend away from male teachers toward an increasingly female teaching force.

Among other women's groups, the General Federation of Women's Clubs had long worked for improved schools through their Education Committee, which took up the task of starting mother's clubs and endorsing kindergartens in public schools. A National Congress of Mothers (a forerunner to the Parent Teacher Association or PTA) formed mother's clubs in nearly every school. Its members focused on improvements for children and looked after the needs of the schools. They brought about "sanitary drinking fountains" and better janitor and food services, hung portraits of great Americans (including southern leaders) in the classrooms, and bought art supplies for the children. When the SEB made its presence known in a state, women's school improvement associations also sprang up. This was true in Virginia, when Mary Munford and Lila Meade Valentine worked with the Co-Operative Education Association in 1902. The same occurred in South Carolina, Georgia, and Alabama. Southern teachers and laywomen also made literacy their special province, staffing "Moonlight Schools" and "Opportunity Schools" designed to teach adults to read. Such programs reached mountain families, miners in camps, and workers in tobacco districts. Southern women tapped into an enormous reserve of energy in aid of school and literacy improvement.

White reformers in the South were often reluctant to address the shameful neglect of the state's black schools for fear of threatening the white crusade for better schools, but funding for black schools and the need for teachers was acute by 1900. In 1895 the census reported only 25,000 black teachers in the entire nation, the great majority of whom were women. More were needed, especially in the South, and this led to the push toward university and teacher-training for black women. Teaching provided great opportunities for black women with education and fortitude, and many of the graduates of universities, colleges, and normal schools went directly into rural areas to teach. Mamie Garvin Fields of Charleston wrote that being a rural teacher on the South Carolina Sea Islands "meant teaching all the time." Taking on tasks that would today be in the province of social workers, teachers helped sharecropper families that could not afford proper clothing and nutritious food for their children and whose health problems were extensive. Such deprived rural areas often had low morale due to a cotton culture that led to debt and never-ending poverty. Public health programs, moreover, did not reach some of the rural places where improvement was needed the most.

Teachers paved the way to better services for these rural areas by placing themselves among the poorest people and publicizing the problems they encountered. Teachers went to places where no schools existed and with the help of the black community built their own schools. Spelman College (for women), co-educational Hampton Institute, and Fisk University all taught carpentry to *women* (100 hours of woodworking at Hampton for women students), who then used these skills to construct schoolhouses. Genevieve Ladson, a teacher in South Carolina wrote, "When I say I built a school . . . I mean I built it, from helping them cut down the trees with my saw, to hammering boards in place." When Ladson began teaching in the late 1920s, the annual state expenditure for each black student was $5.20; the annual expenditure for each white student was *ten times* the amount, $52.60. With such a gross discrepancy in state funding, it was often the case that if the black community wanted to have a school, it would have to build one.

Women educators reached far beyond teaching reading and writing—often without books and to more than a hundred students aged three to eighteen years—for the needs were many and the hands few. Genevieve Ladson joined her community in slaughtering hogs, picking cotton, grinding sugar cane, and harvesting tomatoes. Septima Clark, who began teaching on the Sea Islands in 1916, recalled that by helping women in the community nurse the sick and prepare the dead for burial, she taught them good hygiene and basic health care. Outside of her school hours, she taught the women sewing and suggested appropriate styles of clothing for them to wear. If families had no means to buy material to make clothes, she petitioned her friends in women's clubs and churches for donations. Clark opened up her kitchen to train women how to can and preserve the vegetables they grew, and she founded Opportunity Schools for the older students who needed night lessons. Clark helped the Sea Island men organize fraternal societies and in the process fought against illiteracy because she helped them write and memorize their speeches.

Reform for African Americans from outside the region came almost a decade later than it did for whites with the introduction of the Jeanes Fund teacher supervision program (1907); the Slater Fund program in secondary education (1910), a part of the GEB; and the Julius Rosenwald Fund (1914) which provided a program of rural school construction in the South. GEB funds were mainly limited to endeavors in industrial education, while the Rosenwald Fund offered more training in black leadership and decision making. Slowly state legislatures turned their attention toward more funding for black schools, the creation of high schools, and better facilities and salaries for teachers. These improvements greatly affected those women educators struggling to teach in overcrowded classrooms or in underheated one-room schoolhouses. A National Congress of Colored Parents and Teachers formed in 1908 and later affiliated with the National Congress of Mothers. The two groups shed racial exclusion and occasionally crossed the color line in interracial meetings.

Women found their political voices through education. The mothers' clubs promoted women candidates for school trustees and board membership. To improve local education, women ran for seats on school boards from a clubwomen's platform. Women in some states were granted school suffrage; Kentucky and Louisiana became the first southern states to give women the right to vote for school board members. Voters in Dallas and San Antonio elected two women in each city to their school boards in 1908 and 1909. The voters of Texas elected Annie Webb Blanton as state superintendent of public instruction in 1918 after women had won the right to vote in Texas primaries that July. In the election, Blanton defeated two males, and she stayed in office until 1922, when she made an unsuccessful bid for the U.S. Congress. As superintendent Blanton oversaw the establishment of a free textbook system, teacher certification revisions, an increase in teacher salaries, and a Better Schools Amendment that revised the tax structure for public school funding. Southern women took many paths to political activism, but certainly the educational crusades won them exposure to the process of funding, politicking, and winning. Overall better schools meant better literacy rates and a more educated citizenry, but those who benefited most from school reform were white women. They were more likely to graduate from high school than were men; and a high school education gave them more choices by the 1920s—to follow traditional roles or to find employment and a career.

Women and Labor Reform

Irene M. Ashby, an Englishwoman and labor reformer working for the American Federation of Labor (AFL), visited some twenty-five factories in Alabama between 1900 and 1901. In one textile mill she witnessed a small girl "with bare feet and pale face" upon whose countenance she saw "a worn and anxious aspect" tending a spinning frame and deftly repairing broken threads at both ends of a long line of machinery. Ashby called her a "little gray shadow," yet it dawned on her that, "this child [was] working." As late as 1900, 32,000 children younger than age fourteen worked in textile mills across the South.

Both men and women became involved in the movement to end child labor—the paid employment of children younger than twelve in industries such as the textile mills in the Piedmont and the shellfish canneries on the Gulf Coast. In 1900, children as young as eight worked in the textile mills, usually considered "helpers" for their mothers, a fact that shocked most Progressives. Child labor reformers considered childhood a sacred time when children needed protection from the world for the psychological formation that would take them naturally into adulthood. They believed that premature work in a factory, where the machinery demanded intensity contrary to the ideals of a carefree childhood, led to the retardation of human development. Accidents in the mills maimed some children for life, and labor leaders found that the practice of child labor kept wages in general low and created a class of backward workers. Millwork contributed to high illiteracy rates in the South as parents who needed their children's wages kept them out of school and on the job. Even race entered the picture; if black children, who were not allowed to work in the mills, received more schooling than white children, who would eventually rule the South, they wondered? Middle-class women reformers, mainly clubwomen, took a special interest in mothers and children working in mills. They saw a sad spectacle of unhealthy children and overworked women unable to nurture their children. The reform impulse, therefore, like that for school, prison, and convict lease reform, was motivated by humanitarian and economic concerns, as well as the maternal interest in children and the home. Reformers believed that in order to raise the cultural and economic level of the nation's poorest region, children deserved their freedom in childhood and an education. Many factory children received neither.

Although laws were enacted to prohibit child labor in Alabama, Louisiana, Tennessee, and Virginia in the 1890s, textile owners persuaded the legislators to rescind the laws, and no southern state had regulatory legislation to prohibit children younger than twelve from working by 1900. The drive for child labor reform began in Alabama in 1900 with the help of the American Federation of Labor, clubwomen, and the clergy. The AFL sent Irene Ashby to Alabama, where she found 430 children under the age of twelve working twelve-hour shifts for between fifteen and thirty cents a day. Ashby's work among women's groups and church leaders to promote passage of a child labor bill led her to Edgar Gardiner Murphy, an Episcopal priest and rector of St. John's Episcopal Church in Montgomery. He turned his attention to labor reform after reading Ashby's investigative report of 1901 and brought the problem to the ministerial association, which lobbied the Alabama legislature for regulation of child labor. Meanwhile members of the WCTU had already begun to speak out publicly against child labor. The Alabama Federation of Women's Clubs' leaders, Nellie Murdock of Birmingham and Lura Craighead of Mobile, rallied women supporters to the statehouse on behalf of the child labor reform bill. Even the venerable reformer Julia Tutwiler made an appearance on behalf of the WCTU. The legislature refused to pass a bill to end child labor in 1901, and mill owners, in order to protect their economic interests, launched a vituperative campaign of their own against child labor reform. They insisted that Alabama must first pass a compulsory education act before enacting any sort of child-labor restrictions. Thrusting and parrying like a fencer, Murphy then called for the formation of the Alabama Child Labor Committee (ACLC) in 1901 and went straight to the people of Alabama with newspaper articles and pamphlets reporting the facts on working children. These publications, among the first of their kind in the South, showed with words and photographs the condition of children working in the mills and reported that youngsters under the age of sixteen constituted nearly one-third of the textile labor force. The published reports, *The Case against Child Labor,* and *The South and Her Children* among them, were used in other states' campaigns to end child labor. Ashby continued to speak before clubs affiliated with the AFWC, the WCTU, and the Daughters of the American Revolution (DAR) where she aroused interest in the cause. The AFWC worked alongside of and with the ACLC for passage of a labor bill.

Each time the Alabama legislature met the issue returned. In 1903, after women packed the galleries of the statehouse, the legislators passed a compromise bill that excluded children under twelve from working in the mills but allowed children ten years and older to work if they had a widowed mother or a "dependent father." In 1907, 1915, and 1919, the legislature entertained strengthened versions of the bill. The ACLC actions led to campaigns in other states and the creation of a National Child Labor Conference (NCLC) that standardized labor reform proposals. Every year, the inspectors found children still in the workplace. By 1911 Nellie Murdock became president of the ACLC, combining the power of male reformers with the Alabama Federation of Women's Clubs. The NCLC in 1914 brought in famed photographer Lewis W. Hine and eleven investigators (including ten women) to Alabama to study the child labor problem, and the state adopted a law allowing investigators to check on the status of mills. Finally, in 1919 the Alabama legislature enacted a bill that reduced the work week to forty-eight hours and created a state Child Welfare Department, whose first director was a woman, Lorraine B. Bush. By then most of the opposition to child labor reform had lost momentum as citizens became convinced of the need for young children to be in schools rather than in factories. Much of this change of attitude can be attributed to the hard work of the state's women.

Women in other southern states shared similar concerns. In Louisiana, the Gordon sisters, Kate and Jean, became ardent supporters of child labor reform. As founders of the Era Club in New Orleans, they formed a committee to investigate conditions of child labor and launched a newspaper campaign after the state legislators balked at a child labor law. In 1906 the Louisiana Legislature passed a Child Labor Act that allowed women to become factory inspectors. Jean Gordon served as one such inspector until 1911, and she also served as president of the Southern Conference of Women and Child Labor from 1910 to 1911. The conferences that stemmed from reform efforts pressured state legislatures and standardized approaches to the movement, bringing reformers together and encouraging them in their fight for social justice.

North Carolina and South Carolina, principal centers of the nation's textile industry, passed labor laws reluctantly and only under severe duress from reformers affiliated with the NCLC, women' clubs, and labor unions, such as the United Textile Workers (affiliated with the AFL). By 1914, even these states had modest reform laws in place. Georgia also passed a child labor law in 1906 and ten years later a compulsory education act. Most of the early labor laws put the minimum age of hiring at twelve, and by 1915 at fourteen, but there were loopholes, just as there had been in Alabama. In Texas, clubwomen created their own state-level child labor committee, which persuaded the state commissioner of labor to draft a bill barring children younger than fifteen from factories and mills and younger than seventeen from mines and quarries. They got the bill they wanted in 1911. By 1915 all the southern states had enacted some form of child labor restrictions, and in 1916 Congress passed the Keating-Owen Child Labor Act that prohibited interstate shipment of goods made by children younger than fourteen years of age. Children as young as fourteen continued to work full time, however. The difficulties, as women reformers quickly realized, were not only with the mill owners but also with the parents of working children.

The movement to end child labor brought men and women into open conflict. Cole Blease, governor of South Carolina from 1910 to 1913, allied with his political cohort, "Pitchfork" Ben Tillman, and used racial and gender insults to shame reformers. Blease lambasted male reformers as unmanly and as "nigger lovers." According to historian Joan Marie Johnson, he accused women reformers of "exchanging their dresses for our pants." Such arguments often held weight, for they suggested role changes that threatened the entire society. The loss of male authority seemed at stake as women accused men of exploiting children, while men thought they must defend their right to patriarchal authority. Middle-class southern women countered this argument by denouncing fathers who kept their children out of school, making them work in factories and the fields. They also chastised businessmen and politicians who opposed the passage of child labor laws. Women reformers spoke of the rights of children and the duties of men, attacking an older adage that insisted men had rights while children must perform duties. Some women, particularly those who followed the ideals of the Lost Cause, called upon men to see to their obligations as protectors of women and children. Here is evidence of conservative women acting in defense of children, their activism chiming in with that of the Progressives. These women took the view that poor men who put their children to work in factories rather than giving them an education, or mill owners who profited from child labor were "turning their backs on the chivalric ideal, and neglecting their moral responsibility to look out for the welfare of women and children," writes historian Rebecca Montgomery. But other women reformers eschewed the path of male noblesse oblige and opted instead for state laws that would safeguard children. As women, they assumed the mantle of protectors of children and asked the state to do the same.

The fact remains that some working families resisted labor reforms intended to improve their children's lives, lying about their ages and getting away with it at a time when birth certificates were just beginning to be required for purposes of recording vital statistics. Some historians ascribe parental reluctance to keep older children out of the mills to habit and to the paternalism of the mill owners, who provided housing and amenities for families in the form of churches, welfare programs, and elementary schools (after 1910 states imposed mandatory education for children under twelve, but only for a few months of the year). Supporters of child workers pointed to the fact that farm children also worked long hours and from such a life learned responsibility. Other mill workers were simply glad to have a job and resented labor organizers whose efforts sometimes led to lockouts and disruptions in earnings. Some adult workers confessed that they were coerced by their employers to protest child labor laws, even though they favored schooling for their young ones. Yet economic reality overwhelmed most mill families; in short, mill hands wanted their children to work for the money they brought to the household. If wages had been sufficient for an adult male alone to support his family, resistance to child labor among the workers themselves might have dried up. Even women reformers seemed unable to fix that problem. Despite these obstructions, by 1917 the census showed that children under the age of sixteen in the mills had declined to 6 percent of the workforce. Mill owners began to bend to public pressure to end child labor. In truth, however, child labor could not come to a complete end until federal regulation demanded it. The best course of action would come with the New Deal in the 1930s.

Not all labor concerns involved underage children. The problems of wage-earning women attracted to jobs in southern cities came to the attention of the YWCA, a national cross-class volunteer association designed to aid women workers. Christian women founded branches of the Young Women's Christian Association in southern cities with the help of the national organization. Slow to take root in the South, YWCAs became important there before, during, and after World War I, when more young women left the farm to find a job in the city. At least twelve cities in the South had "colored branches": Richmond, Newport News, Winston-Salem, Charlotte, Columbia, South Carolina, Charleston, and Houston were among the largest. Black and white "Ys" under the national YWCA umbrella served their own constituencies, but unlike the national federation of women's clubs, the Y had the means to introduce white and black volunteers as well as staff members to each other at conferences. In this way the YWCA become a pacesetter in providing contact between middle-class black and white women in the first two decades of the twentieth century.

The main goal of the YWCA was to protect working girls living in cities. The rising numbers of wage-earning girls, whom they referred to as "women adrift," alarmed many southerners. In Atlanta, the city population doubled between 1890 and 1910 to 155,000, but the percentage of white working women rose 200 percent in those same years to 9,352. This comprised 18 percent of all white women in Atlanta, and of these, 80 percent were unmarried; 20 percent were living on their own in 1920. Employment for women in the public sphere was increasing; by the Progressive era 28 percent of all women living in cities were employed. In Houston, women were found working in more than thirty different occupations as early as 1890. Many farm girls ventured into cities to escape the drudgery of rural life and earn needed money. Others sent money back to their families, but many did not earn enough even for their own subsistence. New occupations that had opened up for women, such as telephone operators and store clerks, paid about $3.50 a week. A living wage in 1914 was estimated at $8.00 a week. Middle-class members of the YWCA began to campaign, not for higher wages, which were needed, but for low-cost housing and food for working girls.

Middle-class matrons also worried that young women would need the guidance and support of a women's organization, in place of their families, while on their own in strange towns. Afraid that working girls might be swept into prostitution or sweatshop work, members of the Y met many a traveling young woman searching for work at the train station and led her to decent lodgings, a cafeteria, recreational facilities, and an employment bureau under the auspices of the YWCA. The Y movement not only brought protection to working women but also advanced ideas about education, training, and woman suffrage. To be sure, Bible study was part of the program, but so were social evenings, cafeterias with lunches for 17 cents in 1914, rooms for $2.50–$3.50 a week, reading rooms and libraries, and classes in English, typing, sports, or vocational skills. The most popular feature among the young women was the cafeteria, which in Galveston, Texas, served about 6,000 people a month.

In terms of working conditions, southern women labor leaders moved toward the modest regulatory goal of a sixty-hour work week: ten-hour days, six days a week. In Texas, Eva Goldsmith, of the Texas State Federation of Labor, lobbied the legislature in 1913 for a fifty-four hour work week. Although the bill fell prey to the businessmen's pen, mutilated, as historian Judith McArthur notes, "almost beyond recognition," labor advocates compared Goldsmith to Sam Houston "defending the Texas Republic from the Mexican army." Goldsmith won a position on the Texas State Federation of Labor's Legislative Committee for her efforts and returned to legislative lobbying in 1915 to fight for a minimum wage law for women. Labor Unions in the textile industries, such as the United Textile Workers, fought long and hard for labor reform for women. As with child labor, most southern states would find a modicum of protection for women workers—shorter hours, minimum wages, better conditions—only through federal legislation and the New Deal.

Health Reform and Eugenics

The South was a much germier region than the rest of the United States due to its semitropical climate and latitude, which caused a higher incidence of illness and general malaise. Other factors increasing the incidence of bad health were poverty, the poor quality of health care, and health hazards such as undrained swamps. Mosquitoes carried malaria and yellow fever, causing hundreds of deaths when epidemics hit southern cities such as Memphis and Galveston in the 1860s and 1870s. Thanks to Walter Reed and his discovery of the cause of yellow fever after the Spanish American War in

1898, the South suffered its last nasty episode of the disease in 1905. Cases of smallpox and typhoid fever along with infectious childhood diseases plagued the South, but with the growing acceptance of the germ theory of disease by the turn of the century, medical experts began to search for ways to improve sanitation and public health. State legislatures enacted licensing regulations for physicians, dentists, nurses, and midwives, while passing pure food and drug laws. In addition to the city boards of health and the vigilance of women's civic clubs looking after market, town, and school sanitation, by 1913 the states also had created state boards of public health, bureaus of vital statistics, tuberculosis hospitals, and public health laboratories.

This emphasis on better health care benefited women and children to a great degree. Diseases such as hookworm, cholera, and pellagra affected the weakest and the youngest members of the population, and such debilitating diseases during pregnancy or childhood could have lifelong effects. Reformers concluded that diseases spread by microbes could be remedied, as they were often the result of poor sanitation. The Rockefeller Sanitary Commission for the Eradication of Hookworm Disease found that between 1909 and 1914, in the testing of more than 1 million people, that 44 percent (440,000) were infected with hookworms. The hookworm is a parasite that lives in the soil, enters the body through the soles of bare feet, and lodges in the intestines of the host, robbing her or him of nutrients. Since most often the diseases were spread by human defecation in the fields, or through poor sanitation, the goal of reformers was to convince southerners to adopt modern hygiene, build and use outhouses, and wear shoes. Public health agents demonstrated the newest innovations in privies at county fairs, and the Sanitary Commission treated about 500,000 hookworm patients. When the work of the Rockefeller Sanitary Commission ended, southern women Home Demonstration Agents became educators, teaching residents about health and sanitation, promoting campaigns to kill flies and cover windows with screens, and use hygienic privies or indoor plumbing. In Florida, African

American nurses, in connection with National Negro Health Week established by Booker T. Washington in 1915, traveled across the state to instruct rural families on public health in a bus they labeled the Moveable School. This form of educational outreach primarily helped farming families, and since the South was overwhelmingly rural before 1950, the health measures saved lives, lent more stamina to men and women, and rescued many young people from stunted growth. The South was beginning to take care of its population and address the health needs of its citizens.

At the same time that health reformers addressed the needs of southerners afflicted with contagious diseases or those related to poor nutrition, another, more sinister drive was taking shape to counter what many felt were the ill effects of mental deficiencies. This stemmed in part from the focus of health-reform campaigns on the desperately poor. Many Americans still held to the theories of Social Darwinism, and some reformers saw the South's indigent population, with its inferior education, health, and living standards, as possibly the result of an inadequate gene pool compounded by a poor environment. They held the belief that imbecility or mental defectiveness was a genetic condition, and to improve the populace, they reasoned, reproduction controls should be practiced. Many leading Progressives were caught up in the movement for "eugenics," which means "well-born." They subscribed to the practice of social engineering to produce superior people and reduce the number of inferior people. Kate and Jean Gordon of Louisiana were strong proponents of sterilization laws in order to end the reproduction of "feeble minded progeny." Jean Gordon, who became the director of the Milne Home for Girls in Louisiana, oversaw the sterilization of at least 125 young women. Because eugenicists were essentially countenancing birth control, the Catholic Church and evangelical Protestant groups both strongly opposed their efforts, but other states, such as Virginia and Florida, also practiced sterilization of the mentally retarded. In 1932, twenty-eight states had adopted the practice of compulsory sterilization for the mentally impaired. By the 1970s, when the idea of reproductive rights came under severe scrutiny, 60,000 Americans had been subjected to forced sterilization.

This practice affected girls more than boys; as mentally deficient girls came to maturity, eugenicists feared that their potentially licentious sexual behavior would threaten themselves and the very core of southern society. Reformers drew parallels between mentally deficient girls and prostitutes, claiming that in a 1920 study of 122 Georgia prostitutes, 43 percent were "feebleminded." The solution that many reformers preferred was precautionary sterilization of females for their own protection from male predators, for the good of the gene pool, and to relieve the state of the care of their progeny, which, eugenicists assumed, would be born disabled. Most of the young women who involuntarily succumbed to this treatment were residents of institutions; 60 percent of mentally disabled patients sterilized in Virginia were women as were 80 percent in North Carolina. Once sterilized, and if able to live independently, these young women could be "safely" returned to society, thus relieving the underfunded institutions of the South of their lifelong care. The treatment of women in such a manner can undoubtedly be ascribed to class and gender prejudices and an overzealous desire for social controls. It may also suggest that southerners, like Americans in general, were disturbed by the changing roles of women in their midst.

Gender and Legal Reform

Rights for women and girls came under review during the Progressive era, in part because the agenda for women's reform included the passage of laws aimed at protecting their own sex. Women reformers questioned and then launched an assault on patriarchal authority, which promised to protect the family but all too often failed to deliver. The laws that were passed at the insistence of women reformers granted women greater autonomy while limiting the control historically exerted by men over them. Admittedly these were controversial measures, for not all southern women sought independence from the protection afforded them through male hegemony. Indeed, in the South there were more women than in other parts of the nation who accepted that, however poorly off some women were, as a whole they were better protected when the state held men to a specific standard of patriarchal responsibility.

One example of this is the issue of divorce laws. State legislatures during this period discussed the possibility of more liberal divorce laws, but in many states divorce was a subject that women did not embrace. In North Carolina in 1913, when legislators tried to make dissolving marriages easier or quicker, citizens objected on moral grounds, and women did not champion the cause. Instead, traditional social and religious values prevailed. South Carolinians went so far as to legally deny divorce as late as 1926. There the clubwomen supported the state's ban on divorce, taking a peculiar form of state's rights pride in the notion that theirs was the only state in the nation that did not grant divorces.

Women were much more worried about the age of consent laws for each state. Moral reformers, concerned about the welfare of young girls, insisted on raising the age of consent. In most southern states, a child of ten could legally marry in 1890 with parental consent. The problem with this, as women saw it, was not only that a ten-year old was much too young for intimacy or for marriage, but also it basically allowed men to have sex with children. Under such laws an adult male who had sexual intercourse with a ten-year-old girl could not be tried for the statutory rape of a minor. This glaring insult to female children came under attack by women's groups across the South, and found some remedy during the Progressive era. The Texas legislature raised the age of consent to eighteen in 1918. In North Carolina, however, after forty years of campaigning by women's groups, the state assembly finally brought the age of consent to sixteen in 1923. Women reformers noticed that in those states (such as Colorado) where women had the right to vote, the age of consent was raised in some cases to twenty-one. This prompted Madeline Breckinridge, a suffragist from Kentucky to ask, "Do Southern men protect Southern women at all comparable to the way Western women, granted the right to [vote] protect their own sex?"

Often the campaign for basic women's rights—to property ownership and to their own wages after marriage, for example—languished in state capitals. In state after southern state married women's property rights came under review, in part because of the rising independence among women, but also because women's groups such as the WCTU and women's clubs demanded reform. As early as 1900 in Texas, at the backing of women's rights columnist Pauline Periwinkle (Sara Isadore Callaway), and the Dallas Free Kindergarten and Industrial Association, Lawrence W. Neff, a journalist, compiled *The Legal Status of Woman in Texas* (1905). Women's clubs across the state used this digest as a primer to understand their own legal disadvantages. The result was that women's groups got on the bandwagon to secure a married women's property rights act. Two groups, the Texas Federation of Women's Clubs and the Texas Congress of Mothers, focused exclusively on getting such a bill passed, and they were able to see the enactment of the law in 1913. The married women's property law gave a married woman control over any property or money given or willed to her, although the husband retained management status over their community property. Her personal wages were still considered community property, but a woman's investments or real estate were solely hers. Also, that portion deemed hers by the court was not subject to seizure for her husband's debts—a boon to both husband and wife. This breakthrough for women was just a beginning, for while it did not address issues of making contracts or child custody, it did raise questions about voting. Reformers wondered why, if a woman were entitled to make decisions over her own property, should she not also be given control over her own voice in politics via the ballot?

From humble beginnings in churches and synagogues across the South, black and white women collectively and separately found their way to city halls and state capitols. The local, statewide, and national issues of most concern to women often found support from both men and women Progressive reformers. Although unable to vote, women did affect public policy. Some may view public policy as being determined solely by decisions from officially appointed or elected bodies and individuals, that is, men in powerful positions. Thinking more broadly about political and cultural life and its participants, however, one may define public policy so as to include the actions of private groups and voluntary associations, thereby enlarging the constituency that influenced city life and official public decisions. This is particularly important when considering the history of women's ability to effect change and the long struggle of black women to find within the Progressive movement support for their race, their families, their communities, and themselves. The volunteer activism of women, who fought for improvement in municipal affairs in urban areas, actually constituted political action and ultimately led to the creation of public policy in city halls and in southern statehouses. In addressing issues of importance to women, reformers challenged the very core of society's patriarchal authority over possessions, protections, and the lives of women, children, workers, and prisoners. The women who were ready to question traditional barriers, which in the South went against entrenched cultural values and institutional structures, asked, and in some cases demanded, to be included in the formation of public policy, crossing traditional gender boundaries and tiptoeing into the arena of improved race relations.

CHAPTER FIVE

Women and Politics in the South

On August 18, 1920, Tennessee became the thirty-sixth state to ratify the Nineteenth Amendment, thus ensuring the adoption of a woman's right to vote in the United States. One week later, on August 26, the secretary of state added the Nineteenth Amendment to the U.S. Constitution, thus completing the ratification process and enfranchising—at least in theory—26 million women of voting age, approximately one-half of the nation's adults. Women had sought this momentous goal for at least seventy-two years. The fact that a southern state broke the barrier for women serves as a reminder of the important role the region played in the amendment's ratification.

Six months before ratification of the Nineteenth Amendment, women rolled up their sleeves, and formed a new organization—the League of Women Voters—to educate the newly enfranchised on voting issues. Women formulated political agendas and lobbied to see them adopted through their state legislatures. Political veterans from the woman suffrage campaign alongside newcomers to politics ran for office.

African American women found solidarity in registering to vote and in voting, although their numbers were small due to continuing disfranchisement measures. All told, by 1920 the woman suffrage victory had a profound effect on the South and the nation, for it opened new doors and affirmed the ability of women to reach for a political goal and attain it.

The Strategic South in the Woman Suffrage Movement

The South as a region was indispensable to the success of the passage of the Nineteenth Amendment (also known as the Susan B. Anthony Amendment), in part, because southerners constituted an important voting bloc. In 1920, out of the forty-eight states, thirty-six were needed to ratify the amendment. If thirteen states voted against it, they could have killed it. The southern states constituted the most conservative region in the nation politically, and if they all refused to ratify the amendment, it could have derailed the woman suffrage movement. Carrie Chapman Catt, the president of the National American Woman Suffrage Association (NAWSA) from 1915 to 1920, knew this and began a strategy to counter the possibility of failure. She wrote, "The plan of the antis [antisuffragists] is to find thirteen states which they can hold out against ratification. They have been good enough to give us the list of the states. They are the solid south states . . . ." Considering the former slaveholding states—and one territory—in 1860 to be southern, there were actually seventeen such states that arguably could have blocked the amendment in 1920. This meant that the efforts of southern suffragists were critical in a region that could squash national hopes for women's voting rights. Antisuffragists were especially strong in the South; hence historians have often neglected the study of the southern woman suffrage movement, claiming that it was overwhelmingly unsuccessful with ten southern legislatures taking firm positions against the amendment.

Fortunately for women's rights, southern suffragists comprised a formidable countervailing force to the extreme conservatism of traditional southerners. In seven states associated with the South, notably, Arkansas, Kentucky, Missouri, Oklahoma, Tennessee, Texas, and West Virginia, suffragists ultimately prevailed, and the amendment passed. Energetic and capable women in the South constituted an essential force for reform and expanding democracy at a time when southern legislatures were still passing disfranchisement laws based on race or the inability to pay a poll tax.

Historians have analyzed why many southerners, both men and women, resisted endorsing the right of women to vote. Their reasons usually include the South's inherent conservatism and paternalism (men cast their votes for the women in their families), the ideal of the Southern Lady who was not supposed to soil her hands with the problems of dirty politics, the absence of a strong feminist movement in the South or a link between the antebellum suffrage movement and the abolition of slavery, the strength of the liquor industry that feared women's votes would bring prohibition, and the region's strong belief in states' rights. All of these are probable reasons why some resisted woman suffrage, but the most important reason was race, the fear among southern whites that allowing black women to vote might bring blacks into elected office.

Even southern suffragists who wanted to extend the vote were concerned about race. White southern women reformers were more likely to demand voting rights for white women, while ignoring the rights of black women and men in the South. African American woman suffragists found great difficulty in organizing suffrage societies in the South, yet many black reformers spoke out, sought voting rights for women, and when the amendment passed went straight to the county courthouses and registered to vote.

First-Generation Woman Suffragists, 1890–1910

Although there were a few southern advocates for woman suffrage in the 1860s and 1870s, their efforts died in state constitutional conventions and at the national level with the ratification of the Fifteenth Amendment granting black men the right to vote. Among the first generation of southern suffragists, or those who campaigned during the 1890s, the issue of black voting rights tempered their argument. By 1890 the two rival national women's organizations, the American Woman Suffrage Association and the National Woman Suffrage Association, had merged into the National American Woman Suffrage Association (NAWSA). The two groups had united on terms acceptable to the white South. At first, the NAWSA sought the ballot on a state-by-state basis, complementing the South's interest in states' rights over a federal amendment. At the same time, issues of race emerged. Because the Populist party had threatened the possible unification of poor black and white farmers, white southern Democrats preferred to disfranchise black voters rather than work with them or continue to control their votes. Henry Blackwell, although a former abolitionist and woman's rights proponent, offered a racist solution to both the "problem" of black voters and the desire among southern woman suffragists to gain the vote. He proposed to the Mississippi Constitutional Convention in 1890 to give voting rights to carefully qualified white women in each state. This way, he reasoned, through the numbers of white women voters, southern states would be able to maintain white hegemony. Fearing that the U.S. Supreme Court would declare outright black disfranchisement unconstitutional, woman suffragists adopted this state-by-state plan to give white women the right to vote. Thus did racism and power mongering become a part of the national movement.

The national leaders of the NAWSA acquiesced to this discriminatory tactic in part because they felt it held promise for victory and because they, too, were frustrated by having voting rights extended to "inferior" immigrant men in the North. Hoping to find victory in a "southern strategy," the NAWSA held conventions in Atlanta in 1895 and in New Orleans in 1903. But this proposal to advance the rights of white women while denying the rights of African Americans was unsuccessful, as was winning the vote on a state-by-state basis. Male legislators disfranchised black male voters through the use of literacy tests, grandfather clauses, and poll taxes *and* they did not give—nor was it politically necessary to give—white women the right to vote in any southern state. In fact, not one state gave women the right to vote between 1890 and 1910, although four western states (Wyoming, Colorado, Utah, and Idaho) had done so by 1890. The first wave of NAWSA's movement in the South was tainted from the beginning and ultimately proved a liability. In every southern state, suffrage leaders lost momentum and the movement faltered. The NAWSA then turned its attention toward the West.

It became clear that the "southern strategy" had failed when state legislatures found ways to eliminate black male voters without enfranchising women, and the U.S. Supreme Court actually upheld literacy tests, poll taxes, and the elimination of African Americans from juries in *Williams* v. *Mississippi* (1898). The woman suffrage movement in the South came to a halt, in part because there was not yet a mass demand for the vote among ordinary women at the grassroots level; women's clubs were just beginning to become involved in politics. What gave life to the southern suffrage movement was not white supremacy but the Progressive movement. After the disfranchisement of black men, the racial rhetoric changed to an assured tone that literacy tests, poll taxes, and other disfranchising measures would take care of the "problem" of black women voting. In fact a second generation of woman suffragists emerged from the reforming experience of the Progressive movement, and they led the suffrage charge.

Second-Generation Woman Suffragists, 1910–1920

In this second wave of the movement, between 1910 and 1920, women progressives and suffragists emerged primarily out of women's clubs or from institutions of higher learning. Some favored seeking a federal amendment, and others favored only state amendments, but after 1916, when state woman suffrage amendments failed in the South, suffragists redoubled their efforts to work toward a national amendment to the Constitution. These second-generation suffragists were less inclined to use race as an argument to win the vote for women. While they were well aware of the fears that white men held of black women voting, these suffragists counted on the disfranchisement measures already adopted by the southern states to quell these concerns. For example, in her suffrage notebook of 1913, Erminia Folsom of Austin carefully copied figures representing the number of blacks in Texas by county. She examined in detail the potential strength of black voters but concluded that the state was "safe" from a black voter takeover. She noted that there were only eight counties with "more Negroes than whites. . . ." Even Minnie Fisher Cunningham, president of the Texas Equal Suffrage Association, who was generally regarded as fair minded when it came to matters of race, said that the disfranchisement measures that had successfully kept black men from voting would do the same for black women. This generation of leaders had little reason to use racist demagoguery to make their point. They were confident that blacks would not be voting and, therefore, race was no reason to keep women—white women—from the polls.

Finding arguments for the vote, then, entailed looking toward women's traditional roles as guardians and nurturers of the family. Women at the center of the home "were responsible for the moral tone of a community," writes Anne Firor Scott. In cities across the South, black and white women found affiliation with national women's clubs. Here suffragists borrowed from the many Progressive era women's organizations that emerged at the turn of the century and flourished well into the 1950s. A network of women's voluntary organizations beginning with the Woman's Christian Temperance Union in the 1880s to the National Association of Colored Women, the General Federation of Women's Clubs, the Congress of Mothers, the YWCA, and state branches of each of these organizations set the stage for the emergence of suffragists. These and other organizations gave rise to women's access to public space and public agendas. The result was an unprecedented surge toward improving conditions in urban areas and founding state-level organizations to combat what were considered endangerments to women, children, and families.

In visualizing these "New Women" of the South, it is not difficult to see how many of them moved almost seamlessly into the national woman suffrage movement after 1910. Of course, they believed that women citizens had an inherent right to the vote, but since this argument had been waged without much success for years, they turned instead to more expedient rationales. They argued that women needed the vote in order to accomplish their political agenda of municipal housekeeping, child labor and juvenile reform, protections for working women, and even for enacting prohibition. Engaging fully in party and state politics and avoiding the rhetoric of white supremacy, the southern suffragists created sophisticated political "machines" that knew how to take advantage of opportunities for public approval. This does not mean that there were no divisions within the southern woman suffrage movement. White women divided among themselves over the kind of suffrage law that should be passed and over the best methods of winning the vote. Black and white women divided over issues of race.

After 1913, when the whole nation became more enthusiastic over woman suffrage, the NAWSA focused its attention on a federal amendment, awakening the chords of disunity in southern ranks. The Southern States Woman Suffrage Conference (SSWSC), led by Jean and Kate Gordon of Louisiana and Laura Clay of Kentucky, was so bent on states' rights that it was willing to obstruct a federal woman suffrage amendment. The members of the SSWSC used the arguments of the Lost Cause in part to defend their position, fearful that a federal amendment would bring an intrusion of federal power. This group even sided with the antisuffragists at one point in opposing the ratification of the Susan B. Anthony Amendment. Most followers of the movement saw the SSWSC as too conservative and too willing to obstruct woman suffrage for Lost Cause reasons, and after 1916 they did not gain much support from other suffragists in the South.

The National Woman's Party (NWP), headed by Alice Paul (who had formed the NWP as an offshoot of the Congressional Committee of the NAWSA), offered southern suffragists an alternative to the NAWSA. Discouraged over prospects of winning in the South, Carrie Chapman Catt counseled southern suffragists to campaign for partial suffrage—in presidential or municipal elections. Sue White of Tennessee found this decision counterproductive and joined ranks with the NWP. Most southerners, however, saw the NWP as too radical, especially after its members in 1917 picketed the White House and were arrested and sentenced to the Virginia Occoquan Workhouse. There the women, including Alice Paul, were treated brutally and, after they conducted hunger strikes were force-fed through a tube down the throat. Although winning admiration from many for their fortitude, the women's militancy threatened the movement. Such "unladylike" behavior did not go over well in the South, where women still had to convince male voters that there was nothing radical or frightening about women voting. On the other hand, militancy made the more moderate members of NAWSA seem ladylike by comparison and therefore more deserving of support. Ultimately, the NWP made little headway in the South.

The most formidable opponents to the south-wide woman suffrage movement were the antis. Antisuffragists believed there should be no votes for women at all. In 1915, when the NAWSA elected Carrie Chapman Catt as president, the suffrage movement became much more viable, and opposition to it mounted. Women antis, who openly opposed the Nineteenth Amendment, cited as their reasons biblical precedents, supposed female biological inferiorities, the potential breakdown of the home, the destruction of families, and the violation of states' rights. Antis argued that women were morally superior to men and entering into politics, even to cast a vote, could corrupt women and cause them to lose their feminine influence. One antisuffragist wrote that because polling places were often in saloons, women would be raped at the polls or they would stop breastfeeding their babies and leave home. Cartoons depicted a father wearing an apron, feeding the baby, and cooking dinner while his wife walked out the door wearing her woman suffrage sash. Antisuffragists also catered to white supremacy and used race baiting and fear tactics to oppose woman suffrage. Mildred Lewis Rutherford, Historian General and President of the UDC, became one of the most prominent antisuffragists in Georgia. Beside her in the antisuffrage campaign was Dolly Blount Lamar, another UDC activist. Together, they were able to mount such a strong antisuffrage campaign that Georgia became the first state to vote against the Nineteenth Amendment. Using the vicious rhetoric of white racism, spreading fears among voters that African American women voters would lead to a return of "black rule," they served as handmaidens for the worst of southern traditions. In effect antisuffragists were the accomplices of and the facilitators for Democratic party conservatives who used the argument of white supremacy to retain power and support women's subordinate role within a patriarchal family system.

African American Women Organize for the Vote

African American women supported votes for women, but the NAWSA did not make overtures to black women. In 1912, *The Crisis,* an organ of the NAACP, implied that no black women were included in the organizational hierarchy of the NAWSA in part because black men had not supported suffrage in the past and because southerners were "sensitive" to issues of race. Although forty-one black women, including Ida B. Wells-Barnett, (she had married attorney F. L. Barnett in 1895) marched in the 1913 Washington, D.C., suffrage parade on the eve of Woodrow Wilson's inauguration, they were treated differently from white women and were asked to march at the back of the line. Wells-Barnett refused to comply and waited on the sidelines until her largely white Chicago delegation passed by, at which point she joined them without incident. Whether black or white, all marchers suffered the same humiliating taunts and shoving from men on the sidelines. The parade turned into an embarrassment for President Wilson, who ended up apologizing to the women; however, he still refused to endorse woman suffrage in 1913. Despite the fact that discrimination was displayed against both black and white women from the sidelines at the march in Washington, neither the NAWSA nor the National Woman's Party included black women in their organizational structures. Black women saw themselves on the outside looking in.

African American women, who encountered the double burden of race and sex prejudice in southern society, discovered their need for the vote as they formed civic associations across the South. Such notable clubwomen as Margaret Murray Washington and Adella Hunt Logan of Alabama formed the Tuskegee Woman's Club in 1895, and its members began discussions over voting rights as early as 1897. They and others supported suffrage because they saw it as vital to their interests, and it fit their larger plan of intended progress for the race. The discouragement they experienced from state and national woman suffrage organizations meant that black women would have to find ways to reach out to white women, first in community-building enterprises and later in interracial cooperative groups. As Glenda Gilmore argued, during the period of black male disfranchisement, black middle-class women became diplomats to the white community. Through their own civic leagues, the YWCA, community improvement associations, and volunteer work during World War I, black women sought and won contacts with white clubwomen, ushering in the tentative first steps toward interracial dialogue. Seeking to capitalize on the Progressive movement, black women went before local and state governing bodies to request better services for their communities. African American women recruited potential voters, formed their own suffrage groups, and waited until the Nineteenth Amendment passed. Then they found ways to register to vote.

World War I

During World War I, suffragists alongside other women progressives aided the war effort by cooperating with "Food Will Win the War" campaigns, enlarging Red Cross branches, selling liberty bonds, and working for the military in antivice programs. Suffragists reasoned that their sacrifices for the war would bring them approval from male voters. In 1918 women's clubs boycotted products made in Germany, conducted classes in food preparation and canning, and planted victory gardens. Most followed the patriotic pleas for thrift and sacrifice, carefully monitoring their food buying and serving, and keeping to meatless, wheatless, and gasless days. College students with home economics training were recruited to offer demonstrations in canning and drying food. County and state governments hired professional home demonstration agents to teach women how to can vegetables and fruits from their gardens in what came to be known as "victory kitchens." In Houston, victory kitchen lessons yielded 15,000 cans of vegetables. The efforts to win the war crossed the color line; in East Texas 5,000 African American women and girls learned to preserve food under the direction of four black agents from the U.S. Food Administration. The North Carolina Woman's Committee coordinated all war work in that state among black and white women's organizations in a nonsegregated setting. Home demonstration agents disseminated information to white and black homemakers on how to fight the war through food preservation. In 1917, North Carolina Colored Assistant Emergency Home Demonstration Agents were hired to work in forty-one counties in the state during the summer months. At the end of the war, black women held positions as inspectors as well as home demonstration agents.

Red Cross units attracted patriotic black and white women who replenished older chapters and formed new ones. Here women learned first aid, rolled bandages, and collected supplies and money for hospitals, war refugees, and soldiers. Red Cross chapters sent American soldiers "comfort kits," complete with hand-knitted washcloths and socks. They raised money for soldiers' families and for ambulances and sent books and magazines to the men. Women canvassed neighborhoods selling liberty bonds; these drives brought many volunteers together for the war effort, and in North Carolina alone women sold $9 million worth of bonds.

The YWCA opened "Hostess Houses" on military bases, where men could relax, entertain their families, and converse with female friends. This complemented the goals of the U.S. Army, which wanted to see its young male recruits saved from the siren song of waiting prostitutes. Some women's clubs, under the auspices of their state federations, opened canteens for soldiers stationed nearby and kept the soldiers company in carefully chaperoned settings. The recreational canteens also provided billiards, refreshments, music, and weekly dances with proper young women. The women's clubs financed the expenses, provided the volunteer labor, and found the right kind of girls to be with the soldiers.

Suffrage groups had the opportunity to prove to the nation their patriotic stance by contributing to the war effort in ways similar to other women's clubs, and many of them did. But the Texas Equal Suffrage Association (TESA) found a unique way to help win the war. It commissioned its president, Minnie Fisher Cunningham, to bring to heel city and county office holders in areas where men were stationed. Some of the counties were out of compliance with a directive by Secretary of War Newton Baker to create a vice-free environment, which meant having no prostitutes within a five-mile radius of military camps, posts, and training facilities. In February 1918 the legislature banned the sale of alcohol within ten miles of a military camp, leading to the closure of some 1,000 saloons in Texas. There were fifty such military encampments and posts in the state, and Cunningham, with the support of sixteen organizations, formed a Texas Women's Anti-Vice Committee. Their goals were to see to it that the War Department directives were enforced and to protect soldiers and their wives and children from the spread of venereal disease. Despite their efforts, the women found evidence of evasion, especially in San Antonio, where 70,000 men were stationed and 5,000 prostitutes plied a lively trade. Reports showed that Fort Sam Houston in San Antonio had the highest venereal disease rate of any army camp in the nation. Although poorly funded, the Anti-Vice Committee was able to persuade the War Department to act with vigor, resulting in the closing of red- light districts in Houston, El Paso, Waco, San Antonio, Fort Worth, and Wichita Falls. Following these actions—and concerns for the moral and physical health of the populace—Texas raised its age of consent to eighteen and ratified the prohibition amendment. Their sacrifices and voluntary labor during the war had won women the respect of their male cohorts. Women hoped that after the war their efforts would bring them voting equality.

Ratification of the Nineteenth Amendment

In the national battle to win the vote for women, southern suffragists were disappointed when Carrie Chapman Catt declared most southern states unwinnable and counseled the state leaders to work towards primary or partial suffrage instead. This was not altogether an untenable idea. The state-by-state momentum for suffrage was increasing the pressure on President Woodrow Wilson, and he finally endorsed it on January 9, 1918. Women in western states who already had won the vote threatened to support the Republicans if Wilson did not approve women's right to the franchise. Suffragists reasoned that they had shown their loyalty to the nation during World War I and were entitled to this right of citizenship. The day after Wilson showed his colors for suffrage, the House passed the Susan B. Anthony Amendment, and in June 1919 the Senate did the same sending it to the states for ratification.

Before 1919, Arkansas, Texas, and Tennessee had granted women partial suffrage victories, mostly to vote in the primaries. Catt was wrong, however, to write off the South so callously, because just as it is today in national elections, the South was critical to the suffrage victory. Most tellingly, it was a southern state, Tennessee, that actually put the amendment over the top. Male legislators, of course, ratified the Susan B. Anthony Amendment, and the last male to vote for ratification in Tennessee was Harry Burn. At age twenty-four he was the youngest member of the Tennessee legislature, a Republican from a rural district in the eastern part of the state. The political leaders of his district opposed ratifying the amendment, but Harry's mother wrote him in the heat of the ratification debates, "Hurrah! And vote for suffrage. Don't keep them in doubt.... I have been watching to see how you stood, but have noticed nothing yet. Don't forget to be a good boy and help Mrs. Catt put the "Rat" in Ratification." Harry Burn listened to his mother and promised to vote aye for the amendment if his vote became the deciding one. He kept his promise. Thus in a curious turn of events, the Republican party in a largely Democratic region took credit for granting women the right to vote. Victory, when it came in 1920 with ratification of the Nineteenth Amendment, was bittersweet for white southern suffrage leaders. Of the seventeen states identified with the South, only seven (Texas, Tennessee, Kentucky, Arkansas, Missouri, Oklahoma, and West Virginia) ratified the federal amendment. All of them were peripheral southern states and for various reasons sought "progressive" men to ratify the amendment.

One possible reason that some of these states succeeded in ratifying woman suffrage was that they comprised urban areas that emphasized manufacturing, industry, access to transportation, and growth. In cities such as Dallas, Houston, Nashville, Memphis, Louisville, and Little Rock, women Progressives, through women's clubs and associations, had already tackled city problems such as pure water, sanitation, and disease control. Because they did not have the vote as leverage, they had learned well its value. For these women the franchise had a specific purpose, a way to defend their families and their communities and to promote women's citizenship. Male residents of cities, who were more urbane, better educated, more worldly, and less fearful of the future supported woman suffrage.

Perhaps the most persuasive argument to explain why these particular southern states ratified the amendment stemmed from their relatively low black populations compared to states in the Deep South. In Alabama, Mississippi, Louisiana, Georgia, and South Carolina, the black population in some counties exceeded 50 percent. There, fears of "black rule" harking back to Reconstruction filled antisuffragist rhetoric. Thus race and racism among whites, suffragists included, was a critical factor. In those seven states that ratified the Nineteenth Amendment, fear of black voters did not appear to be as rampant as it was in the states of the Deep South.

Then, too, states with a two-party system created more leverage for women lobbyists, and the strength of the Republican party in Arkansas, Tennessee, and Kentucky led to victory. In the case of Texas, historian Judith McArthur argues that for all the sacrifices women made during World War I, probably nothing would have turned Texas into a suffrage-granting state had there not been a rift in the state Democratic party. Fortunately, Minnie Fisher Cunningham, president of the TESA from 1915 to 1920, and her supporters manipulated to their advantage a split in the party between progressives and conservatives. Texas granted women the right to vote in the primaries in 1918, and women proved their power by voting for William P. Hobby, a somewhat more progressive governor than his predecessor. Texas thereafter became the first state in the South to ratify the Nineteenth Amendment.

The New Woman in Politics

With victory in 1920, the National American Woman Suffrage Association changed its name to the League of Women Voters, Now it dedicated itself to educating women on political issues, how to register to vote, and how physically to cast their ballots. The League became a nonpartisan group, and in doing so changed its character from a confrontational organization fighting for a citizen's right to vote, to a voluntary group seeking to educate the newly enfranchised. One lasting and important result of the suffrage victory came when women veterans of the movement ran for office. In Mississippi, which mounted possibly the strongest opposition to suffrage of any state, two woman suffragists ran for office and won: Belle Kearney and Nellie Nugent Somerville, both of whom were elected to the state legislature in the 1920s. Minnie Fisher Cunningham ran for the U.S. Senate (unsuccessfully) in 1928, while Miriam A. ("Ma")

Ferguson won the governorship of Texas in 1924, the first woman governor in the South and second in the nation to win that office. The ultimate irony was that Ferguson, who many regarded as a shill for her husband and formerly impeached Texas governor James E. "Pa" Ferguson, did not support woman suffrage; the extension of democracy worked in all directions. Thereafter, even antisuffragists who had opposed voting rights used the vote to gain conservative political victories.

Hundreds of thousands of white women came to the polls and cast ballots in the 1920 elections, as did thousands of African American women across the South. In states like Texas that had no literacy test, black women paid the poll tax, registered, and voted. They counted on their status as women to prevent them from attacks by white men at registration or the voting booth. In other states it took more courage for black women to come before the voting registrar to take a literacy test. In such states women organized suffrage parties among their friends and neighbors before traveling to the public place that registered voters. In North Carolina, the state Association of Colored Women's Clubs and the NAACP organized voting drives in the Piedmont and the western part of the state, much to the surprise of Democrats. Charlotte Hawkins Brown, president of the North Carolina Association of Colored Women and principal of Palmer Memorial Institute in Sedalia, hatched a plan to send droves of black women to register to vote in the last two weeks of the state's registration campaign. She and others made sure that black women were prepared to take the literacy test. They waited until the last two Saturdays to register and then surprised the registrars by showing up in large numbers. The registration records from across the state show thousands of black women applying to register (while only a small percentage actually succeeded). Perhaps 1,000 black women paid their poll tax and got past the hurdles to vote. In Tampa, the white registrars were unprepared for the numbers of black (and white) women who showed up to register to vote after the legislature waived the poll tax for women voters in 1920. Others who had been denied the chance to vote refused to be quiet and sent their complaints to NAACP and NWP headquarters. By 1928 many more blacks had registered, including black men, who were pleased that women were voting despite the traditional association of voting with manhood. Sadly, most white clubwomen, who had previously cooperated with black women in municipal projects, argued that whites should try to outnumber black women at the polls. In the arena of politics, there was little interracial cooperation.

Not surprisingly, voting increased in the South as a result of the passage of the Nineteenth Amendment. Despite the imposition of the poll tax, the increase in voters spread from 79 percent in Alabama to 86 percent in North Carolina, with an average 54 percent increase across the South where women were eligible to vote. (Women in Mississippi and Georgia were not eligible by state law to vote in the 1920 presidential election.) Once women began voting, they saw firsthand the fraudulent methods that officials often used to rig elections, including marking extra ballots or destroying ballots. This led to a vigilance campaign among women voters at the polling places.

Martha Robinson of New Orleans was especially outraged at the way democracy was thwarted at the polling booth. She headed the Woman Citizens' Union (WCU), comprised of twenty-two organizations, and began to learn how the well-oiled New Orleans political machine kept running. Members of the WCU began by monitoring elections, starting with the registration rolls and continuing through the long voting day at each of the 262 polling places in the Crescent City. Their aim was to fight voter fraud, and they noted every irregularity. Just by monitoring elections, women learned what they previously had not known about politics, and they were fired up to reform the structure of government, including election proceedings, with voting machines, decent polling places, and civil service laws to end patronage. Women fought for jury service, the right to be included in party decision making, the right to continue primary elections, and the power to run for office. Louisiana women even fought the powerful Huey Long machine by backing anti-Long candidates and encouraging women to work actively for reform in public education.

Males responded in a variety of ways to the voting-poll surveillances, but many party officials went out of their way to win over women to their political persuasion. In those southern states where the Republican party was strongest, women voters represented a real threat to the Democratic party regulars. Women used their lack of party loyalty as a bargaining chip. They also used old and familiar tactics of lobbying in new ways to win their agendas. Before they had been voters, women often had petitioned their legislators in groups and had been forced to have men represent them. After gaining the vote, they realized that assemblymen and senators saw each letter as a potential vote. The volume of letters increased as women's groups developed political strategies for lobbying. In Georgia, women voters sent 12,000 letters in support of a State Board of Health. In Texas the WCTU did the same in support of a minimum wage bill. The League of Women Voters also encouraged lobbying strategies. They announced new agendas during campaigns and asked candidates to reveal their positions on concerns critical to women. With questionnaires, the League forced candidates and office holders publicly to take a stand on issues, providing voters the opportunity to make a choice. If a candidate did not respond to a survey, this along with other candidates' responses were printed in local newspapers and distributed to voters. In some cases, the surveys were used as a quid pro quo to get out the vote for a particular candidate. Thus honesty among candidates improved as women kept up the pressure for disclosure.

The most important evidence of the power of the New Woman voters came with agendas created by women's legislative councils. These were designed to coordinate the lobbying efforts of this newly enfranchised political constituency and bring under one umbrella the desires and needs of such disparate groups as those who represented labor, farm, city, and class interests. The legislative councils worked to send a unified message to the public and state lawmakers, even as they shaped a viable and mutually acceptable agenda. In this way they attempted to speak for the hundreds of thousands of women voters. The Joint Legislative Council of Texas provides an example of one such successful program. Dubbed the Petticoat Lobby by beleaguered assemblymen, it was comprised of women's groups from that state, which included among others the Texas Federation of Women's Clubs, the League of Women Voters, the Mothers Congress, and the WCTU. These groups lobbied the state legislature for five sessions and with that effort made important gains for women, children, prisoners, and dependents in the state. In their initial lobbying results in 1923, they were able to acquire emergency funding for schools, more stringent prohibition laws, studies of schools and prisons, and, most important, sufficient monies to match the federal funds held out by the Sheppard-Towner Act, which furnished medical care to infants and mothers. The Sheppard-Towner Act, passed by Congress in 1921, was the first federal law that offered matching funds for the states to make available health care for mothers and infants. Thus southern legislatures had to make the decision whether to outlay money from their state treasuries in order to accept federal aid. Southern states, at the behest of women voters, did accept the federal grant. The Alabama legislature, after having heard from the Alabama League of Women Voters, appropriated its share of the funds and received $45,000 to create twenty-one health clinics and staff them with nurses.

African American women believed in the power of their votes despite the many obstacles put before them. Knowing that there were black voters in the North unimpeded by voting restrictions, black southerners called upon them and their Republican party representatives to lobby for an antilynching law; they also demanded that elections in the South be supervised by federal marshals. At the local level black women voted their interests for improved public services. In Atlanta, after passage of the Nineteenth Amendment, African American women more than doubled the registered voter pool. The very threat of an overwhelming black vote to defeat a 1921 education bond intended to help only white schools brought city leaders to the negotiating table. Black voters finally forced the city to open the aforementioned Booker T. Washington High School in 1924, and Lugenia Burns Hope, who worked through the Atlanta

Neighborhood Union to bring women to the polls, provided inspiration for the campaign to increase funding for the city's black schools. Similarly, newly enfranchised black women voters in Kentucky helped to defeat a bond initiative intended to enhance a segregated university system—"by a margin of 4,000 votes," according to historian Lorraine Gates Schuyler. In these cases, black southerners found that with women voting they could raise a voting bloc in municipal and bond elections where there was no white primary.

In one rare instance, black and white women formed a pragmatic connection. In Nashville, Tennessee, white women promised certain concessions of support for the black community if black women would vote for a municipal reform agenda in the 1920 election. In part because Nashville was the home of Fisk University and Meharry Medical College, educated black clubwomen found alliance with like-minded white clubwomen. White suffragists created a slate of reform candidates for the city election, and asked women of color to join them. Due to their coalition—and their votes—the city boss of Nashville lost the election. Black women then cashed in their political capital to ask for and receive, among other things, a black probation officer and black nurses in city hospitals. Common interest in good government could make allies of black and white women citizens who voted gender over race. For the most part, however, southern black women voters were at a decided disadvantage with racial disfranchisement, a problem that would not be fully resolved until the 1960s.

The impact of women voters on the South should not be underestimated. Through women's clubs and the newly formed League of Women Voters, women projected an agenda that included the care and protection of children and workers and launched women into the political arena. In some states they monitored polling places, found common cause to rid cities of boss machinery, and urged their assemblymen to take advantage of federal programs to assist mothers and infants. They put forth candidates and backed them; some women even won election at the local and state levels. If they did not already know how to become political, they became so after winning the vote and diving into the ring. This is not to say that white women were ready to form equal social relationships with African Americans, although interracial projects with women and some men moved race relations forward. A woman's agenda was nothing less than a humanitarian attempt to use politics for social good and not necessarily for the acquisition and retention of power.

CHAPTER SIX

Gender, Race, and the "Modern" Decades

According to some historians, the 1920s marked a turning point in the nation's modernization. In the South as well as elsewhere in the United States, a few women altered their styles and dared convention at every turn. Women's roles as wives and mothers changed little, however, even with the access of middle-class people to such new technologies as the radio, electric appliances, and the automobile. Transformations for southern women came through their intellectual, artistic, and cultural endeavors; women writers, artists, and musicians were beginning to speak unpleasant truths about gender and race relations in the South. A few talented black female vocalists and dancers left the South as part of the Great Exodus to find their new land in Harlem or in Europe. Others sought education or exposure to ideas to help them reevaluate the race and class concerns of their home region. For all of those who left the South or hoped to reform it, there were still others who clung to the fabled history of a romanticized older time. Margaret Mitchell, who wrote *Gone with the Wind,* the nation's favorite novel during the 1930s, used stereotyped images of black and white women and men but answered a longing among Americans for an idealized past.

The real South continued to exist with race riots, lynchings, and the rise of an antimodernist viewpoint. Gender and race issues exploded in Atlanta, where events led to bloodletting and the reevaluation of that city's mission. One result was a triumphant revival of the Ku Klux Klan, another the Great Exodus of black citizens no longer willing to stay in the South and be victimized. Southern progressives voiced their shame and despair over the situation, desirous of a saner, safer environment for African Americans, white women, and children of both races. Building on this momentum, tentative first steps toward interracial work began through women's organizations, first in churches, then through the YWCA, and finally in several associations devoted to improving the relationship between the races and ending the tragedy of lynching.

The Thoroughly Modern Southern Woman

While the League of Women Voters and the South's clubwomen continued to seek reform at the hands of their legislators—this time with the vote—a few other women followed the latest fads that pervaded the region through popular culture. Some former southern belles entered bathing beauty contests and flaunted their legs, whereas only a decade earlier, women marching for suffrage had worn ankle-length dresses with long sleeves and hats dripping with feathers. The worldly 1920s southern woman bobbed her hair, raised her skirts, wore red lipstick, and drank illegal whisky and gin. Southern women now drove cars and went on dates unchaperoned. More young women went to colleges and universities, where they found fraternity men attractive companions at football games and dances. According to Paula S. Fass, the modern peer culture emerged at this time from college campuses—mostly from fraternities—and southern university women became sorority divas with an Old South flavor. The image of college women in the 1920s riding in roadster rumble seats while their escorts sported raccoon coats and hip flasks was countered in reality by more traditional southern mores. Women's colleges tried to put a check on some of these independent attitudes, for ladylike decorum was still a necessary, if unofficial, requirement for graduation. Black colleges, most of them co-ed, set specific rules for women that were stricter than those for men. On many a campus young women were not allowed to play cards, dance, smoke, or drink. At all-white Winthrop College in South Carolina, to be caught smoking in 1930 could lead to dismissal for a term. Sororities for black and white women were at times both snobbish and industrious in encouraging good grades and community service work.

Among working women, another lifestyle unfolded during the decades surrounding World War I. This was especially true among young, wage-earning white and black women who discovered city life full of pleasures to be found in dance halls and jazz clubs. Atlanta's Decatur Street clubs catered to the black working class—taking workers away from the drudgery of domestic or menial labor to the independence and daring of the city's nightlife. Here the music was fluid and varied—ragtime and lowdown blues. As historian Tera Hunter explains, "African Americans could pursue entertainment at will—an important distinction from slavery." The nightlife on Decatur Street arose during the late 1890s, but by 1906 segregated saloons, cheap hotels, gambling houses, pool rooms, cafes, and dance halls attracted adventurous working-class men and women—both black and white—creating an explosive racial and sexual mix. Decatur Street night life led to rumors of Chinese opium dens and white slavery, but some of Atlanta's all-white police force enjoyed off-duty hours there alongside drifters, jobbers, and con artists. After 1906, and the horrendous race riot that left twenty-five blacks dead, Decatur Street became a center for vaudeville, becoming more a formalized theater district in the 1920s. At the other end of the spectrum for more conservative African Americans was Auburn Avenue, where well-dressed families promenaded on Sunday mornings and considered it "a place to go at night and dress up," recalled Alice Adams, a domestic worker.

Black Atlantans discovered vaudeville's allure and went to see the Whitman Sisters, the highest paid black dance performers on the circuit, and Ethel Waters (Sweet Mama Stringbean), whose performing career stretched into the 1950s. As early as the 1910s the South launched some of the best black talent in the nation, and both black- and white-owned theaters gave these artists performance space while audiences voted approval with their attendance. Among the most influential of these venues was the Eighty One Theater, a white-owned operation on Decatur Street that welcomed such artists as Ma Rainey and Bessie Smith, the Empress of the Blues. Josephine Baker, who later stunned audiences in Paris and became an outspoken diplomat for black equality during the 1950s, entertained Atlantans by dancing, singing, and cross dressing. The Whitman Sisters presented tap dancing in such a way as to begin a cakewalk fad during the 1920s. The talents of these performers became nationally known, and some dancers who trained with the Whitman Sisters took their technique to Broadway just when musical theater began to draw audiences. A new age of women in the public eye came to the South with the 1920s—on stage, in recordings, in beauty pageants, and in films.

Southern Music: The Gendered Art

Jazz reportedly got its start in New Orleans, but music historians, who say that jazz is the descendant of black and white folk music, dispute that. It appeared all over the South and for a time was synonymous to most Americans with pop music. By the 1920s the South's jazz was celebrated in cities like New York and Chicago. Louis Armstrong, who got his start playing cornet in New Orleans, found his opening with King Oliver's Creole Jazz Band in Chicago in 1922, and by 1925 he had made his first recording. Luminaries like Duke Ellington rose from backgrounds in minstrelsy and vaudeville to great fame as jazz virtuosi. By the 1930s the radio popularized jazz, and southern music found its way to northern and western audiences eager for the energy and life this music projected. While jazz groups hired both men and women performers, jazz solo instrumentalists were nearly always men. Thus it was the blues that emerged onto the national scene in the 1920s that gave women artists the limelight.

The blues may have been seen as a man's art at first. W. C. Handy, "father of the blues," encountered folk blues from his travels through Mississippi in 1902. The blues grew out of black work songs, field shouts, spirituals, and hymns. Handy began to collect traditional melodies and blue notes, arranging them for his own band. His success led him to Memphis, where he published his first blues piece in sheet music form in 1912; after that he went on to make Beale Street famous with his dance band. The origins of the dance tune the "Fox Trot" can be traced directly to his composition, "The Memphis Blues." The general public perceived blues as a novel type of ragtime with the unusual features of three-line stanzas and blue notes, a form of flattened, lower-pitched notes used almost exclusively in blues music. Thomas A. Dorsey, a blues artist generally considered the "father of gospel music," composed gospel songs using blue notes, but most blues were not so much connected to the spiritual side of life as to the mundane and to a sense of joy overwhelmed by a feeling of hopelessness. Men were more likely to introduce this music because the material conjured images of relationships with women whose lives were rough, seamy, and loose. Men could sing about women this way, but women singers took a risk on stage with lyrics that spoke of sex, drinking, and violence. Traditional stereotypes of black female promiscuity led black middle-class women to protest their reification as sex objects. Female blues singers dared bourgeois convention when they entertained in carnivals or vaudeville acts, dividing their emphasis either between instrument or voice, but performing with a forcefulness and an honesty that suggested that their own lives were wild, passionate, and sad. By telling such poetic tales of passion and desire in the 1920s, women blues singers defied the rules of respectability carefully cultivated by Progressive era reformers. Despite the controversy, or perhaps because of it, when the world discovered the blues, a few notable women artists rocketed to stardom.

Beginning in 1920, Mamie Smith became the first African American woman to record the blues—"Crazy Blues." This record sold 1 million copies within a year, thanks in part to black Pullman porters buying them and reselling them during their travels at a 100 percent profit. The majority of consumers were black, and they found in this "race record" not only enduring entertainment but also pride in the fact that this music, which stemmed from southern juke joints and country road houses in remote rural locales, was spreading to urban audiences nationwide. Smith's recording began a ten-year boom in black music, and she became the first black superstar to step onto a national stage. Mamie Smith was not, however, alone in achieving success, as blues and jazz entertainers such as Ma Rainey and Bessie Smith, who hailed from Georgia and Tennessee respectively, found their own paths to stardom. Bessie Smith soared in popularity when she made 160 recordings and a film based on W. C. Handy's "St. Louis Blues." Gertrude "Ma" Rainey, considered the "Mother of the Blues," recorded more that 100 songs and was among the first to introduce blues into her musical routine. The advent of recordings and radio, and the consumption of these media by a nation hungry for what was new and hip, led to the empowerment of black women artists. Literary critic Hazel Carby argues that "women's blues" is a "discourse that articulates a cultural and political struggle over sexual relations," especially within a patriarchal society, but which celebrates women's sexuality and sensuality through music. The most expressive example of this can be found in Ma Rainey's "Prove it on Me Blues," the song in which she asserts her preference for women, flaunting it before the heterosexual world. Women blues singers worked their way to a privileged place of independence and public notoriety. Among the majority of black women, they stood out as royalty—Bessie Smith was called "Empress of the Blues." Having dared convention with their sensuality in song, they ensured a mass market for African American's women's artistry.

Entertainment in the 1920s was beginning to show signs of interracial appreciation and gender neutrality. A gifted woman singer was as likely to earn recognition and advancement as was a male performer. The songs they sang, especially the blues, spoke honestly of relationships between men and women that were dysfunctional, destructive, even brutal, but always real and passion fueled. In describing the poverty, weariness, and disappointment of living day-to-day in the segregated South with its rigid gender codes, the blues allowed the world to hear another version of life in the region—one not clouded by denial.

In "Yonder Comes the Blues," Ma Rainey voiced for thousands of women their frustration of enduring relationships squeezed by the vise of racial prejudice and exploitation. Yet, by singing her lament, Rainey rose beyond the ordinary.

> I worry all day, I worry all night,
> Everytime my man comes home he wants to fuss and fight,
> When I pick up the paper and try to read the news,
> Just when I'm satisfied, yonder comes the blues.
>
> I went down to the river each and every day,
> Trying to keep from throwing myself away.
> I walked and walked' til I wore out my shoes,
> I can't walk no further, yonder comes the blues . . .
>
> Some folks never worry, things all go all right
> Or lay down on that sofa, weep and cry all night
> When I get a letter, it never brings good news
> Every time I see the mail, babe, yonder comes the blues
>
> Go back blues don't come this way
> Oughta give me something else beside the blues all day
> Every man I love, I've been refused
> And when I want some loving yonder comes the blues
>
> People have different blues and think they're mighty bad
> But blues that bother me are the worst I've ever had
> I've been disgusted and all confused every time I look around
> yonder come those blues.

Women Writers and Southern Literature

If jazz and the blues were not enough to fuel the South's modern image, there was the literary renaissance of the 1920s, 1930s, and 1940s. In a November 1917 issue of the *New York Evening Mail,* the journalist H. L. Mencken from Baltimore published his famous essay, "The Sahara of the Bozarts," in which he excoriated the South for its backwardness and for giving little of cultural value to the world; in his view the region was a desert of the Beaux Arts. As if in response to Mencken, southerners surprised the world and produced a literary Renaissance unequaled in the history of the region. Undoubtedly, the greatest writer to emerge in the twentieth century was William Faulkner who used local, family, and Mississippi history to write his devastating critique of southern culture.

The great impetus for women writers in Dixie was not only the region's blatant disregard for female equality but also its embrace of the ideal of the Southern Lady. The woman suffrage movement made great strides toward forcing southerners to rethink their stance on women, race, and class, and southern women writers took advantage of that opening. Earlier writers such as Kate Chopin and Ellen Glasgow had protested the enduring "burdens of ladyhood." Writers, such as Julia Peterkin in *Scarlet Sister Mary,* followed suit, disregarding the polite veil of silence that surrounded women's domestic lives and speaking honestly of their sexuality. In a similar vein, women stepped down off the pedestal in *The Hard Boiled Virgin* (1926) and *Dead Lovers Are Faithful Lovers* (1928), both by Frances Newman.

The black writer and anthropologist Zora Neale Hurston, considered a part of the Harlem Renaissance, had her roots in northern Florida. She returned there from 1927 to 1932, after studying with anthropologist Franz Boas at Barnard College, to gather folk tales and study black dialect. Much of her talent and energy went toward the study of African Americans as a distinct rural cultural group with a rich folk tradition, but her most memorable work was a novel, *Their Eyes Were Watching God* (1937). In this haunting story Hurston portrayed the life of Janie

Crawford, who left a bleak North Florida town to find an even bleaker future married to a heartbreak husband who harnessed her to a plow and expected her to perform a life of servitude. Janie rebelled to become an independent black woman with a taste for a younger man surprisingly named Tea Cake. Hurston's feminism through her fictional characters found expression at a time when black women were combating not only racism but also the confines of patriarchy within African American culture. Her work was criticized by such distinguished intellectuals as Howard University Professor Alaine Locke, whose essay on the "New Negro" written in 1925 called for an end to the stereotypes of blacks that had kept them from achieving equality. He saw in Hurston's novel carefree characters that spoke in the dialect of the South and thereby catered to white audiences fascinated with "pseudo primitives." He missed her point, however, that whites were not the only oppressors of black women; black men and black community gossips worked to dampen women's independence. After Hurston's initial success, the novel lost appeal amidst the upheavals of World War II and the civil rights movement, but with the rise of second-wave feminism in the 1970s, *Their Eyes Were Watching God,* made a poignant comeback. The novel influenced such luminaries as Toni Morrison and Alice Walker, whose main character Celie in her 1983 Pulitzer Prize–winning novel *The Color Purple* bears an uncanny resemblance to Janie Crawford.

Though there are many women writers who could claim prominence among the literati, none took the South to task more forcefully for its hypocritical stance on race and gender than did Lillian Smith. Her first book, *Strange Fruit* (1945), portrayed a love relationship of unequal power between a white man and a black woman; it ended badly with the lynching of an innocent man, hence the title, which was immortalized also in song. Her second book, a memoir called *Killers of the Dream* (1949), characterized the South as a "dark and tangled forest full of sins and boredom and fears." The sins she described were those of parents who taught their children racial prejudice, instructed them that sex was sinful, and admonished them not to cross the color line in support of black rights, for that would displease God and family. In evaluating her own book she wrote, "I say nothing that people in their hearts do not already know but I try to say it in such a way that their imaginations will be stirred and some of their energies released that are now tied up in conflict."

Katharine Du Pre Lumpkin's autobiography, *The Making of a Southerner* (1947), is the work of an intellectual whose education, first in the South and later in the North, provided her with awakenings and epiphanies denied those whose lives were mired in the social mundanity of southern life. Subtly she begins to tell the history of her family, the plantation filled by working slaves, the division of slave families after the master's death, the rising interest in the Confederate cause, and the aftermath of the Civil War. Lumpkin writes in a matter-of-fact style at the beginning of her book in order to entice the southern reader to continue without displaying her hand. Once well into her story, the reader discovers that she is no apologist for the Old South or the Lost Cause, with which she was completely familiar. Rather, hers is an indictment of white male superiority, racism and class values, and of her own timidity in facing interracial cooperation through her work with the YWCA. Both Lillian Smith and Katharine Du Pre Lumpkin remained in committed relationships with women partners but were unable to disclose publicly their sexual orientation. These facts, nonetheless, shaped their lives. Lillian Smith owned and managed a girl's camp and thus isolated herself from southern society even as she criticized it. Katharine Lumpkin found little regard for the company of others in her later years after a successful career as a sociologist and writer.

While Smith and Lumpkin found much to criticize in the South they inherited, Margaret Mitchell, as noted earlier, glorified the region's history in her 1936 Pulitzer Prize–winning Civil War–era novel. *Gone with the Wind* became an instant best seller and was made into a blockbuster film (one of the first in full color) in 1939. The book came out in July and by December had sold 1 million copies; it had sold as many as 28 million by 2008. The movie, viewed by 25 million people in the first six months of its release, was still a favorite among the majority of Americans according to a poll conducted by the American Film Institute in 1998. It ranks among the top twenty films in box-office receipts, before taking inflation into account. The movie won eight academy awards: including best film, best actress for Vivien Leigh as Scarlett O'Hara, and best supporting actress for Hattie McDaniel as Mammy, the first "Oscar" for an African American actor. Although honored in Hollywood at the Academy Awards ceremony, neither McDaniel nor any of the African American actors were invited to the official premier events for the film in segregated Atlanta. In an uncanny presaging of historical change, however, a "slave choir," in costume performed before an Atlanta Junior League ball to celebrate the opening of the film. Among those in the children's choir was a very young Martin Luther King, Jr.

Gone with the Wind was revived in 1976 for television and became "the highest-rated single network program ever broadcast," according to historian Catherine Clinton. The sets, the characters, and the script have been thoroughly analyzed and criticized, yet the public still reveres the film. Part of the reason for this may be the character Scarlett—her manipulative nature, her ambition, and most of all her independence. Beautiful but tempestuous, even violent, she uses the Southern Lady model when she needs it but enters a man's world and acts with force when confronted with destitution. In the end, she achieves monetary success by working hard and marrying well but she remains unhappy. The fact that other female characters in the novel, such as Melanie, epitomized the Southern Lady (in her case finding great joy in her marriage to Ashley Wilkes), suggests that even in 1936 most white women in the South would have a difficult time finding happiness outside the role of the Southern Lady. Overly sentimental and unrepresentative of the true nature of African Americans, flawed in its representation of the southern class system (most antebellum white southerners did not own slaves or live in mansions), the story remains a classic in part because many were nostalgic for an idealized romantic South. More benign in its depiction of race and race relations than the overtly racist *The Birth of a Nation* (1915), *Gone with the Wind* nonetheless has shaped the American imagination about the history of the South, festooning southern women with the mantel of ladyhood and shackling southern black women with the image of "Mammy."

Re-creating a White Man's South

Many of the social changes wrought by World War I and the decade of the 1920s seemed alien, atheistic, and dangerous to a majority of families living on farms, working in factories, or trying to cling to a middle-class existence in small towns across the South. For those who eschewed the so-called modern tendencies, there was not much hope for the future as represented by the disillusioned writers, dissolute black songsters and blues players, beauty queens, moonshiners, and dance-hall operators. Moreover, for conservative southerners the changes that women had achieved seemed to threaten their concepts of southern manhood and notions of pure womanhood. Traditionalists feared and resented advances made toward civil liberties by African Americans, for their economic and social progress challenged notions of white superiority. What southerners needed, they opined, was a return to the true values of the South—the old-fashioned virtues of religion, the biblical assertion that a man is the head of the household, and the premise of white supremacy and black subordination.

White evangelical religious groups that considered personal morality one of the benchmarks of civilization supported these antimodernist views. The new cultural media, primarily film, presented challenges to their belief in the sanctity of the home and placed, according to historian Ted Ownby, "the purity of women—ever the cornerstone of evangelical morality—under siege in new ways." Movie theaters replaced religious revivals as the new form of entertainment; and the automobile took families for a Sunday drive rather than to church. Films such as *The Great Romance*, *The Parisian Tigresse*, and *What Every Woman Wants* tempted a new generation to see women as sexual beings—even the daughters of respectable middle-class families. Cars facilitated the chance for young people to experiment sexually, away from parental eyes. Studies of human sexuality conducted by Alfred C. Kinsey and others show that the idea of girls "holding the line" was fast disappearing, as a majority of women interviewed in the 1930s reported having engaged in premarital sex.

Many evangelical Christians fumed against the invasion of secular values into their homes and worried that science would destroy religious faith. Several historical events catalyzed their opinions and indicated the malcontent that lurked just beneath the surface of southern progress. One of these was the 1925 John Scopes "Monkey" Trial in Dayton, Tennessee, wherein the court decided to uphold the state law prohibiting the teaching of the theory of human evolution in public schools. The other was the turn toward an institutionalized and vicious form of race purity that stemmed from the old notion of the protection of white womanhood. By the 1920s the attitudes of antimodernists—a good many of them evangelicals—had morphed into a distorted version of "100 percent Americanism" rife with notions of nativism, racism, and male dominance.

For North Carolinian Thomas Dixon such ideas had gained currency as early as the 1880s when he studied history at Johns Hopkins University under the tutelage of Herbert Baxter Adams. American democratic roots reached back to Teutonic concepts of law, according to Adams, who also supported notions of Social Darwinism. He concluded that African Americans and other so-called inferior peoples were incapable of self-government or rule. From these thoughts, Dixon created two historical novels that inflamed race relations at the turn of the century; *The Leopard's Spots: A Romance of the White Man's Burden, 1865–1900* (1902) and *The Clansman: A Historical Romance of the Ku Klux Klan* (1905). In both novels the subject was Reconstruction and the damage done to the white South by granting political rights to African Americans. For Dixon and for many southerners an ideological progression ensued: once endowed with political rights, blacks would advance to social equality, which would lead black men to consort with or desire to marry white women. The driving force that fueled these fears was the potential for sexual liaison between white women and black men. *The Clansman* sold more than a million copies, and in it the Ku Klux Klan of the 1870s came to represent all that was valiant and noble in white southern manhood. The book became a play that reached many audiences, and when it came to Atlanta in 1905 it caused a near riot between white and black audience members. *The Clansman* played in Atlanta for months prior to a vicious gubernatorial campaign and an explosive black-on-white rape accusation charged by Annie Poole against Frank Carmichael. Rather than waiting for an arrest and a trial, a party of white men murdered Carmichael in "a roar of gun powder." The Democratic candidate for governor, Hoke Smith, using racist invectives, fomented so much fear and hatred that he handily won the election. Inflammatory news reports of more black-on-white rapes set off another such explosion. September 22, 1906, saw Atlanta erupt in a race riot in which twenty-five blacks lost their lives.

Middle-class whites tried to distance themselves from the bloodshed of the riot, although leading black Atlantans, such as John and Lugenia Burns Hope, Addie Hunton, Walter White, W. E. B. Du Bois, and Reverend Henry Hugh Proctor, charged that "respectable" white Atlantans had done little to stop the violence and were responsible if not directly culpable for the massacre. In sensing the need to protect African Americans, Lugenia Hope founded the Neighborhood Union. Addie Hunton, who presided over the black Atlanta's Women's Club in 1906, insisted that whites allow black men to protect black women from white sexual transgressors, but she also maintained that the uplift of the race depended on the agency of black women to disprove the stereotypes of black women as sexually permissive. W. E. B. Du Bois continued his plans for a national association to challenge racism in the United States culminating in the establishment of the NAACP, and Walter White joined him in that life-long endeavor. Henry Proctor became the leading spokesperson for interracial dialogue and cooperation in Atlanta after the tragedy.

There remained among whites, however, a continuing fear about the advancement of African Americans in the South, the interacting of black men with white women, and the alleged need to protect white women from their assaults. White men saw their manhood at stake in the protection of their wives, daughters, sisters, and sweethearts, leading to further trouble and hardship. Then in 1915, Hollywood entered the arena. Film director D. W. Griffith, a southerner by birth, had been raised on a poisonous interpretation of Reconstruction in the South. This rendition asserted that African Americans ruled the southern states (black rule), whites were punished and made destitute by black ineptitude, venal men from the North (Carpetbaggers) took advantage of the prostrate South, and the saviors of the region were noble Confederate veterans who rode at night in hoods to defend innocent women from these interlopers. For Griffith, the novel *The Clansman* held enormous appeal, and he created what critics claim is the single most important American film of all time, *The Birth of a Nation*.

In this film, black Reconstruction legislators are shown lazing about the statehouse, eating fried chicken, resting their shoeless feet on mahogany desks, and carrying forth placards that read, "Equal Rights, Equal Politics, Equal Marriage." Renegade blacks who were former Union soldiers terrify the white citizenry, and one even attempts to marry or possibly rape the youngest daughter of the noble Cameron family. Chased to the top of a cliff, the young woman leaps to her death to protect her chastity. Another African American character from the North, cunning in his bid for power, wins the lieutenant governorship and plots to build a "Black Empire" with an unwilling white woman, the daughter of his northern mentor. As events reach a crisis, the newly formed Ku Klux Klan rides in to save white womanhood from the savage beasts, and the closing scenes show an ethereal Christ overseeing the noble order of the Klan. In the end there is a reunion of the North and the South in the way northerners came to accept the "noble South's" version of the war and its aftermath. When President Woodrow Wilson viewed the film in the White House, he is reported to have said, "It's like writing history with lightning."

The film caused an uproar among African Americans. The NAACP condemned it for its racist depiction of blacks. Critics called it "the meanest vilification of the Negro race." After it played in Boston and Philadelphia, police had to quell riots, which led other cities—Chicago, Denver, Pittsburgh, St. Louis, and Minneapolis—to refuse to screen it. The film was re-released in 1924, 1931, and 1938; each time lawsuits were taken out against it, which then led to more box-office receipts. As an antidote to *The Birth of a Nation,* Oscar Micheaux, an independent African American filmmaker, produced *Within Our Gates* in 1920, which depicted an entirely different perspective on race and gender. Micheaux, born in Illinois and raised in Kansas, was the son of former slaves. As such, he understood the pressures that African Americans endured. *Within Our Gates* is the oldest extant film produced by an African American. In it the audience finds a strong black woman, a teacher at a struggling black school in the Deep South who goes to Boston to help raise funds for the school. She succeeds in raising the funds from a northern woman philanthropist, but not until the subject of paternalism toward blacks has been explored. In the course of finding money for the school, she meets a respectable black optometrist with whom she falls in love. The guilt of her past, however, interferes in their romance. It seems that her adopted family of black tenant farmers was falsely accused of murder and then lynched. She herself was nearly raped by the white man who had fathered her—probably by raping her mother. In terrible flashbacks, the audience learns about the lynching and the sexual assault. These grim events match the violent behavior of men toward women in *The Birth of a Nation,* but in an opposing racial framework. Whites were nearly as alarmed by *Within Our Gates* as blacks had been by *The Birth of a Nation.*

The release of *The Birth of a Nation* in 1915 coincided with one of the most celebrated lynching cases in southern history: the Leo Frank case. In 1913, Atlanta was the scene of yet another violent incident involving a white girl. Mary Phagan, a thirteen-year-old worker at the National Pencil Factory, came on a Saturday to collect her wages from her employer, Leo

Frank. She never made it home, and later her body was found in the basement of the factory. Mary's fate was a worry to Georgians who read in it danger for young women moving from rural areas to cities and entering the workforce. Mary Phagan had moved with her family from Marietta, Georgia. Unable to make a living on the farm, they settled in a section of Atlanta full of working-class whites, whose fortunes now depended on the industrialists, some of them from the North. Members of the working class did resent their economic circumstances, but their resentment was most often directed toward their employers or the industrial system that paid poor wages and left proud yeoman farm families feeling degraded and young working girls unprotected.

Leo Frank was arrested and charged with the murder, and although he denied the accusation, popular opinion turned against him because he was a Jew from the North. The black janitor, Jim Conley, who many now think most likely committed the crime, became a witness for the state instead of a suspect. The fact that Atlantans did not prosecute a black man is a curiosity in a state that lynched black men at will, but as Mary Phagan's minister said, "it was as if the death of a black man 'would be poor atonement for the life of this innocent little girl.'" The trial was a travesty of justice. Tom Watson fanned the flames of hate through his newspaper, vilifying Frank as "the typical young libertine Jew." Frank was convicted and sentenced to hang, but Governor John M. Slaton commuted the sentence to life in prison, hoping that eventually there might be an acquittal. Before that could happen, however, a group from Mary Phagan's home county kidnapped Frank from prison and lynched him in Marietta, Georgia. Calling themselves the Knights of Mary Phagan, they took up the banner in defense of public order and white womanhood.

In that same year, 1915, "Colonel" William Joseph Simmons, a former Methodist minister and revivalist, took a band of thirty men to the top of Stone Mountain, Georgia, to reinstate the "Invisible Knights of the Ku Klux Klan." Some of his followers may have been the lynchers of Leo Frank. Fanned by the fears of an imperfect society, the Klansmen vowed to return the nation to its Anglo-Saxon roots—or to pure Americans who presumably would be better able to protect young women from alleged northern exploiters and black rapists. Klan membership languished until Mary Elizabeth Tyler and Edward Clarke were hired to expand the organization. These two had gained their promoting and organizing skills by working in the Anti-Saloon League and the Chamber of Commerce. They used typical booster techniques to attract Klan members, charging a $10 initiation fee to join. The organizers kept about 60 percent of the dues to form a national organization, so their anti-Semitic, negrophobic, nativist sentiments made them rich. Their slogan of "100 percent Americanism" was aimed at foreigners, Jews, Catholics, labor-union organizers, and blacks. The Klansmen stood for the sanctity of the home and sometimes whipped errant white men for cheating on or beating their wives, or they humiliated wayward women by exposing their sexual "sins." In an attempt to regain control of their world, members of the KKK asserted their masculinity. They did this by evoking the historical memory of a violent group of men hailed as heroes for bringing white redemption to the South.

The members of the Klan were city and small-town businessmen, farmers, and evangelical ministers, the "frayed white-collar class" of the 1920s South. They had close connections to evangelical denominations—the Baptist, Methodist, and some Presbyterian churches—and their initiation into the Klan was similar to a religious baptism. Klansmen would at times march down the aisle of a white church during the Sunday service, deposit money in the collection plate, and march out again as if to announce their connection to a holy cause. By 1925 the national KKK probably had 4 million members; some 275 lynchings were attributed to them. They tried to, and in some states did, take over politics by enrolling "respectable" middle-class men and women voters as supporters of their political agenda, which was to return the South and the nation to its Anglo-Saxon roots.

Some women joined Klan auxiliaries and affirmed the "reactionary populist" agenda. But others, seeking greater freedom in their lives, including working in the cities, visiting dance halls, dating, and becoming sexually active, found that the Klan was a quasi-religious restraining association that used fear and intimidation against not only Catholics, labor organizers, immigrants, and blacks but also women who veered from southern traditions of conservative social behavior. The clash of values over respect for an older, male-dominated order and a newer, female-liberated one could not have been more apparent.

Black Southerners and the Great Migration

African Americans became the main targets of Klan violence. Approximately 50,000 blacks had served in World War I, but the so-called peace in 1919 saw a far worse form of violence against blacks and black soldiers: there were seventy lynchings, ten veterans were still in uniform; five were burned at the stake. Southern whites fearful of black aspirations used vigilante groups and the Klan to intimidate recently released black soldiers. Returning troops, having proved their manhood in defense of their country, found that whites were determined to return them to a subordinate place. C. F. Richardson, editor of the black-owned *Houston Informer,* had this to say about African Americans and their service during World War I: "The black man responded to the call, firstly because he was an American citizen; secondly, because he knew that the world could not be made and maintained safe for democracy without at least bursting asunder some of the fetters that bound his race in 'democratic' America. . . . The black soldier fought for democracy."

When black soldiers came home to lynchings and riots—southern whites rioted in Longview, Texas; Knoxville, Tennessee; Charleston, South Carolina; and Washington D.C.—they knew their ability to protect their families, their homes, and their own lives was at stake. Postwar violence, along with an oppressive sharecropping system, Jim Crow laws, the emasculation of former black soldiers, and disfranchisement spurred the Great Migration of African Americans out of the South and into northern cities. There they did not always receive a warm welcome, but they were able to vote and their increased political presence eventually brought pressure against national racist policies. Between 1916 and 1921, 500,000 southern blacks packed up and headed to what Porgy, from George Gershwin's opera *Porgy and Bess,* called "the heavenly lan'." ("Oh Lawd, it's a long, long way.") In moving north, southern blacks did not leave their southern ways behind; with the flowering of jazz, blues, and black fiction, they became consumers of the recordings of Mamie Smith, Ma Rainey, and Bessie Smith. They listened to the big band of Duke Ellington and read novels by young black writers. The new immigrants to the North formed communities in exile, and southern blacks began the process of using democratic means to challenge race discrimination. They joined the NAACP, voted for the party that gave them a fair break, urged members of Congress to nullify the federal appointments of segregationists, and took cases of discrimination to court. Migration and resettlement were responses to white violence that had led the South down a trail of sorrow.

Interracial Beginnings and the Anti-Lynching Campaign

White and black women who remained in the South also responded to the bloodshed—by organizing interracial meetings. The twilight of the Progressive era ushered in a movement for interracial cooperation, and Progressive women were among its leading lights. Beginning in the Methodist Episcopal Church, South, and extending with evangelical promise to the YWCA, women with religious conviction met together in interracial groups to explore ways to ease tensions between the races and give African Americans "a place in American life." Those words were spoken by Lugenia Burns Hope in July 1920 at Tuskegee Institute to one of the first delegations of white women to attend a conference there with black women. That same year, Will Alexander, a Methodist minister, YMCA worker, and leader of the newly formed Commission on Interracial Cooperation (CIC) at the urging of Estelle Haskins and Carrie Parks Johnson, two white Methodist activists, helped to plan a larger meeting among black and white women in Memphis for October 6–8, 1920, called the Woman's Inter-racial Conference. Ninety-one women from churches, the YWCA, and women's clubs attended that meeting, where many for the first time, heard three African American women address them as their equals. Margaret Murray Washington of Tuskegee Institute, Elizabeth Ross Haynes of the YWCA, and Charlotte Hawkins Brown of Palmer Memorial Institute in North Carolina eloquently and firmly laid before their white audience the plight of African American women and men in the South. Brown called upon white women in the audience to "control your men . . . that so far as lynching is concerned. . . . If the white women would take hold of the situation [then] lynching would be stopped." Brown also vanquished the threadbare myth that all black women were promiscuous, and therefore unworthy of any respect. Black women wanted to be addressed as "Miss" or "Mrs." and certainly to be protected from sexual exploitation by white men. Such honest and forthright words were spoken that day perhaps because Brown had been accosted on the way to the convention by a group of white men and forcefully removed to the Jim Crow day coach of her train after she had paid for a Pullman berth. The members of the audience did not take umbrage at being made to hear this report; instead they rose to their feet and began singing a hymn of Christian solidarity. It was in Brown's words, "the greatest step forward . . . taken since emancipation." After that initial meeting, the CIC formed a Woman's Committee (later the Department of Women's Work of the CIC) and women's committees began to organize across the South, dominated mostly by Methodists. The YWCA and the Woman's Committee of the CIC continued their mission, and soon interracial work became acceptable to middle-class whites, breaking down barriers and finding common ground. By the end of the decade, however, progress within the CIC seemed stymied like a sailboat without wind. Male ineffectiveness and dominance within the organization was partly to blame; men reformers just did not see the value of women's full participation in the CIC. Carrie Johnson complained that "the men will meet and work out what they want and pass it on to the women." Even Will Alexander, who had encouraged the formation of the Woman's Committee, feared that due to their emotions, "women couldn't be trusted to take leadership roles." At the state and local levels, interracial work stumbled, as progress was slow and subtle notions of superiority infected the groups. A decade would pass before women were ready to confront the hard issue of organizing to stamp out lynching that had been thrown before the audience by Charlotte Hawkins Brown in 1920.

When white women took action against the savagery of lynching, they turned the tide against the southern tradition that had held them on a pedestal and as objects to be protected from black men. As Jacquelyn Dowd Hall writes in *Revolt Against Chivalry,* "Of all aspects of racial etiquette, those governing sexual relations aroused the strongest emotions and carried with them the severest sanctions." The myth of the black rapist emerged with a vengeance in the first two decades of the century. The subsequent rise in brutality that accompanied lynching—torture, castration, mutilation, and burning—was shocking proof of the underlying fears many southerners held of the great changes in society, among them the advance of African Americans in education and in economics, the increase in working women, and even woman suffrage in the South. Still pervasive in society was the image of African American men as subhuman.

Lynching never was exclusively a response to rape. An accusation of rape or attempted rape of a white woman by a black man was the cause in only 23 percent of lynchings between 1882 and 1946. As Jacquelyn Hall reports, crime studies tell the true story. More white on white or black on black rapes occurred during this period. Yet, the fear of rape, the taboo against interracial love affairs, and the threat of lynching served to keep two groups—African Americans and white women—under the control of white men through anxiety and intimidation. It was this realization that led some white women in the South to reject the so-called code of chivalry. They saw lynching as an unjust extralegal system of terrorism, and they refused to be named in the cause of such lawlessness.

Jessie Daniel Ames, who had been treasurer of the Texas Equal Suffrage Association, first president of the Texas League of Women Voters, and delegate at large to the national Democratic party, decided to take action. She became interested in interracial cooperation as a result of her introduction to the disparities in educational facilities for black and white children, and in 1924 she assumed the directorship of the Texas Council of the Commission on Interracial Cooperation. It was through the CIC, as Director of its Women's Committee, that she founded the Association of Southern Women for the Prevention of Lynching (ASWPL) in 1930 with twelve other members. Their headquarters was in Atlanta, the scene of the 1906 race riot, the Leo Frank trial, and the site of the rise of the second Ku Klux Klan.

Hoping to prevent lynchings before they occurred, she and the other founders enlisted the aid of twelve women in each of the thirteen southern states that participated in ASWPL. Their purpose was to create state councils of women who were active in Protestant churches and Jewish synagogues to act as state leaders and educate whites on the real causes of lynching, such as economic jealousy, interracial quarrels, and control measures. These women were to work with their church groups and women's clubs because, according to Ames, "an educational campaign against lynching should become part of the program of all organizations of women of the South, as did the child labor amendment and prohibition." The ASWPL leaders were never entirely open to interracial work although they did encourage black women also to work for an end to lynching; instead they sought white rather than black women as members because they thought that other whites would not accept their arguments if black members joined. Their goal was to enlist the aid of white women in every southern state and county and help them see that the prevention of lynching was their responsibility.

To that end, members of the ASWPL were encouraged to elicit pledges to stop lynching from political candidates, sheriffs, judges, and governors. Ames and her followers reluctantly but valiantly went to the site of lynchings and inquired into their causes; between 1933 and 1935 Ames personally investigated twenty lynchings reputedly caused by an attack on a white woman. Newspaper editors, whom she carefully cultivated as her allies, then disseminated her reports in print, and potential members gained firsthand information about lynchings. In counties across the South, ASWPL members campaigned against lynching by writing letters, keeping statistics, forming councils, and courageously facing lynch mobs. Because white women were the intended objects of protection by white men, in standing before a white mob and asking it to disband, they had about as much power as a sheriff with a shotgun. By 1940 there were 109 women's associations with 4 million members who had endorsed and joined ASWPL's campaign to end lynching. According to Jacquelyn Dowd Hall, "these included the women's auxiliaries of the major Protestant denominations, national and regional federations of Jewish women, the YWCA, and the Business and Professional Women's Clubs." Five states with the worst lynching records won the utmost attention of these groups: Mississippi, Georgia, Texas, Louisiana, and Florida. Although Ames and the ASWPL never endorsed a federal antilynching law, in 1939 the number of lynchings had been reduced to three; by 1942, mob murders had decreased to the point that the women disbanded their association. Just as women reformers before the turn of the century had turned to their churches and synagogues for the organizational structure to aid the poor with welfare relief, as well as tend to orphans, the elderly, and the ailing with benevolent institutions, in the twentieth century women in organized religious groups, clubs, and professional associations catalyzed the movement to end lynching. These women presaged the civil rights era, when the momentum for a "second reconstruction" would find victory.

The social transformation of the 1920s with regard to music, dance, fashion and mores remain in popular memory. Substantive changes during this era, however, heralded the awakening of greater gender and race equality in southern culture. For homegrown talent, the South could hardly be matched. Musicians of all stripes found means to express their craft. The music was new to many, and radio carried blues, jazz, and country music—by both male and female artists–to the millions listening. The reputation of the South went from that of a cultural desert to an oasis as writers, black and white, revealed the region's convoluted race, class, and gender conflicts. Not everyone wanted to hear the truth, and some sought to drown out the voices of progress with a bugle call to the past. The South was a racial pressure cooker; white men were serious about keeping their position of dominance. Their fear of its loss led to race riots, kangaroo court trials, lynchings, and the organization of 4 million KKK members. Women tentatively and somewhat timidly reached across the racial divide, first between women in church groups and the YWCA, and later with full meetings between white and black women's organizations. Finally, the request made by black women to stop lynching was heard and ultimately heeded. Where there had been 4 million KKK members, there now stood 4 million southern white women willing to support those who would go before a mob and call off the lynching party. Southern women no longer wanted to be controlled by white men. And they no longer wanted to be "protected" by the savagery of lynching.

CHAPTER SEVEN

The Great Depression and the New Deal

The Great Depression started a decade earlier in the South than it did in the rest of the nation. During World War I, cotton, textiles, and coal had been in high demand and prices had soared, so southerners were dismayed that by 1920 their economy was heading toward a slump. Cotton farms, textile mills, and coal companies experienced the squeeze as orders dropped and their inventories remained stable. Many southerners had an early taste of the economic conditions the rest of the nation would experience in the 1930s. Because of wage and hiring discrimination, women workers often found themselves on the edge financially. As in all economic cycles, women and minorities were the last to be hired and the first to be fired. Farmwomen did what they could to continue to feed their families, clothe their children, and bring in their crops, hoping from year to year for better prices. By 1933, with the inauguration of Franklin D. Roosevelt, help was on the way through FDR's New Deal, but not for everyone. The Agricultural Adjustment Administration (AAA) policies saved large farms but nationwide pushed 3 million tenant farmers and sharecroppers off of the land. This severely affected farm wives as many nonlandowning families, ejected from their homes, headed toward towns and cities in search of work. It also affected men, whose attitude about providing for their families bolstered their sense of manhood. To lose not just work but a livelihood struck at the root of male gender expectations. Mill workers celebrated the new textile codes enacted through the National Industrial Recovery Act (NIRA), but they soon found a dark side to its policies and experienced the frustration tied to union organizing. While the New Deal relief agencies created work for thousands of southern women, a pattern of race, sex, and wage discrimination begun at the federal level intensified at the local level in the hands of white male administrators. African Americans did not receive the same subsidies or work opportunities that whites did. Educated white women fared better in obtaining supervisory jobs, but black and poor white women were tossed mostly crumbs from the New Deal table. With so few options available, a minority of southerners turned their hopes toward more radical organizations, such as the Socialist or the Communist party. Middle-class women reformers, however, saw in the Roosevelt reforms an opportunity to bring the land of their birth and its people out of the morass, and they took advantage of the opportunities offered by New Deal agencies to enter professional careers. When the 1930s had ended, the South stood poised for the biggest transformation in its history—the coming of World War II, the advancement of a civil rights movement, and changing roles for women.

The Depression Comes Early to the South

During World War I, the value of southern agricultural products increased, and cotton farmers and textile manufacturers enjoyed high prices for cotton and cloth. While at war, the United States helped feed and clothe its civilian population, its armed forces, and the civilian populations of its European allies and their armies. During these years, lending institutions softened loan regulations, and more farmers had access to capital to increase their land holdings, buy more livestock, or purchase new or better equipment. Farm extension agents, sponsored both by the state governments and the U.S. Department of Agriculture, taught farmers how to increase their yields. Times were flush until the war ended, when farmers found themselves caught in a bind. They had borrowed money when prices for their products were high and had increased their yields, but the age-old problem of overproduction resurfaced shortly after the war.

The economic decline for southern farmers started as early as 1920. The importance of this downturn can be seen in the number of southerners who still worked the land in the late 1920s: 42.8 percent. Nearly two-thirds of these people lived in rural areas, and their economic hardships necessarily affected the entire region. In Tennessee, for example, the value of crops sold dropped by nearly one-half between 1919 and 1924. Thereafter (between 1924 and 1929) prices dropped again by nearly one-half, finally bottoming out at 18 percent of their value in 1919. Cotton, which had sold for 16 cents a pound in 1929, brought only 4.6 cents a pound in 1932. To add to the farmers' burdens, many states increased property taxes. In Tennessee, property taxes went up 175 percent between 1913 and 1922, so as prices for crops plummeted, many who owned land found that they could no longer afford to pay the taxes or their loans and mortgages. The 1922 Annual Report of the U.S. Department of Agriculture stated, "Certainly no other industry could have taken the losses agriculture has taken and maintain production, and we have no evidence to show that any other group of workers would have taken the reduction in wages in the spirit in which farmers have taken their reduction." Community businesses also suffered as farm income declined; the result was that banks and counties forced the sale of farms, leaving some farmers homeless. By 1925, just 40 percent of all southern farmers owned their own land, but it was harder for black farmers to do so. Only 20 percent of African Americans in the South owned their own land, and holding onto it proved tenuous. The areas hardest hit by the loss of land ownership were the farmlands of the Lower South, the Mississippi Delta, and the Blackland

Prairies of Texas, where tenant farmers constituted 70 percent of the rural workforce. In 1932, one-quarter of Mississippi was for sale, and African American sharecroppers, at the bottom of the economic ladder, suffered greatly from hunger and malnutrition. How did farmers live through the downturn? Some sold part of their land or lost all of it and became tenants. Some gave up farming and moved to towns to find work; others stuck it out and hung on to whatever they could. Anxious southerners hunkered down and raised their own food, hunted squirrels, rabbits, possums, and birds, fished rivers and bays, and went without store-bought goods. In part it was the family unit that pieced together a mode of survival to stay on the land, with women devising a critical component of this strategy.

The status of farmwomen depended on their position to the land either as sharecroppers, tenants, or owners. Class and race distinctions continued to separate landowning families from croppers and tenants, and white landowning women clung to their higher status. Even in the midst of the Depression, when cotton remained the major crop for most parts of the Deep South, more-fortunate farm wives worked only in the home. When asked about fieldwork, one Texas woman, the wife of a large landowner, glaringly replied, "I *never* picked cotton!" Clearly, her response suggests she felt this task was beneath her, as picking cotton was menial work reserved mainly for landless hired workers or the poorest of landowning farm families. In actuality, however, many women worked in the tobacco and cotton fields, as illustrated by Margaret Jarman Hagood in her 1939 book, *Mothers of the South: Portraiture of the White Tenant Farm Woman*. In fact, among white farmwomen in Texas, at least half of them worked in the fields. Among black women in Texas the percentage was much higher: 87 to 90 percent of them spent time making a crop. The difficulties mounted for tenant and sharecropping wives when families sought better lands or moved at year's end to another farm. On average, tenant or sharecropping farm families moved every two years, making rootlessness a way of life for many wives. Moving could mean the loss of good neighbors, trusted merchants or shop owners, and consistency of schooling for the children. Women, even if they were reluctant to acknowledge it, relied on the support of extended family, friends, and neighbors. The landowning wife, having the stability of place, might have found life during the Depression rough, but at least she had advantages beyond class status that tenant and sharecropping women lacked.

Staying alive during those difficult years depended as much on the resourcefulness of women in the home as it did on the income realized by the men of the family. Farmwomen had no choice but to produce more at home, buy less from the store, use free services that existed in towns, such as libraries and extension demonstrations, and produce surplus homemade goods for sale. Delilah Woodruff, who lived in a cabin on a twenty-acre mountain farm near Pigeon Forge, Tennessee, found ways to meet the needs of her husband and four children through the downturn. The family was fortunate; her husband worked for the Little River Lumber Company building railroads and, except for the occasional layoff, brought in a steady income. When the Depression hit, the Woodruffs lost all their savings in the 1932 bank failure. Again, relatively speaking, they were lucky; their house and land were paid off, so they started over. Delilah helped rebuild their savings by taking in four or five paying boarders, men who worked at the lumber camps. In addition, she grew all her own vegetables and herbs (for medicinal purposes), which she preserved along with seasonal fruits by drying them since the knowledge of canning techniques had not yet reached the mountains. She bartered surplus eggs and butter for items such as salt, sugar, and coffee that could not be produced on the farm. After the yearly hog killing she smoked the meat and made sausage, which she packed in corn husks. Because the family owned their own land, the Woodruffs had space for cattle, which yielded milk products, and for sheep, which produced wool that Delilah spun and knitted into socks. Women like Delilah sewed their own clothes, made their own bread, did their own laundry, and created their own family entertainment with small household pump organs while the men often played fiddles and banjos. For families such as the Woodruffs, hard work, good health (an illness of just one adult could sink a family), thrift, and good luck made all the difference. While men and women shared equally the hard work that needed doing, the farming-household economic system meant that the wife's job was as critical as that of the husband.

Textile workers experienced a different kind of hardship during the economic downturn of the 1920s. The need for cotton cloth declined with the end of the war, and textile firms struggled to survive; some did so only with the introduction of a synthetic fiber—rayon. Except for hosiery workers, who saw an increase in wages due to the demand for women's hose, workers found their wages low and their jobs threatened with replacement by labor-saving machinery. Management forced those who kept their jobs to endure speed-ups and stretch-outs, which entailed tending to machines "by the acre," meeting increasing production quotas, and "going all day in the unbearable heat with their clothes stuck to their bodies like they had been dipped in a pool of water." The pay for women textile workers dropped to less than five cents an hour in the 1930s. These conditions led workers to conduct walkouts and strikes, first in 1927 in Henderson, North Carolina, and then in 1929 in Elizabethton, Tennessee. Young women, who constituted 40 percent of the workforce, initiated the 1929 strike, but the entire workforce of 3,000 followed, complaining of low wages and factory rules too hard to abide. The county government sided with the owners and stationed National Guardsmen armed with machine guns on the roofs of plants. The women strikers taunted the guardsmen, counting on men's protective attitudes to keep them from harm. The United Textile Workers Union, hoping to capitalize on the strike, sent the women home, yielding to middle-class notions of propriety against women workers taunting soldiers. Still, strikers were in danger, as industrialists and their special police kidnapped the union organizers and searched vehicles for suspected unionists. The strike ended without any gains for the workers. The AFL attempted to organize workers under the United Textile Workers, and the strike mood swept over the mountains into the Piedmont.

The most notorious strike took place at the Loray Mill in Gastonia, North Carolina, in 1929, and ended in the death of a union balladeer, Ella Mae Wiggins, composer of the song "Mill Mother's Lament." Lines from her ballad resonated with the women strikers and their grievances: "How it grieves the heart of a mother, you every one must know. But we can't buy for our children, our wages are too low." Strikes continued despite the risks. In Marion, North Carolina, six strikers died. Another strike at Danville, Virginia, in 1930 continued for four months; its eventual defeat crippled the union. Jobs were disappearing, and unemployed laborers lined up, waiting for any work they could get at any pay. In the aftermath of the union movement, women's organizations took to their legislatures and repeated their demands for laws to protect women and children. The Gastonia uprising was so important that it gained the attention of the radical journalist and union organizer Mary Heaton Vorse. In her 1930 novel *Strike!* Vorse gave an account that informed readers across the country of the difficult conditions women textile workers faced.

The Wall Street Crash of 1929 ended up exacerbating conditions for southern farmers and industrial workers. To make matters worse, by 1931 a continual drought had dried up crops and soil erosion had turned the prairie lands of Oklahoma, Arkansas, Texas, and Kansas into a Dust Bowl. This drove many farmers off the land from 1934 to 1935, with "Okies" and "Arkies," such as the fictional Joad family, hauntingly depicted in John Steinbeck's graphic novel *The Grapes of Wrath,* loading their meager belongings on top of their jalopies and heading west to California. Arriving there, they found that the Depression had created a collective meanness among growers in the West, rivaling that of any landowners in the South.

During the 1930s, per capita income fell by 44 percent in the South, while the rest of the nation experienced a drop of 46 percent. Southerners, however, began with lower wages and incomes. Poverty was endemic in the South; one in three southern white workers was without a job. While the unemployment rate reached 25 percent nationally with 15 million out of work, the unemployment rate for blacks went as high as 75 percent. African American men in industries such as mining and lumbering lost their jobs first as employers tried to cut the payroll. Birmingham steel mills cut workers' pay by 50 percent. Private companies in Memphis fired 6,000 working women, vowed not to hire any more women, and gave their jobs to men. Probably 1 million Americans became vagrants, hopping freight trains, begging at back doors for food, and sleeping in hobo villages called Hoovervilles, while President Herbert Hoover haplessly presided over the worst depression the nation had ever seen. Some southern state governments were so close to defaulting on their debts that they paid their remaining employees with scrip and implemented sales taxes. Some municipalities declared bankruptcy. More than one-third of U.S. banks failed or disappeared in mergers, while 60 percent of bank assets were lost to bad loans and the inability of debtors to pay. Nobody guessed that the Great Depression would last ten years.

Southern state and city governments were slow to find relief money in the years between 1930 and 1933, and what monies were available soon ran out. In South Carolina some 400,000 people, constituting 25 percent of the state's population, needed assistance. In Houston 60,000 people, or 16 percent, were on relief. As one official said, it would have been worse except that we are "turning away as many Negroes as we can." San Antonio, Texas, with its population of whites, African Americans, and Mexican Americans, was a city hit hard by the Depression. Of its 280,000 residents, 31 percent were on relief. Mexican migrant farm laborers, finding little work in the fields, came with their families to San Antonio, where jobs were scarce and support networks weak. For Mexican American women times were especially uncertain. If they were viewed as illegal immigrants, they could be denied relief, or worse, deported to Mexico. In any case, by the spring of 1932 most city governments had run out of relief funds, and private philanthropic measures, such as those offered by the Red Cross, were inadequate to ease the pain. One Arkansas widow wrote the Red Cross in 1931 with what must have been a familiar request, "I wish if you will please send me some clothes. Just enough to wear to the cotton patch."

Franklin D. Roosevelt and the New Deal

Meanwhile Americans in 1932 had a choice to re-elect Herbert Hoover, whose policies did not stem the worsening tides of the Depression, or to vote for a jaunty, aristocratic Democrat from New York. Franklin Delano Roosevelt won the presidency by a landslide with the help of southern Democrats, but just after his election in November 1932 the nation experienced the nadir of the Great Depression. In the five months before Roosevelt's inauguration, the United States banking system collapsed, and desperate bank depositors tried to withdraw funds that banks did not have. The result of this run on the banks was that four-fifths of them closed, some because of bankruptcy. Overall, the hardest hit region was the South.

It is no wonder, then, that the first measure taken by FDR on March 6, 1933, was to close all the banks and declare a bank holiday. Next the president sent Congress an Emergency Banking bill on March 9 that passed after just four hours of deliberation. This bill probably saved the nation's banking system and allowed solvent banks to reopen. Roosevelt's reassuring words, given in the first of his thirty so-called fireside chats (radio broadcasts), "that it is safer to keep your money in a reopened bank than under the mattress," convinced southerners to put their money back into banks. Their savings accounts would find protection in June 1933 under the new Federal Deposit Insurance Corporation. Labeling his administration's policies to combat the Depression the New Deal, Roosevelt prompted Congress in the first 100 days of his administration to pass fifteen major pieces of legislation that would bring to the nation relief, recovery, and reform.

The New Deal not only brought the beginnings of recovery to southerners who had money to put in the bank but also paved the way for federal intervention in state affairs, something southern politicians dreaded and feared would erode their power. Most southerners found Roosevelt their hero, but southern politicos found themselves walking a tightrope: trying to keep federal funds flowing to their constituents while opposing some of the progressive ideas of the New Deal, which they considered an imposition on states' rights. Roosevelt often felt hamstrung by southern senators and congressmen, many of whom were returned to Congress year after year by small southern state electorates (due to disfranchisement). These politicians chaired powerful congressional committees and became floor leaders. At the time, Democrats in Congress wielded more power than they had for more than a decade, and Roosevelt needed their votes to pass his New Deal legislation. Therefore, FDR felt he could not afford to bring up matters of race in Congress, including the anti-lynching bill advocated by many women reformers, without jeopardizing his critical agenda. FDR knew he had to work with them, but no southern whites became a part of his inner circle. African Americans did, however. Roosevelt invited Mary McLeod Bethune, founder of Bethune-Cookman College in Florida, to direct the Division of Negro Affairs at the National Youth Administration (NYA) between 1935 and 1943. She became part of Roosevelt's "black cabinet," an informal group of New Dealers, mainly community leaders, who were always pressing for progress on matters of race: for integrated federal administrative boards; training of African Americans in skilled jobs; more black policymakers in New Deal agencies; and blacks to head projects. Bethune enjoyed enormous prestige among educators and among African Americans hoping to find equity through the New Deal. In 1935 she became president of the National Council of Negro Women, which brought together black women's associations, and there she served as a liaison between black women's organizations and the White House. Eleanor Roosevelt had suggested the appointment of Bethune to the NYA, and Eleanor actually was the force behind the National Youth Administration, which provided hard-to-find summer jobs for young people in high school and college so they could continue their education during the Depression. The NYA was unusually egalitarian in hiring across race and gender lines, an idea promoted by the black and white administrators running the program. As Eleanor Roosevelt was always looking out for the most oppressed in the nation, and because she was able to work within a less restrictive environment than had her husband, she became the conscience of the New Deal—FDR's eyes and ears, persuading him in directions that his political enemies often opposed. She was particularly interested in the South and especially its women and young people.

The New Deal in the South

At first, relief agencies such as the Civilian Conservation Corps (CCC) catered only to men, a practice based on the idea of the male as breadwinner. The first CCC camp opened in April 1933 near Edinburg, Virginia. Named Camp Roosevelt, it was supervised by the Department of War with the help of the Forest Service, and it recruited young men, paid them $30 a month ($25 of it sent directly home to their families), and trained them in carpentry, heavy equipment repair, and other marketable skills. Other men earned high school diplomas while working for the CCC. Eventually, the CCC, administered by four federal agencies, established 100 camps in the South and employed young men between the ages of eighteen and twenty-five to plant trees, build reservoirs, clear firebreaks, create parks, and drain swamps, among many other projects. In South Carolina, work accomplished by the 50,000 CCC employees led to the creation of sixteen state parks and a statewide park system. By giving southern men a role in providing for their families after the nation's rate of unemployment had reached 25 percent, the federal government fortified the traditional conviction that earning a living was a man's job. The fact that women were excluded from CCC camps demonstrates the existence of a division of labor by gender, and yet the realities of southern women's need for employment still waited to be addressed. Complaints on that score led to the creation of camps for 8,000 young women under the Federal Emergency Relief Administration (FERA) and the Works Progress Administration (WPA), but Hilda Smith, director of the program for women, griped to Eleanor Roosevelt, "The CCC camps with their millions of dollars for wages, educational work, travel, and supervision constantly remind me of what we might do for women from these same families. As [is] so often the case, the boys get the breaks, the girls are neglected." On the other hand, because the boys' pay was sent home, mothers, sisters, and other female relatives received money for rent, shoes, clothing, and food.

The CCC camps were racially segregated, and national administrators allowed only 10 percent of its CCC positions to be filled by black youths, ironically those who suffered the highest rate of unemployment. Nationwide, 250,000 African American men worked in 150 segregated CCC camps. States like Mississippi, Georgia, Florida, Arkansas, and Alabama were threatened with getting no camps at all if they did not hire their quota of blacks. Residents of counties where CCC camps for African Americans were established often complained of being disturbed by a large presence of black men. Protestors near Washington, D.C., for example, noted that the camp was set up in an area where white "women are left alone." The director of the CCC, Tennessean Robert Fechner, usually removed camps for African Americans when protests ran too high. A pattern developed in the administration of agencies that were designed in Washington and administered by officials at the local level. Southern politicians, administrators, and functionaries at the grassroots level often discriminated most severely against black women and men and to a lesser degree against white women in awarding federal money for jobs, training, and resources. One estimate shows that African Americans were given less than half of the amount of relief funds awarded to whites, even though the former constituted three times the numbers in need. Hence, the New Deal's record was less than perfect when it came to equality for African Americans and women.

Southern women sent letter after letter to government agencies, the Red Cross, and even directly to Eleanor Roosevelt begging for relief or work of any kind. These letters represent a long history of communication between southern women and government, one that began during the Civil War, when wives and mothers complained that their menfolk were not with them to plow the fields, chop cotton, or gather the crops. Desperate once more for help, this time with jobs, relief, or social welfare programs, southern women put pen to paper to remind federal agents and Red Cross workers that men were not the only ones who could use work to benefit their families.

The Federal Emergency Relief Administration (1933), the Civil Works Administration (1934), and the Works Progress Administration (1935) brought jobs directly to southern women. While the federal government directed and provided the salaries, state-level administrators managed the work programs. Harry Hopkins, head of both the CWA and FERA, created a women's work program in each agency under the leadership of Ellen S. Woodward from Mississippi. At a White House Conference on the Emergency Needs of Women in November 1933, Woodward cited widespread unemployment in the South. One example came from Birmingham, Alabama, where 6,000 female clerical workers were out of work and in one instance 5,000 women lined up to apply for seventy-five sales clerk jobs at a city department store. Woodward's first task was to set up a Women's Division with an all-female staff in each state. State directors were mostly middle-class white women workers and administrators who remained in New Deal work even after the FERA ceased to function; many became administrators for the WPA after 1935. Their backgrounds were varied; some had been in nursing, while others had been home demonstration agents or held jobs in business. Still others came from the YWCA, settlement-house work, social work, the Red Cross, state women's club work, and the Democratic party women's division. These women gained experience in administering questionnaires to applicants for relief, thus learning one aspect of the field of social work. Loula Friend Dunn, a regional supervisor with FERA for eleven states, found her work frustrating at first and complained about the die-hard opposition of southern office holders to state participation in federal work relief. Dunn, a reformer at heart, eventually found an influential position as commissioner of public welfare in Alabama. Woodward herself had a background in social welfare work, having served as executive secretary of the Mississippi State Board of Development. Thus New Deal agencies had the effect of shaping careers for middle-class southern women with backgrounds in social work, club work, and charitable work.

Ellen Woodward made a list of the paid jobs that women could do in these relief agencies. She considered any type of work that paid a salary as "women's work," even manual labor if it included the equivalent of a man's wages. This idea was important since WPA administrators allowed pay differentials between men and women, citing women's work as being less taxing than men's. The WPA also created regional pay differentials. The federal wage guideline in these agencies was based on the cost of living according to regions; the South received the lowest rate. This meant that for southern women, the average salary was 32 cents an hour, less than the national average of 46 cents an hour. Salaries notwithstanding, Woodward found that the neediest women were those with virtually no skills other than doing agricultural work, and they comprised 80 percent of the supplicants. Some did not know how to sew, so the WPA instituted sewing rooms for women to learn to sew and make items for the states to distribute to the needy. In San Antonio, the WPA offered sewing jobs to white, black, and Mexican American women. Lorena Hickok, the agency's reporter, after visiting a WPA sewing room, noted with satisfaction the improvements for sharecropping women: "Working in pleasant surroundings, having some money and food have done wonders to restore their health and morale." These women more than paid for the expense of the program. In Mississippi, women made $250,000 worth of clothing and were paid $200,000 for their work. In Atlanta, recipients of work aid through the WPA made 4 million garments for distribution.

Woodward chose training for women in typical female jobs such as sewing, canning, clerical work, nursing, and other health-care positions; she introduced child-care training through nursery school programs, music education, research, and stereotypically for black women, housekeeping work. African American women preferred to work in occupations that required skilled employment, such as dressmaking, but whereas 23 percent of WPA workers were black, only 7 percent of WPA seamstresses were black women. More often they experienced discrimination and were asked to do menial or heavy work, which often paid less, while white women were given better-paid skilled or lighter jobs. The federal regional wage guideline further depressed the wages based on race. Thus southern black women could not earn what white women could in federal jobs because of their race and their region. Even more frustrating for black women was the interference of local politicians who managed to see that federal relief work for them was suspended entirely during cotton-picking time, forcing women back into the fields at low wages. Efforts to investigate reported cases of discrimination often failed because local officials denied their complicity, and victims feared losing their jobs with the FERA, CWA, or WPA.

After 1935 the WPA went beyond offering typical domestic jobs and provided work for women writers, historians, artists, actors, and musicians. The Four Arts Projects: Art, Music, Writers, and Theater, enrolled skilled women in all of these programs and more. Despite the widening job opportunities, women hired by the WPA and its sub-agencies did not go beyond 27 percent of the total numbers working for the agency nationally. This was better than the hiring rates of the earlier New Deal years, when out of 2 million jobs created by the FERA and CWA, in 1933 and 1934, only 100,000, or 5 percent, went to women distributed throughout thirty-five states. In part this gender discrepancy could be explained by the fact that some work programs were intended just for heads of families, for which a few women might qualify, but the other reasons pertained to typical gender expectations, that men participated in public work and brought home the bacon while their wives stayed home to cook it. This sensibility was made more prevalent when in 1932 Congress passed the Economy Act, Section 213 of which mandated that only one spouse of a married couple could hold a federal job, resulting in three-quarters of married women with a spouse in a federal job losing their government employment. Protests came from such prestigious groups as the League of Women Voters, but some states and local governments copied the discriminatory federal act, and justified it by calling working married women "undeserving parasites" of government payrolls. Thus in states like Missouri, married women teachers lost their jobs, under the assumption that men would step into such roles as kindergarten teachers. This was especially hard on married African American women teachers, whose incomes were lower than those of whites to begin with and whose husbands' incomes may not have supported them adequately. Some men actually benefited from this ruling; of the total number of teachers in public schools, male teachers increased from 19 to 25 percent in the 1930s.

The WPA stayed in operation until 1943, when it was phased out due to full employment during the war years. All types of women found jobs through this and other work relief agencies, not only those who had received training and drawn a salary working for the agency, but also those women who had administered the programs. Yet the New Deal agencies did not reach as many women as men, due to conservative gender policies regarding women's public roles. Black women, the neediest of all, found access to skilled relief work more limited on account of race and gender prejudices.

Down on the Farm

To combat agricultural overproduction would take an act of Congress, and in May 1933 that body finally acted. As a result of the creation of the Agricultural Adjustment Act and the Bankhead Cotton Control Act of 1934, farming in the South changed forever. The Agricultural Adjustment Administration encouraged farmers to reduce crops such as tobacco, corn, cotton, rice, wheat, peanuts, sugar, and products such as milk. In return, crop farmers received federal subsidies for their unplanted lands. The goal was to reduce supply in order to raise the price of farm produce, and it worked. In Georgia, where cotton prices had dipped to 5 cents a pound, with federal measures they soared in 1936 to 15 cents a pound. While the federal farm policies helped the largest farmers, they also brought about farm consolidation and the development of agribusiness. In areas such as the Mississippi Delta, some landowners received as much as $10,000 from the AAA for reducing their crops. With that federal money, owners mechanized their operations and turned their sharecroppers into day laborers, hiring them only when needed. Tenant farmers and sharecroppers, most of whom were African Americans, were turned off the land as owners took rented land out of production, kept their government checks, and continued to plant other lands for more income. The result was a disaster for renters and sharecroppers, many of whom were evicted and ended up in cities seeking relief jobs or charity. Between 1932 and 1935, 3 million people were forced to abandon farming as a result of the AAA. Black farming families in North Carolina declined from nearly 75,000 to 58,000 (75 percent were sharecroppers or tenants); in other words, 17,000 families had to shift for themselves during the Depression. In the Mississippi Delta, according to historian James Cobb, "the percentage of cropland harvested by tenants of all sorts fell from 81.9 percent in 1930 to 58.2 percent in 1940." Federal subsidies did not help small landowners much either. The benefits of reducing crops on small farms added up to between $7 and $20 in payment, hardly enough to bring prosperity. Men still had to work the fields and find a job off the farm for added income. Women still had to make do with the barest of essentials.

The Resettlement Administration (RA) created in 1935, replaced later by the Farm Security Administration (FSA) in 1937, was intended to mitigate the negative effects of the AAA. It gave loans to small farmers and made large landowners improve facilities for migrant farm workers. The most widely recognized work accomplished by the RA and the FSA, however, was publicity. These agencies hired photographers to document the need that still existed in the nation, especially in the South and among southern refugees in the West. Although the South contained 31.5 percent of the national population, it was represented in 42.4 percent of the entire FSA collection of photographs, giving the region unprecedented pictorial coverage, and allowing the rest of the nation to become aware of the South's poverty, resilience, and need for change. Walker Evans, Arthur Rothstein, Margaret Bourke-White, Russell Lee, and Dorothea Lange, through their photographs, hoped to convince Americans that agencies such as the WPA were vital in continuing to help the poor and dispossessed. Dorothea Lange's most famous photographs were of women whose faces and postures of despair and resilience seared into the American memory and helped to keep New Deal agencies in public favor.

Fewer than 5 percent of farms in the rural South had electricity. The Tennessee Valley Authority (TVA) in 1933, the Lower Colorado River Authority (LCRA) in 1934, and the Rural Electrification Administration (REA) in 1935 slowly brought electricity to remote areas of the South. Congressman Lyndon Baines Johnson secured federal grants and loans to build the hydroelectric plants that would eventually send electricity to 800,000 people in rural areas. Wiring farms with electricity was a massive undertaking, and even with the federal infusion of money, by 1941 only four out of ten farms in the South had electricity.

Johnson knew well what life was like on a farm without electricity. He had been raised in the Texas Hill Country and watched his mother toil without the labor-saving devices employed by women in cities. Farms without electricity were places of constant drudgery that made women old and stooped before their time. Without electric lights, the family burned kerosene lamps at night or in the morning to milk the cows. The lamps gave off only dim light for reading or sewing and often brought on headaches, and the task of cleaning the smoky lamps fell to women and children. When a farm had no electricity for a water pump, water had to be drawn from a well by hand. Windmills could have helped to pump water into a tank, but in 1937 a windmill cost $400, too much for most families. Wells were often as far as 300 feet from the house and ran between 50 and 100 feet deep. Someone in the family, the wife or an older boy perhaps, went every day to haul water, pulling up about four gallons, or thirty-two pounds, of water and carrying it to the house. It took 40 gallons of water per person per day to cook, clean, and wash dishes; for a family of five that meant the daily hauling of 200 gallons. On wash day the need for water was even greater. Since there was no electricity for a washing machine, the wife made a fire in the yard outside the house. She chopped the wood and built the fire to heat the wash tub; then she filled the cauldron and three more tubs with water. The first washtub was used for scrubbing with lye soap and a scrub board; this was used for all the men's overalls, typically caked with a week's worth of dirt, as well as for dirty diapers. Scrubbing was back-breaking work that required stooping, bending, and twisting. Next she would wring each piece to get the dirty water out and put the laundry in the cauldron of boiling water, punching the whole lot with a stick or broom handle to agitate the load until it seemed reasonably clean. If she were really lucky, she might have a hand wringer attached to the tub. At that point she lifted the clothes out and dunked them in a rinse tub; then she would wring out the water and swish the whites through a vat of bluing to counteract yellowing, and next through a vat of starch, giving the clothes one last wring. Finally she hung them out to dry. A farmwife usually did four loads of washing a week, but larger families required as many as eight loads. In winter outdoor washing was cold and miserable and in summer water had to be boiled despite the temperature reaching the inferno level.

The next day, ironing day, somebody again chopped the wood and fired up the stove. Irons—sad irons—weighed about seven pounds, and there were always at least two of them heating up on the top of the stove. If the housewife were lucky she had irons with wood handles, if not she used a hot pad to pick up the iron and begin the day-long process of ironing miles of sheets, shirts, and dresses. Burns from a hot iron produced nasty blisters. As salt was used to scrape the soot off the face of the iron it would sting blistered hands mightily. If one speck of soot landed on a white sheet, the sheet had to be washed again. After finishing a day's work, farmwives stoked the cook stove with wood and started supper.

Farmwives planted vegetable gardens and fruit trees to provide food for the whole summer, but they still had to conserve food for the winter. In the Texas Hill Country, where summer temperatures often reached 100 degrees, women had to heat up the kitchen to preserve garden produce in jars. First the jars and lids had to be sterilized, then filled with parboiled tomatoes, peaches, pickles, or green beans. Finally canners boiled the filled jars again to seal the lids. Yet these long summer days in a hot kitchen ensured food on the table all winter, and as households depended on the produce preserved by women, wives took pride in larders filled with canned and dried goods.

Lyndon Johnson drew on his memory of farm life in his own childhood when he ran in a special election for Congress from Texas's 10th Congressional District in 1937. He went to the "forks in the creeks" of his district and explained to the voters the merits of the Rural Electrification Administration, urging them to vote for him and for electricity. LBJ was an ardent supporter of Roosevelt and the New Deal because he had seen firsthand, as director of the Texas National Youth Administration, that the federal government had much to offer farming families, especially farm wives. Although he conversed with men, he really was explaining how electricity would change women's lives—their washing, ironing, cooking, canning, dishwashing, and cleaning. With electric well pumps, wives would no longer have to tote so many gallons of water each day; it would save their backs. Eventually, a farm family could buy the same electric labor-saving appliances that urbanites enjoyed. It was mostly men who voted; the poll tax had eliminated thousands of eligible women voters (although in 1937 the U.S. Supreme Court ruled that women could pay a lower poll tax than men). If, however, LBJ could convince the men to vote for him, he could promise their wives some of the conveniences of city living. Getting farmers behind the program was not easy, and cooperatives had to be established to qualify for loans from the REA, but Johnson, who won that 1937 election, went to FDR himself to see to it that an electric cooperative with money from Uncle Sam was up and running by 1938 for Texas Hill Country residents. Every customer had to pay $5 to the cooperative as well as pay the cost of wiring their homes, money that was dearly earned by farmers. By November 1939, however, 2,892 Texas farm houses had lights ablaze; Johnson had seen to it that farm wives could put their sad irons to good use—as door stops.

Women, Textiles, and the NRA

Textile workers found that the policies of the National Recovery Administration (NRA) in 1933 (and later the Fair Labor Standards Act [FLSA] in 1938) gave them better hours and eventually better pay. Gladys Griffin, a textile worker in Greensboro, North Carolina, reported, "The best thing that ever happened to working people was when President Roosevelt got in. He was the only president I've ever known that helped the poor people. . . . Roosevelt raised the legal age for work and got those younguns out of the mill. He cut our hours down from twelve hours a day to eight . . . and the mill owners couldn't cut our pay."

Under the provisions of the NRA, this was the way it began, but the happy attitude among workers did not continue. The NRA did restrict mills to the eight-hour day with no pay cut, but mill owners still had the authority to decide the workload, and employers were allowed to pay women less than men even if they did the same work. Letters to Washington by mill hands reported the extreme stretch-outs that industrialists and their time-efficiency experts imposed on the workers. Women mill workers, who benefited most from the raise in minimum wages under the NRA, were the first to find their workday made unbearable. One sixteen-year-old girl lamented in a letter to Eleanor Roosevelt and Secretary of Labor Frances Perkins that her mother, a widow with fifteen children,

> was running 22 Looms making from 19 to 22 dollars a week . . . then in 1931 1932 they streched out and put her on 40 Looms her average wages was 11 and 12 dollars per week

> then they streched her out on 50 and 60 Loom and She countent make production they turned her off would not Let her work there. She was with us Little children for the mercy of the world to feed.

The employers' trick of stretching out the work over multiple looms or spinning machines and then underpaying or firing mostly women with children for not keeping up and making quota was one way the industry evaded the NRA protection codes for workers. As in sweatshops, the dire working conditions affected women first, and the stretch-out became the most contested point in labor disputes.

The NRA called for the cooperation of labor unions and management, but it did not protect workers from owner retaliation. When Laura McGhee joined the United Textile Workers and paid her dues, she found herself out of a job; this occurred after she put in thirty-five years of "the best work that any worker could do." In addition to management harassment of union members, the "sexual dimension of economic power," as it is expressed by historians, was especially disturbing. Men cursed at women and left vulgar notes on their machines. Bosses sexually harassed young women workers and fired them if they did not succumb to their overtures, but the NRA codes offered women no protection from sexual misconduct by supervisors or co-workers. Black workers were also denied full protection since their work came under the category of cleaners or sweepers rather than of textile workers. The Textile Code provision of the NRA exempted cleaning, scrubbing, and outside jobs, those normally held by African Americans.

By July 1934 such dismal work conditions in northern Alabama led to the walkout of 20,000 hands from several mills; by September with the help of the United Textile Workers, employees closed down hundreds of mills in textile centers from Maine to Alabama. The strike spread to other industries, including mining, iron, and steel. Called the General Strike of 1934, it was the largest single strike in the nation's history. A total of 400,000 workers walked away from their jobs (84,000 in Alabama alone), and violence inevitably broke out with National Guard soldiers, local police, thugs, and vigilantes hired by industry. Yet the unionists were resourceful. In Durham, North Carolina, World War I veterans protected the picketers. Women formed committees to sustain the strikers, such as a strike "sick committee" or "commissary committee." Women took on traditional roles while leaving the military-like operations of the strike to the men. Black women members of the nascent Communist party in Birmingham, Alabama, either wives or daughters of heavy-industry workers who had joined the party out of frustration with the inequitable labor conditions, formed auxiliary committees and worked with the unions behind the scenes. They discouraged scab laborers from crossing the picket lines, fed strikers from their gardens, and withheld sex from husbands who were tempted to go back to work before the strike was settled. In Atlanta, young white female strikers, who readily admitted to being communists, were arrested and charged under the state's insurrection law. Ultimately the strike, which lasted only twenty-two days, failed, and the United Textile Workers could neither sustain nor protect workers from retaliation at the hands of mill owners. By 1935, the U.S. Supreme Court declared the National Industrial Recovery Act unconstitutional, but passage of the 1935 Wagner Act, with the National Labor Relations Board (NLRB) it established, led to unionization attempts at the mills through the newly created Congress of Industrial Organizations (CIO). The CIO gained a beachhead in the southern labor struggle, but this did not necessarily lead to more secure jobs for women. Workers' memories of the General Strike, and their experience of evictions and retaliations, led to a chill on union organizing in southern mills.

Labor advocates had long wanted to raise wages and reduce the working hours of women textile workers and black women in other southern industries. The National Consumers' League (NCL), an organization founded during the 1890s, comprised roughly 15,000 middle-class women whose goal was to raise wages and improve the working conditions of women. Their strategy at the turn of the century was to boycott products made in poor and unsafe labor conditions. By the 1930s the NCL had set its sights on southern women workers. The NCL Board hired

Lucy Randolph Mason, a descendant of the venerable eighteenth-century Virginia statesman George Mason, to organize a southern committee. She did this successfully, forming branches in Virginia, North and South Carolina, Tennessee, Texas, Kentucky, and Louisiana, in part by using her Southern Lady image and always dressing stylishly as she made her rounds. The plan was to lobby state governments to adopt a nine/forty-eight law (nine hour days, forty-eight-hour work week) and minimum wage laws for women (later for men), to see the ratification of a federal child labor law, and to improve state labor departments. The NCL committees engaged local churchwomen, labor unions, and academics in their cause, and it was this interaction with local representatives that brought forth a drive for countering poor labor conditions. The groups most *uninterested* in labor reform by the 1930s due to increasing conservatism were the General Federation of Women's Clubs and, unsurprisingly, the United Daughters of the Confederacy and the Daughters of the American Revolution.

Southern born and bred Consumer League advocates took up the labor cause where clubwomen had left it and were not afraid to speak out about labor laws for women or to cut through the states' rights arguments voiced against federal intervention or the presence of "outside agitators." Thus a new breed of "liberal" southern women was off and running in defense of women laborers. They spoke to their legislators in ways reminiscent of women club leaders seeking reform before World War I. In Louisiana, for example, Consumer League women were so agitated with Huey Long for speaking out against the NRA's minimum-wage law that they joined the women's campaign and lobbied the legislature to see him removed from the Senate. As a consequence of their actions, in 1938 Louisiana passed a women's minimum-wage law.

Southern Consumer League women found that they were not alone in supporting federal laws to improve conditions in the South, and they forged alliances with a coterie of southern women. These were educated women who had been a part of the woman suffrage movement, the Democratic party structure, the YWCA, the League of Women Voters, or the Association of Southern Women for the Prevention of Lynching. Because they foresaw a time when race and sex equality could prevail, they developed ties to such interracial groups as the Urban League (an African American organization) and the Southern Conference for Human Welfare (SCHW). The SCHW in 1938 brought together in Birmingham, Alabama, 6,000 progressive-minded southerners of both races as well as First Lady Eleanor Roosevelt to seek, in the words of journalist John Egerton, "ways to make their region a healthier, better educated, better paying, less violent, more charitable, more equitable, more democratic place." The Southern Consumer League members favored the federal government's social welfare agenda. At the same time they saw male politicians as often corrupt, incompetent, and resistant to change. League women trained other women for the possibility of appointment to local office to replace male party hacks. They supported women such as lawyer Helen Douglas Mankin, who in 1946 was the first woman elected to Congress from Georgia, a contest she won with the help of African American voters. From their concerns for the future, then, a middle-class activist women's network coalesced that sought more federal protection, more accountability from state and local government, and much better interracial cooperation. In the end, the 1938 Fair Labor Standards Act ended child labor and mandated a minimum wage that granted workers 25 cents an hour, regardless of race or gender. For women mill workers this constituted an instant raise, and for some it meant a doubling in wages.

Bubbling Radicalism

At the same time that the Southern Consumer League organized on behalf of laboring women in the Southeast, in Texas some of the poorest working women were finding strength through labor-union organizing. In 1938 in San Antonio, Mexican American pecan shellers staged the largest strike in the city and, according to historian Zaragosa Vargas, "the most massive community-based strike waged by the nation's Mexican population in the 1930s." Texas sold about 40 percent of the nation's pecans, and San Antonio was the state's center of production, with 400 under-regulated pecan-shelling factories. The largest producer, The Southern Pecan Company, sold an estimated 15 million pounds a year valued at $1 million. In unventilated, dust-laden, dirty work sheds, where the tuberculosis rate exceeded the national average, Mexican Americans, considered a cheap labor pool by employers, toiled at crudely made benches (with no back rests). Women constituted more than half the workforce; and whereas men earned fifty cents per 100 pounds of cracked pecans, women earned six or seven cents a pound of shelled pecans. In strictly assigned jobs, men cracked the shells while women were consigned to pick out the nut meat. As historian Julia Blackwelder relates, "pickers' fingers became swollen and sometimes infected from the continuous handling of the broken shells." Girls as young as eight years old worked with their mothers; one family—two girls and their mother—were able to earn a total of $5.00 a week. Another girl, age seventeen, earned no more than $2.00 per week. These were some of the lowest wages in the nation. Because pecan shelling was deemed an agricultural enterprise, it did not come under government codes that could have raised wages for nonfarm workers. Often the employers simply paid their workers in food allotments from the company's commissary. To worsen the situation, San Antonio became flooded with out-of-work Mexican farm laborers seeking jobs at any wages. Women acutely felt the sting of racial and gender discrimination in wages, segregation, and poor housing as most Mexican Americans lived in the poorly serviced west side of the city.

In 1935 the Texas Pecan Shelling Workers Union affiliated with the CIO, and by February 1938 the pecan shellers called a strike after their employers declared wage cuts by a few cents per pound. Then 12,000 workers—the majority of them women—left their work benches for three months. This had not been the first strike fomented by underpaid Mexican American workers, but it was the largest. Labor activist Emma Tenayuca, who had been working to improve labor conditions for Mexicans in San Antonio since 1933, took on a principal role in the strike, leading picketers, storming the mayor's office, and getting arrested for staging marches and demonstrations. She had already founded two local branches of the International Ladies' Garment Workers Union, and under the Unemployed Councils and the Workers' Alliance of America, communist organizations designed to aid the unemployed, she led the community in protests and demonstrations. Moved by the extreme discrimination experienced by thousands of Mexican Americans in Texas and by the deportation of many others by the U.S. Immigration Service, Tenayuca joined the Communist party in 1937, mainly because it was the only organization that expressed notions of racial and gender equality in the 1930s. Her self-professed communist ties radicalized the strike, and while she sat in jail after her arrest, other women activists, such as Manuela Solis Sager and Minnie Rendon, took up the cause. City officials and the San Antonio police acted with surprisingly harsh measures against the strikers. Police sprayed tear gas on picketers eight different times, arrested women and children indiscriminately, and turned fire hoses on them when they protested inhumane prison conditions. Finally, union and city leaders, after intervention by Governor James Allred, conducted a negotiated settlement for the pecan-shelling workers. The strike is remembered as a movement uprising, an important marker in the struggle for dignity—especially for gender and race equity—among the state's lowest paid workers. Although the Fair Labor Standards Act passed in 1938 demanded minimum wages for all hourly workers, the pecan-shelling industry subsequently mechanized its operations and laid off any remaining workers. Nonetheless, in her own words, Tenayuca recalled, "What started out as an organization for equal wages turned into a mass movement against starvation, for civil rights, for a minimum-wage law, and it changed the character of West Side San Antonio."

The Communist party was attractive to many African Americans living in the South for the same reason it had appealed to Emma Tenayuca; it was one of the only organizations that endorsed full racial and gender equality, justice in the courts, and economic opportunity for the most dispossessed. It had already made a reputation for defending innocent blacks against the maw of injustice, especially that found in Alabama in 1931. When nine black boys, aged thirteen to twenty, were arrested in Scottsboro, Alabama, for riding the rails, and then were accused of raping two white women who had been riding in a nearby gondola, it was the Communist party that brought the case to the attention of the world. The innocence of the men seemed apparent from the beginning, but when the women accused them of rape, fearing that they might be arrested for crossing state lines for immoral purposes (the Communist party labeled them "notorious prostitutes"), the case took on the properties of a legal lynching. One of the women, Ruby Bates, recanted her testimony against the men, but the court still did not throw out the case, indeed the trials led to conviction and the death penalty. The International Labor Defense (ILD), supported by the Communist party, appealed the sentence and took the case to the U.S. Supreme Court, where twice the high court overturned the convictions. Even after multiple trials, the Scottsboro Boys remained in prison. The Alabama justice system kept them until gradually they were released or escaped (one of the defendants, Haywood Patterson, made a dramatic escape and wrote to tell about it in *Scottsboro Boy*).

As shameful an incident of injustice as the trials were, the episode had something important to say about issues of gender and black-on-white rape in the South, a story that had been part of the fabric of southern society since the Civil War. On the one hand, although a crowd of angry white men had gathered outside the jail, the nine boys were not lynched, as well could have happened had the two women in the case been from Scottsboro or if the governor had not sent twenty-five men from the National Guard Armory to protect the prisoners. On the other, it exposed the real lives of white working-class women during the depths of the Depression. Victoria Price and Ruby Bates were job hunting, riding in boxcars, hoboing with men, and apparently engaging in casual sex in labor camps. The medical examination confirmed their previous sexual activity, yet the very fact that authorities insisted on a medical examination indicates the initial doubt over their testimony. At the beginning at least, their whiteness did not protect them from suspicion of lying. After Bates's recantation and subsequent work with the ILD to publicize the injustice to the nine, southerners had stopped believing her, although she and Price remained the reason for the boys' continued incarceration. Finally, the case publicized the fact that southern justice when it came to black men was hardly justice at all—something that had been known regionally but now became exposed to the outside world. The Communist party can be credited with saving the lives of the nine young men, but it could not save them from the Alabama prisons. Not coincidentally, as the case was making headlines, quietly in Atlanta, white women members of the Commission on Interracial Cooperation (CIC) were forming the Association of Southern Women for the Prevention of Lynching; their goal was to prevent lynching and see to it that the accused persons were tried legally. Violation of the rights of the accused, the world learned, could be found in southern courts as well as in a lynching bee. The CIC, unfortunately, did not publicly endorse blacks serving on juries or black voting rights, two actions that could have improved southern justice for African Americans.

The same year that Emma Tenayuca joined the Communist party of Texas and four of the youngest Scottsboro boys were released from jail, young communists from the Southern Negro Congress along with a host of other organizations across the South founded the Southern Negro Youth Congress (SNYC, 1937). The SNYC included the Boy Scouts and the Girl Scouts of America, representatives of historically black colleges, and the YWCA. Its participants addressed issues that stretched beyond the workplace—to civil rights, sexism, and racism. Their concerns, such as police brutality leading to the deaths of black arrestees, wrongful imprisonment, and lack of voting rights inspired them to demand justice and raise the consciousness of those who would defend democracy in the South. When members of the SNYC convened for the first time in Richmond, Virginia, in an integrated meeting of blacks and whites, liberals and communists, men and women, they did so with the conviction that their voices for equal education, equal wages, voting and jury rights, and an end to lynching represented a broadcast message for a New South. Such notables as Mary McLeod Bethune and Charlotte Hawkins Brown, whose lives had been dedicated to education and the advancement of people of all races, served on the SNYC advisory committee. Choosing the theme of "Freedom, Equality, Opportunity," they focused on voting rights and unity. Organizing chapters in ten states in the South, their membership climbed to 11,000, and they continued to meet year after year until 1949. Out of the Great Depression and the New Deal, then, came a song for the future, one that included women's voices and foretold of a South rising out of its poverty and racial and gender prejudices.

Historians agree that the South was the most economically depressed region in the nation during the 1920s and 1930s. Southern women coped as best they could with the downturn of the economy from the start of the 1920s through the end of the 1930s, nearly twenty years of struggle and challenge. In 1937, President Franklin D. Roosevelt during his second inaugural address stated, "I see one-third of a nation ill-housed, ill-clad, ill-nourished." As late as 1938 Roosevelt labeled the South the nation's number-one economic problem and a region overrun with handicaps—too many farmers on too little land, overproduction of cotton, chronically low wages in industry, a conservative outlook on women's and men's roles, and a racial caste system that denied full purchasing power to one-third of its population. The New Deal, with its attempts to find and rescue the indigent, unemployed, and untrained, countered these ills with relief in the form of work agencies such as the CCC, FERA, CWA, WPA, and NYA. It helped southerners recover economically and improve their lives through such massive projects as the TVA and REA. It brought reform with the NRA, FLSA, and AAA, ending low wages and child labor and bringing higher farm prices and a slow death to sharecropping. The Second New Deal of 1935 brought Social Security benefits and introduced the National Labor Relations Board through the Wagner Act, making it possible, although still difficult, to organize workers in textile mills. All of these laws affected women; for white women the number and kind of jobs available increased along with Social Security benefits; for black women the same cannot be said, as 90 percent of them worked as domestics or agricultural laborers and were not covered under the 1935 Social Security Act. Minimum wage laws enacted by the Fair Labor Standards Act did not apply to black women who worked as maids in private homes or as part-time field workers. Thus black women's status declined in comparison to even the poorest white women who, because they were white, were more likely to receive aid, access to training programs, or employment in industries mandated to give benefits and minimum wages.

New Deal policies, enacted with the goals of saving capitalism and returning the region to full employment, were, in the end, not entirely successful. Large landowners in southern states manipulated AAA policies to increase their landholdings, modernize their farming procedures, and minimize their dependence on tenant and sharecropping labor. The effect was to marginalize small or landless farming families. Black farming women especially suffered great disparity as they experienced discrimination of race and gender. In politics, state and local office holders, from governors to county commissioners, often acted to bring whatever federal largesse they could find to their state or locality, but these officials—the great majority of whom were white men—maintained control over its dispersal. Federal policies in fact helped to solidify roles for women within families according to racial and class designs.

Historians disagree over the failures and accomplishments of the New Deal, but for those living in the hard times of the Depression, prospects for the future seemed only marginally brighter with regard to gender and race equality. By 1935 middle-class progressive women's groups were emerging to form volunteer agendas or work in programs to cope with the national emergency. These women found places in New Deal agencies, union organizing, social welfare work, volunteer organizations, and radical politics. Their interest in interracial work continued the dialogue between the races begun in the 1920s, even while local officials in the South tried their best to maintain the racial caste system. Some of the New Deal programs enacted by Congress literally rescued a generation of southerners from continued destitution, but there is no denying the fact that federal policies toward helping women and minorities were too weak to override the innate conservatism of the South except through denial of funds or court action for noncompliance. Radical alternatives also came about as a result of inadequate attention to injustice, and these along with the federal government's actions eventually would prove effective in combating discrimination. In the short run, however, the New Deal could only lend a measure of hope to those who sought greater gender and race equality.

EPILOGUE

Southern Women and World War II

The New Deal and all of its programs, agencies, and relief dollars did not end the Great Depression. It helped people cope with the worst of it and rearranged whole sections of the nation with 3 million farmers departing the land. New Deal programs left labor unions poised to challenge the old habits of industrialists, but they included women and African Americans only minimally. The Depression finally ended after the United States entered World War II in 1941, and that war opened up a whole new chapter for the South.

World War II became America's largest and most all-encompassing war. Fought on two fronts, with 16 million inductees, it changed the nation, and it certainly changed the South. The war led to unprecedented sums of money coming to the southern states when the federal government invested more than $7 billion in military bases and industrial plants in the region. Industry received another $1 billion from private sources. The war, with its massive defense spending, went beyond what the New Deal could do, bringing jobs, money, renewed hope, and a measure of prosperity.

The southern states received more military bases than did any other region during the war, and eight of the nine largest army bases were in the South. This was due in part to climate and geography: the South offered mild winters, clear skies for airstrips, and readily available land. The political influence of southern congressmen was another strong factor. After the war many of these bases were expanded, thus bringing more military personnel to the South. In places such as South Carolina, the presence of the military actually had a liberalizing effect on the state, especially after President Harry Truman integrated the armed forces in 1948. Because 4 million soldiers were stationed in the South during World War II, a great many federally paid jobs became available for women; they worked on the bases in administrative and clerical positions as well as in food and other services.

The South did not receive as many war-industry plants as did other regions because these went to areas of the nation where industrialization was already well established. Still, the number of factory and production workers in the South more than doubled to almost 3 million at this time. Most of the defense plants closed after the war, but the one at Oak Ridge, Tennessee, built to process uranium for atomic bombs, remained open. It required 110,000 workers during its construction and 82,000 during its peak production period in 1945. Mississippi, as early as 1936, began to subsidize industrial plants with its Balance Agriculture with Industry program, and by 1944, the state's twelve plants operated at maximum production, with the shipyard at Pascagoula employing 18,000 workers. Defense industries also made investments in steel and iron milling, petrochemicals, oil and oil pipelines, aluminum and tin milling, and aircraft industries and shipyards, especially in Newport News, Norfolk, Charleston, Tampa, Mobile, Pensacola, Pascagoula, New Orleans, and Houston. This translated into work for pipe fitters, welders, and steel burners; 20,000 workers had defense jobs in eight plants in New Orleans alone. As early as 1942, Consolidated-Vultee in Fort Worth took to making B-24 "Liberator" bombers, while Bell Aircraft in Marietta, Georgia, produced B-29 "Superfortress" bombers. The industrial capacity of the South grew by 40 percent between 1939 and 1947. With the Fair Labor Standards Act and minimum wage, southern industries could no longer pay below the norm. In Mississippi, one of the poorest states, per capita income doubled during the war years. Prior to the war, women in the workforce usually earned $5.00 a week. During the war their average salary leapt to $40.00 per week.

The war brought huge demographic shifts to the South. Between 1940 and 1945, 22 percent of the region's farming population left the land. The combination of the New Deal "enclosure acts" and the pull of military and industrial work led to further abandonment of farming by millions of southerners. For former sharecroppers and renters, the industrial salaries proved a bonanza. The war also offered mobility to southerners, for they could leave the South and farm life, assured of finding work in other places. More than 1.5 million southerners left the region during this time, two-thirds of them African Americans. At the same time, more than 6 million nonsoutherners came into the region either with the military or in civilian jobs. This had a bearing on the culture of the South; for example, to outsiders segregation was confusing. A northern woman who had recently arrived in the South, seeing signs for "white only" and "colored only" laundries wondered why some laundries only washed white clothes whereas others only washed colored clothes. Although many people from other sections of the nation moved south either for war work or military training, many of them stayed in Dixie, infusing the region with new ideas and traditions—especially pertaining to desegregation—that challenged white southerners' assumptions about race and gender.

Women's roles expanded during the war, and their economic status changed in important ways. Nationally, 350,000 women joined branches of the armed forces; while 1,100 civilian women joined the Women Airforce Service Pilots (WASP) and ferried aircraft from factories to bases. As many as 4 million women worked outside the home in 1940 and by 1945 as many as 5 million did so. The national percentage of women in the workforce leapt from 24 percent before the war to 36 percent by its end. In the South, about the same percentage of women entered the workforce. Women boosted food production by 32 percent over the preceding decade. Wages for white women increased eight-fold at this time. Everywhere in the nation, government propaganda attempted to persuade women to join the workforce because there was a literal shortage of "manpower." Posters and leaflets persuaded women that patriotism required them to enter the workforce to take the place of men at the front—their participation would win the war faster. Federal promoters, however, tugged at women's heart strings rather than promoting equal job opportunities. One poster depicted a woman receiving a war letter from her sweetheart; it proclaimed, "Longing won't bring him back sooner. . . . GET A WAR JOB!"

In the South, war recruitment went hand in hand with job training, and federal programs in welding, pipe fitting, plumbing, carpentry, and electricity were made available to southern women in late 1942 when labor shortages surged. Universities in the South, with the aid of federal grants, offered free courses in engineering, chemistry, or physics, and by December 1942, 30 percent of the enrollees under this program in Alabama were white women. Recruitment for defense contract work now aimed at a relatively untapped source of labor—white middle-class married women with children. Recruiters encouraged middle-class housewives to join the workforce because, they advertised, if you could run a sewing machine, you could burn a design in steel. For the most part, women took the jobs because defense work paid better than any job previously held or even contemplated. Riveting and welding were certainly no harder than plowing and harvesting the fields, which some southern women still had to do. Women flooded cities such as Mobile where more than 10,000 worked during the war. There, according to historian Mary Martha Thomas, about 7,500 women worked for the Mobile Air Service command and "inspected the [airplane] engines, repaired the fuselages, welded parts together, riveted sheet metal, and prepared the engines for combat use." In Mobile, as in most southern cities, as many as 85 percent of women working in defense industries were white.

Black and white women experienced World War II in different ways. Throughout the United States black women fled domestic service in private homes for war work, and the percentage of African American women working as domestics declined between 1940 and 1944 from nearly 60 percent to 44.6 percent. About 18 percent of black women worked in industry—perhaps twice as many as before the war. The number of black women who worked on farms also declined by half. All told, 600,000 black women entered the paid workforce during the war years. Yet despite these national statistics, African American women found few opportunities for advancement in the South. At first, training programs for war work with whites were denied black women in Alabama despite FDR's Executive Order 8802 prohibiting discrimination in industries or institutions under war contract. Not until separate training schools opened did black women find admission to these programs. Yet training did not necessarily lead them to well-paid jobs. Of the black women working in Mobile, not one worked "as an operative in a defense plant in 1944," according to Mary Martha Thomas. Those who found jobs in the shipyards of Mobile were hired to clean out the ships and perform such heavy work as picking up scrap iron or loading boxcars. In Baltimore a few African American women found work on the Glenn Martin Aircraft Company assembly lines, but they worked in a small segregated subassembly plant. Others in that city found jobs as street cleaners after 1943 when all the available black male labor had been exhausted. The majority of black women worked as janitors, cooks, laundresses, bus girls, and domestics. The rationale for discrimination was based on the entrenched notion that women workers had to be separated by race as whites demanded. In the cotton mills, a few black women (5.3 percent of the textile workforce) found jobs as unskilled laborers, but at the Dan River factory in Virginia, the managers who had hired black women workers in 1944 fired them after white women textile workers threatened a strike if they did not do so. Thus, employee resistance to integrated workplaces allowed companies to back off from hiring black women in positions equal to whites.

In addition to hiring discrimination, there was a blatant pay discrepancy. Nationally, domestic service jobs earned black women an average of $16.50 a week whereas defense-plant operatives could earn as much as $43.45 a week. If African American women wanted skilled jobs during the war, they almost had to leave the South. Videll Drake did just that. Working as a maid and a waitress at the prestigious Hockaday School in Dallas, she managed to earn a meager $7.75 a week. After she moved to Los Angeles and found a job as a riveter with National American Aviation, she started out earning $24.00 a week. One exception to the pattern of low-paying jobs for black women in the South could be found at the Tuskegee Army Flying School that trained black pilots for the war in Europe. There African American women found work as secretaries and typists, as dispatchers and electricians; they worked in ground crews and in the areas of aircraft repair and maintenance. Many others trained as nurses in a nine-month course offered through the Cadet Nurse Corps at John Anderson Memorial Hospital in Tuskegee. The shortage of nurses prompted some city hospitals in northern states to hire black nurses, and late in the war the Army and Navy Nurse Corps integrated, providing jobs for women trained in the South. Despite the advances in some areas, the end result for most black women working during the war years in the South was that they were the last hired and then only in jobs that employers thought befitting their station and gender. White women found many more opportunities in well-paid industrial jobs, but black women made only minimal advancements.

In other arenas, women volunteered their time and efforts for the war. Volunteerism, through churches, clubs, and civic associations, had long been part of women's lives. In the South two-thirds of the women did not take on paid work, yet many from this group did what they could for the war effort. Under the Civilian Defense Program every state established a Citizens' Defense Corps, in which women volunteers worked in war-bond, used-clothing, salvage, and recruitment drives. Other women signed up as spotters, learning to observe the style, make, and model of planes flying overhead, while noting the number of engines, as well as altitude and direction. The volunteers reported their sightings to the Aircraft Warning Service. Many spotters made sure that those flying overhead were not enemy planes, thus preventing false alarms. Other women joined the Citizens' Service Corps, which coordinated volunteer activity and encouraged community activism on behalf of the war; still others joined the Red Cross, where they rolled bandages, trained as nurses' aides, and made clothing for the soldiers. In Alabama, black women formed their own Red Cross chapters and directly helped black soldiers. Women volunteered in segregated United Service Organizations (USOs) across the South, performing typical female jobs such as washing and ironing soldiers' uniforms, sewing on insignias, and hostessing events at USO stations.

Clubwomen also contributed to the war effort in myriad ways. The Texas Federation of Women's Clubs embarked on several ambitious projects, one of which was to save silk stockings, a resource used in the production of parachutes and gunpowder bags. One woman from Mission, Texas, wrote in 1942, "If you still need silk stockings for war purposes please advise me where to send them. . . . I have many pairs and I will be glad to give them to help fight the Japs." In that year alone, Texas clubwomen salvaged 8,000 pounds of silk. Even more impressive was the energy displayed in selling war bonds. Nationally, clubwomen raised $185 billion in seven different organized bond drives. Competition helped fuel the efforts as clubs were given incentives and goals to fulfill. In Texas, a "Buy a Bomber" program urged women to sell bonds to fund naval bombers, fighters, and patrol planes. Eight naval planes constituted an armada that cost $1.5 million to build, and these were available for sponsorship. In a furious effort between November 1943 and April 1944, Texas clubwomen sold $10.6 million worth of bonds. This qualified them to fund nearly seven armadas of naval war planes—the building of a whole fleet of planes funded by Texas clubwomen!

With victory in sight in 1945, industries began the transition to a peacetime economy, and women, especially African

American women, who had held industrial jobs were laid off. Employers, government advertisers, and union representatives began to chant in unison that men returning from the war needed jobs, and women were to leave the workplace to make room for them. They reiterated the traditional roles for women as wives and mothers, and told them that it was time to go home, welcome their husbands, and have children. The nation had no end of gratitude for women workers, but now their industrial skills—welding, pipe fitting, burning steel, riveting—would not be needed in the postwar economy. One widow with small children from Missouri, who had left plowing fields to take up welding during the war, found that even with the highest levels of training, she could not get a job as a welder after the war. She ended up washing dishes in a diner for seventeen years.

Although women trained for and took jobs formerly reserved for men, historians differ over the results of women's employment in the South during the war. Many say it made little long-term difference in their lives because when the war ended, men took the available peacetime jobs and women returned to homemaking or to typical "women's jobs." There certainly were fewer opportunities for African American women in industry and administrative work. A continuation of policies formulated during the years of the New Deal followed in World War II. Administrators in Washington, D.C., set policies designed to maximize the war effort but now were reluctant to implement new changes that would have brought black women out of the lowest economic category. White women in Dixie fared better than did their black counterparts during the war, just as they had during the Depression, but permanent change in working equity for white and black women remained elusive until the passage of the 1964 Civil Rights Act, which added race and sex to categories of illegal discrimination.

Other historians note that the seeds of change were planted during the war and trace a thread of resistance to southern race and gender mores. One million black soldiers served in the U.S. military, the majority from the South. They served in segregated armed forces, except for the Navy, which quietly integrated its ships. All of the officer training programs were integrated except those belonging to the Army Air Force. The Tuskegee Airmen, a Negro branch of the U.S Army Air Force, saw action with the 332nd Fighter Pilot Squadron in combat missions. From their air base in southern Italy, they flew sorties into Europe and North Africa. With such outstanding examples of black fighting men, spokesmen talked about winning the "Double V"—victory against America's enemies abroad and victory against racism at home. Once again, African American men, called upon to serve their country, were well aware of the hypocrisy in a nation that would call on them to risk their lives overseas to defend democracy while at the same time denying them equal rights at home. The NAACP called for integrating the armies and ending discrimination in education and voting. A group of sixty influential African Americans who formulated the Durham Manifesto in 1942 wanted "A New Charter of Race Relations" that extolled equality in all areas of life but especially for "the manhood and security of the Negro." An important crack in the wall of American indifference to equality occurred when President Harry Truman through Executive Order 9981 integrated the military in July 1948. African American women gained from these changes as well, since segregated units affected their participation in the military.

As to African American progress in industry, at the urging of A. Phillip Randolph of the Brotherhood of Sleeping Car Porters, President Roosevelt signed Executive Order 8802 in June 1941, making it illegal to discriminate against minorities in companies with defense contracts. The order also created the Fair Employment Practices Committee (FEPC) to which complaints were brought when employers or labor unions treated blacks unequally. Although stymied by its lack of enforcement power, the FEPC, nonetheless, represented a hard-won concession from the federal government, validating the idea that black and other minority workers needed protection from white supremacy. This led the way toward more lasting and effective agencies such as the Equal Employment Opportunity Commission created in the 1964 Civil Rights Act to end race and sex discrimination in the workplace.

In the realm of politics, good news came from the U.S. Supreme Court when in 1944 it struck down the white primary in *Smith* v. *Allwright*. African American activists, such as Grace Towns Hamilton of Atlanta, helped establish the All-Citizens Registration Committee to put forth a massive voter-registration drive in that city in 1946. The result was a tripling of black registered voters from 7,000 to 21,000. Through these efforts, African Americans gained power as a voting bloc in municipal elections, including the election of Atlanta mayors. Voter registration and the turnout rate in primaries accelerated in the states of the peripheral South, where voting restrictions were not as binding as were those in the Deep South. This presaged a time in 1965 when Congress would pass the Voting Rights Act, allowing all southern women and African Americans the franchise.

Black and white women activists started planning for the day when integration would be achieved in schools, public facilities, and the workplace, and when young women would find no obstacles to their ambitions. Younger and some older female voices emerged in the postwar transformation to challenge age-old assumptions about women's work. As discussed previously, Katharine Du Pre Lumpkin in 1946 published *The Making of a Southerner,* illuminating the legacy of the Civil War and its attendant racial strife on the history of the South. Lillian Smith began to turn toward full-time writing, and in 1944, brought out *Strange Fruit* and in 1949, *Killers of the Dream,* a damning critique of the segregated South that also speaks to the inner lives of women. Sarah Patton Boyle, a white Virginian, stunned the region when she published an article in the *Saturday Evening Post* in 1954 entitled "Southerners Will *Like* Integration." This brought Boyle immediate ostracism from elite whites as well as hate mail and cross burnings in her front yard. She concluded her critique of the South in 1962 with an autobiographical account, *The Desegregated Heart,* that spoke of her own painful journey from that of a privileged white female interested in the welfare of African Americans to a liberal proponent of integration.

Writers were not the only heralds of a new postwar South. In 1955, Septima Clark, a dedicated teacher and activist, joined

Montgomery protester Rosa Parks at the Highlander Folk School in Tennessee, where they learned methods of nonviolent resistance. Virginia Durr, a white activist and friend of Parks, spent the years after 1945 defending equal rights in Montgomery. Fannie Lou Hamer, a sharecropper in Sunflower County, Mississippi, found her voice amidst the civil rights movement two decades after the war, creating with others the Mississippi Freedom Democratic Party (MFDP). Ella J. Baker from North Carolina, a graduate of Shaw University, worked during the war years for the NAACP and in 1960 helped students, among them Diane Nash of Fisk University, organize the Student Non-Violent Coordinating Committee (SNCC). She would continue her role as consultant and activist for civil rights, working with Fannie Lou Hamer in the formation of the MFDP. There were many more women whose names are just now being recorded by historians who found new winds blowing through the South. They, and those who may never be known, took their chances to influence the direction of their region.

As historian Pete Daniel wrote, "For many southerners, World War II was the great divide. The war challenged their provincialism, offered employment, and reshaped society. After the war, they could not fit their experiences or expectations back into the South of the 1930s." The war was a great divide for southern women as well, for now there were choices before them. Nor could women simply remove themselves from shaping the future of the region. In the post–World War II years, more women began to speak out on matters of white male supremacy, women's inequality, and the effects of race discrimination—stifling roles that had kept the South in a suspended state of advancement toward democracy. Slowly and painfully a few southerners struggled toward greater freedom while conservatives from the Civil War to World War II continued to play the race or gender card. By 1945, however, the voices of such state's rights groups as the United Daughters of the Confederacy, powerful in their devotion to Lost Cause memory, began to subside; these were replaced by new voices, some strident in the defense of the "southern way of life" (a euphemism for segregation and patriarchal dominance), others eager to bring on a civil rights movement so sweeping it would challenge the conscience of the entire nation. The legacy of a war that had ended eighty years before still lingered, but in the turbulent years between 1865 and 1945, there can be no doubt that women's agency challenged the old order even as that order resisted yet ultimately yielded to change.

BIBLIOGRAPHICAL ESSAY

Preface

Excellent overviews of women's history are almost too numerous to cite, but certainly one might start with Mary R. Beard, *Woman as Force in History: A Study in Traditions and Realities* (New York,1946); Gerda Lerner, *The Majority Finds Its Past: Placing Women in History* (New York,1979); Berenice A. Carroll, ed., *Liberating Women's History: Theoretical and Critical Essays* (Urbana, IL, 1976); Joan Kelly-Gadol, "The Social Relations of the Sexes: Methodological Implications of Women's History," *Signs* 1 (Summer 1976): 809–82; Joan Wallach Scott, "Gender: A Useful Category of Analysis," *American Historical Review* 92 (December 1986), 1053–75; and Manuela Thurner, "Subject to Change: Theories and Paradigms of U.S. Feminist History," *Journal of Women's History* 9 (Summer 1997): 122–46.

Introduction

For first-hand accounts and reminiscences of the Civil War written by women see John F. Marszadek, ed. *The Diary of Miss Emma Holmes, 1861–1866* (Baton Rouge, LA, 1979); Sarah Morgan Dawson, *A Confederate Girl's Diary*, edited by James I. Robertson, Jr. (Bloomington, IN, 1960); Judith W. B. McGuire, *Diary of a Southern Refugee During the War* (New York, 1867); Eliza Frances Andrews, *The War-Time Journal of a Georgia Girl* (New York, 1908); John Q. Anderson, ed., *Brokenburn: The Journal of Kate Stone, 1861–1868* (Baton Rouge, LA, 1972); Sallie A. Brock Putnam, *Richmond During the War: Four Years of Personal Observation* (New York, 1867); Beth G. Crabtree and James W. Patton, eds., *Journal of a Secesh Lady: The Diary of Catherine Ann Devereux Edmonston, 1860–1866* (Raleigh, NC, 1979); James I. Robertson, Jr. ed., *The Diary of Dolly Lunt Burge* (Athens, GA, 1962); Mary A. H. Gay, *Life in Dixie during the War, 1861–1865* (Macon, GA, 1892); Cornelia McDonald, *A Diary with Reminiscences of the War and Refugee Life in the Shenandoah Valley, 1860–1865* (Nashville, TN, 1934); Elizabeth Allston Pringle, *Chronicles of Chicora Wood* (Cary, NC, 2007); Emma LeConte, *When the World Ended: The Diary of Emma LeConte* (New York, 1957); and Gertrude Clanton Thomas, *The Secret Eye: The Journal of Ella Gertrude Clanton Thomas, 1848–1889* (Chapel Hill, NC, 1990). Perhaps the most well known of all Civil War diaries is that of Mary Boykin Chesnut, *Diary from Dixie* (New York, 1905). For a full explanation of the evolution of her diary see C. Vann Woodward, ed., *Mary Chesnut's Civil War* (New Haven, 1981); Elisabeth Muhlenfeld, *Mary Boykin Chesnut: A Biography* (Baton Rouge, 1981); and Michael P. Johnson, "Mary Boykin Chesnut's Autobiography: A Review Essay," *Journal of Southern History* 47 (November 1981): 584–92. These and other narratives are analyzed in Sarah E. Gardner, *Blood and Irony: Southern White Women's Narratives of the Civil War, 1861–1937* (Chapel Hill, NC, 2004); and

Anne Goodwyn Jones, *Tomorrow is Another Day: The Woman Writer in the South, 1859–1936* (Baton Rouge, LA, 1981).

For histories of the lives of women during the war see Drew Gilpin Faust, *Mothers of Invention: Women of the Slaveholding South in the American Civil War* (Chapel Hill, NC, 1996); Mary Elizabeth Massey, *Bonnet Brigades* (New York, 1966), reprinted as *American Women and the Civil War* (Lincoln, NE, 1994); Edward D. C. Campbell, Jr., and Kym S. Rice, eds., *A Woman's War: Southern Women, Civil War, and the Confederate Legacy* (Richmond, VA, 1996); Catherine Clinton, ed., *Southern Families at War: Loyalty and Conflict in the Civil War South* (New York, 2000); George C. Rable, *Civil Wars: Women and the Crisis of Southern Nationalism* (Urbana, IL, 1989); Marli F. Weiner, *Mistresses and Slaves: Plantation Women in South Carolina, 1830–80* (Urbana, IL, 1998); Kirsten E. Wood, *Masterful Women: Slaveholding Widows from the American Revolution through the Civil War* (Chapel Hill, NC, 2004); Victoria E. Bynum, *Unruly Women: The Politics of Social and Sexual Control in the Old South* (Chapel Hill, NC, 1992); Anne J. Bailey, *War and Ruin: William T. Sherman and the Savannah Campaign* (Wilmington, DE, 2003); and Jacqueline Glass Campbell, *When Sherman Marched North from the Sea: Resistance on the Confederate Home Front* (Chapel Hill, NC, 2003). On women's work during the war see Jane E. Schultz, *Women at the Front: Hospital Workers in Civil War America* (Chapel Hill, NC, 2004); Phoebe Yates Pember, *A Southern Woman's Story: Life in Confederate Richmond*, ed. Bell Irvin Wiley (Jackson, MS, 1959); Cheryl A. Wells, "Battle Time: Gender, Modernity, and Confederate Hospitals," *Journal of Social History* 35 (Winter 2001): 409–28; and E. Susan Barber, "Cartridge Makers and Myrmidon Viragos: White Working-Class Women in Confederate Richmond," in Janet Coryell, et al. eds., *Negotiating Boundaries of Southern Womanhood: Dealing with the Powers That Be* (Columbia, MO, 2000), 199–214.

The historical literature on women and gender for this transitional period from war to Reconstruction is growing; see LeeAnn Whites, *The Civil War as a Crisis in Gender,*

Augusta, Georgia, 1860–1890 (Athens, GA, 1995); Laura F. Edwards, *Scarlett Doesn't Live Here Anymore: Southern Women in the Civil War Era* (Urbana, IL, 2000); Leslie A. Schwalm, *A Hard Fight for We: Women's Transition from Slavery to Freedom in South Carolina* (Urbana, IL, 1997); Jean E. Friedman, *The Enclosed Garden: Women and Community in the Evangelical South, 1830–1900* (Chapel Hill, NC, 1985); Monica Maria Tetzlaff, *Cultivating a New South: Abbie Holmes Christensen and the Politics of Race and Gender, 1852–1938* (Columbia, MO, 2002); Nancy Bercaw, *Gendered Freedoms: Race, Rights, and the Politics of the Household in the Delta, 1861–1875* (Gainesville, FL, 2003); and Laura Opendahl, "A History of Captivity and a History of Freedom: Race in a Civil War Household of Single Women," in Thomas H. Appleton, Jr., and Angela Boswell, eds., *Searching for their Places: Women in the South Across Four Centuries* (Columbia, MO, 2003), 122–43.

Chapter One

The histories of the postwar South are numerous. Certainly one should begin with Eric Foner, *Reconstruction: America's Unfinished Revolution, 1863–1877* (New York, 1988); Leon F. Litwack, *Been in the Storm So Long: The Aftermath of Slavery* (New York, 1979); Gavin Wright, *Old South, New South: Revolutions in the Southern Economy Since the Civil War* (New York, 1986); Roger Ransom and Richard Sutch, *One Kind of Freedom: The Economic Consequences of Emancipation* (Cambridge, UK, 2002, 1977); and Jacqueline Jones, *Labor of Love, Labor of Sorrow: Black Women, Work, and the Family from Slavery to the Present* (New York, 1985). The debate over the Fifteenth Amendment in the words of woman suffragists can be found in Carrie Chapman Catt and Nettie Rogers Shuler, *Woman Suffrage and Politics: The Inner Story of the Suffrage Movement* (Seattle, 1969, 1926). For a discussion of the androcentric nature of married women's property rights, see Suzanne Lebsock, "Radical Reconstruction and the Property Rights of Southern Women," *Journal of Southern History* 43 (May 1977): 195–216.

For documents of the transition from slavery to freedom see Ira Berlin, Barbara J. Fields, Thavolia Glymph, Joseph P. Reidy, and Leslie S. Rowland, eds. *Freedom: A Documentary History of Emancipation, 1861–1867*, Series 1, vol. 1, *The Destruction of Slavery* (Cambridge, UK, 1985); Ira Berlin, Steven F. Miller, Joseph P. Reidy, and Leslie S. Rowland, eds. *Freedom: A Documentary History of Emancipation, 1861–1867*, Series I, vol. II, *The Wartime Genesis of Free Labor: The Upper South* (Cambridge, UK, 1993); Ira Berlin, Thavolia Glymph, Steven F. Miller, Joseph P. Reidy, Leslie S. Rowland, and Julie Saville, eds. *Freedom: A Documentary History of Emancipation, 1861–1867*, Series I, vol. III, *The Wartime Genesis of Free Labor: The Lower South* (Cambridge, UK, 1990); and Ira Berlin, Joseph P. Reidy, and Leslie S. Rowland, eds., *Freedom: A Documentary History of Emancipation, 1861–1867*, Series 2, *The Black Military Experience* (Cambridge, UK, 1982). See also Laura F. Edwards, "'The Marriage Covenant Is at the Foundation of All Our Rights': The Politics of Slave Marriages in North Carolina after Emancipation," *Law and History Review*, 14 (Spring 1996), 81–124; Edwards, *Gendered Strife and Confusion: The Political Culture of Reconstruction* (Urbana, IL, 1997), and Nancy D. Bercaw, *Gendered Freedoms: Race, Rights, and the Politics of Household in the Delta, 1861–1875* (Gainesville, FL, 2003).

For African Americans on their entry into freedom in their own words see George P. Rawick, ed., *The American Slave: A Composite Autobiography* (Westport, CT, 1972) and Supplement Series 1 and 2 (1978, 1979); Ira Berlin, Marc Favrreau, and Stephen F. Miller, eds., *Remembering Slavery: African Americans Talk about Their Personal Experiences of Slavery and Freedom* (New York, 1998). For transitions from slavery to freedom see Steven Hahn, *A Nation Under Our Feet: Black Political Struggles in the Rural South from Slavery to the Great Migration* (Cambridge, MA, 2003); Laura F. Edwards, "Status Without Rights: African Americans and the Tangled History of Law and Governance in the Nineteenth-Century South," *American Historical Review*, 112 (April 2007): 365–93; Maud Cuney Hare, *Norris Wright Cuney: A Tribune of the Black People* (New York, 1913); Douglas Hales, *A Southern Family in Black and White: The Cuneys of Texas* (College Station, TX, 2003); and Willard B. Gatewood, *Aristocrats of Color: The Black Elite, 1880–1920* (Bloomington, IN, 1990).

For the history of women, gender, and farming in the post–Civil War South see Sharon Ann Holt, *Making Freedom Pay: North Carolina Freedpeople Working for Themselves, 1865–1900* (Athens, GA, 2000); Margaret Jarman Hagood, *Mothers of the South: Portraiture of the White Tenant Farm Woman* (Chapel Hill, NC, 1939). A valuable resource for firsthand accounts of tenant farming in Texas can be found in William A. Owens, *This Stubborn Soil* (New York, 1966). On childbirth and birth control see Marianne Leung, "'Better Babies': Birth Control in Arkansas during the 1930s," in Virginia Bernhard, et al., *Hidden Histories of Women in the New South* (Columbia, MO, 1994), 52–68; Leung, "Making the Radical Respectable: Little Rock Clubwomen and the Cause of Birth Control during the 1930s," *Arkansas Historical Quarterly* 57 (Spring 1998): 17–32; Johanna Schoen, *Choice and Coercion: Birth Control, Sterilization, and Abortion in Public Health and Welfare* (Chapel Hill, NC, 2004); and Harold L. Smith, "Class, Gender, and Race in the Origins of the Texas Birth Control Movement," paper delivered to the Texas State Historical Association, March 2006.

For gender and textile and tobacco manufacturing in the South, start with Jacquelyn Dowd Hall, et al., *Like a Family: The Making of a Southern Cotton Mill World* (Chapel Hill, NC, 1987); Victoria Byerly, ed., *Hard Times Cotton Mill Girls: Personal Histories of Womanhood and Poverty in the South* (New York,1986); Dolores E. Janiewski, *Sisterhood Denied: Race, Gender, and Class in a New South Community* (Philadelphia, 1985); and Bryant Simon, A *Fabric of Defeat: The Politics of South Carolina Millhands, 1910–1948* (Chapel Hill, NC, 1998). See also Allen Tullos, *Habits of Industry: White Culture and the Transformation of the Carolina Piedmont* (Chapel Hill, NC, 1989). For a valuable look at the early enthusiasm of economists for cotton mills see Broadus Mitchell, *The Rise of the Cotton Mills in the South* (Baltimore, 1921). This view is countered by C. Vann Woodward's classic *Origins of the New South, 1877–1913* (Baton Rouge, LA, 1951).

For a history of gender and interracial unionism see Daniel Letwin, *The Challenge of Interracial Unionism: Alabama Coal Miners, 1878–1921* (Chapel Hill, NC, 1998); and Letwin, "Interracial Unionism, Gender, and 'Social Equality' in Alabama Coalfields, 1878–1908," *Journal of Southern History* 61 (August 1995): 519–54. Other valuable histories of interracial unionism are Brian Kelly, *Race, Class, and Power in the Alabama Coalfields, 1908–21* (Urbana, IL, 2001); Eric Arnesen, *Waterfront Workers of New Orleans: Race, Class, and Politics, 1863–1923* (New York, 1991); and Daniel Rosenberg, *New Orleans Dockworkers: Race, Labor, and Unionism, 1892–1923* (Albany, NY, 1988).

Chapter Two

Helpful histories of women's contribution to the Lost Cause collective memory and history are W. Fitzhugh Brundage, *The Southern Past: The Clash of Race and Memory* (Cambridge, MA, 2005); Karen Cox, *Dixie's Daughters: The United Daughters of the Confederacy and the Preservation of Confederate Culture* (Gainesville, FL, 2003); Cynthia Mills and Pamela H. Simpson, eds., *Monuments to the Lost Cause: Women, Art, and the Landscapes of Southern Memory* (Knoxville, TN, 2003); and Sarah E. Gardner, *Blood and Irony: Southern White Women's Narratives of the Civil War, 1861–1937* (Chapel Hill, NC, 2004). This should be followed by reading Jane Turner Censer, *The Reconstruction of White Southern Womanhood, 1865–1895* (Baton Rouge, LA, 2003). For a stunning history of the power of Lost Cause collective memory over emancipationist memory see David W. Blight, *Race and Reunion: The Civil War in American Memory* (Cambridge, MA, 2001). See also Nina Silber, *The Romance of Reunion: Northerners and the South, 1865–1900* (Chapel Hill, NC, 1993); and David Goldfield, *Still*

Fighting the Civil War: The American South and Southern History (Baton Rouge, LA, 2002). For an overview of the Lost Cause see Gaines Foster, *Ghosts of the Confederacy: Defeat, the Lost Cause, and the Emergence of the New South, 1865–1913* (New York, 1987); Charles Reagan Wilson, *Baptized in Blood: The Religion of the Lost Cause* (Athens, GA, 1980); Thomas L. Connelly and Barbara L. Bellows, *God and General Longstreet: The Lost Cause and the Southern Mind* (Baton Rouge, LA, 1982); and Paul M. Gaston, *The New South Creed: A Study in Southern Mythmaking* (New York, 1970).

On Winnie Davis see Cita Cook, "Winnie Davis (1864–1898): The Challenges of Daughterhood," in Martha H. Swain, Elizabeth Anne Payne, and Marjorie Julian Spruill, eds., *Mississippi Women: Their Histories, Their Lives* (Athens, GA, 2003), 21–38. Several very fine dissertations in the field of memory and memorialization are Antoinette G. van Zelm, "On the Front Lines of Freedom: Black and White Women Shape Emancipation in Virginia, 1861–1890" (Ph.D. dissertation, College of William and Mary, 1998); and Kelly McMichael Stott, "From Lost Cause to Female Empowerment: The Texas Division of the United Daughters of the Confederacy, 1896–1966" (Ph.D. dissertation, University of North Texas, 2001). See also Caroline E. Janney, *Burying the Dead but Not the Past: Ladies' Memorial Associations and the Making of the Lost Cause* (Chapel Hill, NC, 2007); and Sarah H. Case, "The Historical Ideology of Mildred Lewis Rutherford: A Confederate Historian's New South Creed," *Journal of Southern History* 68 (August 2002): 599–628. For a firsthand account of the construction of southern memory, see the *Lost Cause* magazine, an organ of the UDC; and Katharine Du Pre Lumpkin, *The Making of a Southerner* (Athens, GA, 1991, 1946).

On the origins and evolution of Jim Crow see Jane Dailey, Glenda Elizabeth Gilmore, and Bryant Simon, eds., *Jumpin' Jim Crow: Southern Politics from Civil War to Civil Rights* (Princeton, 2000); Grace Elizabeth Hale, *Making Whiteness: The Culture of Segregation in the South, 1890–1940* (New York, 1998); Joel Williamson, *The Crucible of Race: Black-White Relations in the American South Since Emancipation* (New York, 1984); an abridged version, *The Rage for Order: Black-White Relations in the American South Since Emancipation* (New York, 1986); Leon F. Litwack, *Trouble in Mind: Black Southerners in the Age of Jim Crow* (New York, 1998); Beverly Guy-Sheftall, *Daughters of Sorrow: Attitudes toward Black Women, 1880–1920* (Brooklyn, NY, 1990); Jane Dailey, "Deference and Violence in the Postbellum Urban South," *Journal of Southern History* 63 (August 1997): 553–90; and Bryant Simon, "The Appeal of Cole Blease of South Carolina: Race, Class, and Sex in the New South," *Journal of Southern History* 62 (February 1996): 57–86.

On disfranchisement see Michael Perman, *Struggle for Mastery: Disfranchisement in the South, 1888–1908* (Chapel Hill, NC, 2001). For first-hand accounts of disfranchisement and segregation see William H. Chafe, Raymond Gavins, and Robert Korstad, et al., *Remembering Jim Crow: African Americans Tell About Life in the Segregated South* (New York, 2001). For discussion of race theorists see John Higham, *Strangers in the Land: Patterns of American Nativism* (New Brunswick, NJ, 1955).

On lynching see Christopher Waldrep, ed., *Lynching in America: A History in Documents* (New York, 2006); W. Fitzhugh Brundage, *Lynching in the New South: Georgia and Virginia, 1880–1930* (Urbana, IL, 1993); Brundage, ed., *Under Sentence of Death: Lynching in the South* (Chapel Hill, NC, 1997); William D. Carrigan, *The Making of a Lynching Culture: Violence and Vigilantism in Central Texas, 1836–1916* (Urbana, IL, 2004); and William D. Carrigan and Clive Webb, "Muerto por Unos Desconocidos (Killed by Persons Unknown): Mob Violence against Blacks and Mexicans," in Stephanie Cole and Allison Parker, eds., *Beyond Black and White: Race, Ethnicity, and Gender in the U.S. South and Southwest* (College Station, TX, 2004), 35–74. For gender and lynching see Ida B. Wells, *Southern Horrors: Lynch Law in All Its Phases* (New York, 1892); Mildred I. Thompson, *Ida B. Wells-Barnett: An Exploratory Study of an American Black Woman, 1893–1930* (Brooklyn, NY, 1990); Jacquelyn Dowd Hall, *Revolt Against Chivalry: Jessie Daniel Ames and the Women's Campaign Against Lynching* (New York,1979); and Stewart E. Tolnay and E.M. Beck, *A Festival of Violence: An Analysis of Southern Lynchings, 1882–1930* (Urbana, IL, 1992). Tolnay and Beck have revisited the lists of lynching victims compiled by the NAACP (*Thirty Years of Lynching in the United States, 1889–1918*) and supplements, listings by the *Chicago Defender*, as well as a Tuskegee University study compiled in 1968 (Daniel T. Williams, *Amid the Gathering Multitude: The Story of Lynching in America. A Classified Listing*). They revised the figures downward in many cases from that compiled by these various groups. But they did not include in their calculations Texas, a state with the third greatest numbers of lynchings in the South. For this reason, I chose to use the NAACP figures that included Texas. In the years between 1882 and 1930, Tolnay and Beck calculate that in Mississippi 538 were lynched, 509 of whom were black. In Georgia 458 were lynched, 435 of whom were black.

Chapter Three

For a discussion of women's roles in churches and the community begin with Anne Firor Scott, *The Southern Lady: From Pedestal to Politics, 1830–1930* (Chicago, 1970, 1995); and Scott, "Most Invisible of All: Black Women's Voluntary Associations," *Journal of Southern History* 56 (February 1990): 3–22. See also Evelyn Brooks Higginbotham, *Righteous Discontent: The Women's Movement in the Black Baptist Church, 1880–1920* (Cambridge, MA, 1993); Sally G. McMillen, *To Raise up the South: Sunday Schools in Black and White Churches, 1865–1915* (Baton Rouge, LA, 2001); Elizabeth Hayes Turner, *Women, Culture, and Community: Religion and Reform in Galveston, 1880*–1920 (New York, 1997); Paul Harvey, *Redeeming the South: Religious Cultures and Racial Identities among Southern Baptists, 1865–1925* (Chapel Hill, NC, 1997); Elna C. Green, *This Business of Relief: Confronting Poverty in a Southern City, 1740–1940* (Athens, GA, 2003); Catherine Prelinger, ed., *Episcopal Women: Gender, Spirituality and Commitment in an American Mainline Denomination* (New York, 1992). Sarah Dudley Pettey, "What Role Is the Educated Negro Woman to Play in the Uplifting of Her Race?" in D.W. Culp, ed., *Twentieth Century Negro Literature* (Miami, 1969). For a firsthand account of the WCTU see Belle Kearney, *A Slaveholder's Daughter* (New York, 1900).

On Farmers' Alliances see Edward L. Ayers, *The Promise of the New South: Life after Reconstruction* (New York, 1992), which covers not only the Farmers' Alliances and Populism but also the cultural and intellectual climate of the South until 1906. For women's roles see also Marian K. Barthelme, *Women in the Populist Movement: Letters to the* Southern Mercury (College Station, TX, 1997); and Julie Roy Jeffrey, "Women in the Southern Farmers' Alliance: A Reconsideration of the Role and Status of Women in the Late-Nineteenth-Century South," *Feminist Studies* 3 (Autumn 1975): 72–91.

For women's educational institutions and women's influence in the South see Amy Thompson McCandless, *The Past in the Present: Women's Higher Education in the Twentieth-Century American South* (Tuscaloosa, AL, 1999). Many sources exist to explain the history of African American education in the South. One should begin with James D. Anderson, *The Education of Blacks in the South, 1860–1935* (Chapel Hill, NC, 1988). For the Association for the Study of Negro Life and History see Jacqueline Anne Goggin, *Carter G. Woodson: A Life in Black History* (Baton Rouge, LA, 1993). For African American women's history in the reform era see Glenda Elizabeth Gilmore, *Gender and Jim Crow: Women and the Politics of White Supremacy in North Carolina, 1896–1920* (Chapel Hill, NC, 1996); Stephanie J. Shaw, *What a Woman Ought to Be and to Do: Black Professional Women Workers during the Jim Crow Era* (Chicago, 1996); Cynthia Neverdon-Morton, *Afro-American Women of the South and the Advancement of the Race, 1895–1925* (Knoxville, TN, 1989); Dorothy Salem, *To Better Our World: Black Women in Organized Reform, 1890–1920* (Brooklyn, NY, 1990); Floris Barnett Cash, *African American Women and Social Action: The*

Clubwomen and Voluntarism from Jim Crow to the New Deal, 1896–1936 (Westport, CT, 2001); Paula Giddings, *When and Where I Enter: The Impact of Black Women on Race and Sex in America* (New York, 1984); and Elsa Barkley Brown, "Womanist Consciousness: Maggie Lena Walker and the Independent Order of Saint Luke," *Signs* 14 (Spring 1989): 610–33. For discussions of the image of the Southern Lady see Anastatia Sims, *The Power of Femininity in the New South: Women's Organizations and Politics in North Carolina, 1880–1930* (Columbia, SC, 1997).

Chapter Four

Women and Progressivism in the South, once a subject neglected by historians, is now one of the most explored topics in the field. See Dewey W. Grantham, *Southern Progressivism: The Reconciliation of Progress and Tradition* (Knoxville, TN, 1983); Edward L. Ayers, *The Promise of the New South: Life after Reconstruction* (New York, 1992); William A. Link, *The Paradox of Southern Progressivism, 1880–1930* (Chapel Hill, NC, 1992); Anne Firor Scott, *The Southern Lady: From Pedestal to Politics, 1830–1930* (Chicago, 1995, 1970); Scott, *Natural Allies: Women's Associations in American History* (Urbana, IL, 1994); Cynthia Neverdon-Morton, *Afro-American Women of the South and the Advancement of the Race, l895–1925* (Knoxville, TN, 1989); Dorothy Salem, *To Better Our World: Black Women in Organized Reform, 1890–1920* (Brooklyn, NY, 1990); Floris Barnett Cash, *African American Women and Social Action: The Clubwomen and Voluntarism from Jim Crow to the New Deal, 1896–1936* (Westport, CT, 2001); Sharon Harley and Rosalyn Terborg-Penn, eds., *The Afro-American Woman: Struggles and Images* (Port Washington, NY, 1978). On domestic politics see Paula Baker, "The Domestication of Politics: Women and American Political Society, 1780–1920," *American Historical Review* 89 (June 1984): 620–47.

There are several urban studies that focus on women and gender. For Atlanta, see Jacqueline A. Rouse, *Lugenia Burns*

Hope: Black Southern Reformer (Athens, GA,1989); Darlene R. Roth, *Matronage: Patterns in Women's Organizations, Atlanta, Georgia, 1890–1940* (Brooklyn, NY, 1994); Georgina Hickey, *Hope and Danger in the New South City: Working-Class Women and Urban Development in Atlanta, 1890–1940* (Athens, GA, 2003); Sarah Mercer Judson, "Building the New South City: African American and White Clubwomen in Atlanta, 1895–1930" (Ph.D. dissertation, New York University, 1997). For Texas cities see Elizabeth York Enstam, *Women and the Creation of Urban Life: Dallas, Texas, 1843–1920* (College Station, TX, 1998); Jacquelyn Masure McElhaney, *Pauline Periwinkle and Progressive Reform in Dallas* (College Station, TX, 1998); and Elizabeth Hayes Turner, *Women, Culture, and Community: Religion and Reform in Galveston, 1880–1920* (New York, 1997). Other cities represented are Nancy A. Hewitt, *Southern Discomfort: Women's Activism in Tampa, Florida, 1880–1920s* (Urbana, IL, 2001); Sandra Gioia Treadway, *Women of Mark: A History of the Woman's Club of Richmond, Virginia, 1894–1995* (Richmond, VA, 1995); and Marsha Wedell, *Elite Women and the Reform Impulse in Memphis, 1875–1915* (Knoxville, TN, 1991). For a fascinating study of sex and race, including a detailed history of Storyville, see Alecia P. Long, *The Great Southern Babylon: Sex, Race, and Respectability in New Orleans, 1865–1920* (Baton Rouge, LA, 2004). General studies of urban reformers include Don H. Doyle, *New Men, New Cities, New South: Atlanta, Nashville, Charleston, Mobile, 1860–1910* (Chapel Hill, NC, 1990); and Elisabeth Lasch-Quinn, *Black Neighbors: Race and the Limits of Reform in the American Settlement House Movement, 1890–1945* (Chapel Hill, NC, 1993).

For women and reform before and during the Progressive era at the state level see Glenda Elizabeth Gilmore, *Gender and Jim Crow: Women and the Politics of White Supremacy in North Carolina, 1896–1920* (Chapel Hill, NC, 1996); Anastatia Sims, *The Power of Femininity in the New South: Women's Organizations and Politics in North Carolina, 1880–1930* (Columbia, SC, 1997); Sarah Wilkerson-Freeman, "Women and the Transformation of American Politics: North Carolina, 1898–1940"

(Ph.D. dissertation, University of North Carolina at Chapel Hill, 1995); and Joan Marie Johnson, *Southern Ladies, New Women: Race, Region, and Clubwomen in South Carolina, 1890–1930* (Gainesville, FL, 2004). For states farther west of the Carolinas see Mary Martha Thomas, *The New Woman in Alabama: Social Reforms and Suffrage, 1890–1920* (Tuscaloosa, AL, 1992); and Judith N. McArthur, *Creating the New Woman: The Rise of Southern Women's Progressive Culture in Texas, 1883–1918* (Urbana, IL, 1998).

For child labor reform see Shelley Sallee, *The Whiteness of Child Labor Reform in the New South* (Athens, GA, 2004). For women's educational reform see Amy Thompson McCandless, *The Past in the Present: Women's Higher Education in the Twentieth-Century American South* (Tuscaloosa, AL, 1999); Rebecca S. Montgomery, *The Politics of Education in the New South: Women and Reform in Georgia, 1890–1930* (Baton Rouge, LA, 2006); Montgomery, "Lost Cause Mythology in New South Reform," in Janet L. Coryell, et al., eds., *Negotiating Boundaries of Southern Womanhood: Dealing with the Powers That Be* (Columbia, MO, 2000), 174–98; James L. Leloudis, *Schooling the New South: Pedagogy, Self, and Society in North Carolina, 1880–1920* (Chapel Hill, NC, 1999); Leloudis, "School Reform in the New South: The Woman's Association for the Betterment of Public School Houses in North Carolina, 1902–1919," *Journal of American History* 69 (March 1983), 886–909; William A Link, *A Hard Country and a Lonely Place: Schooling, Society, and Reform in Rural Virginia, 1870–1920* (Chapel Hill, NC, 1986); Stephanie J. Shaw, *What a Woman Ought to Be and to Do: Black Professional Women Workers During the Jim Crow Era* (Chicago, 1996); Walter J. Frasier, Jr., R. Frank Saunders, Jr., and Jon L. Wakelyn, eds., *The Web of Southern Relations: Women, Family, and Education* (Athens, GA, 1985); and Debbie Mauldin Cottrell, *Pioneer Educator: The Progressive Spirit of Annie Webb Blanton* (College Station, TX, 1993). For a history of African Americans that incorporates the role of ideas in the postwar South see Michele Mitchell, *Righteous Propagation:*

African Americans and the Politics of Racial Destiny after Reconstruction (Chapel Hill, NC, 2004).

For married women's property rights see Kathleen Elizabeth Lazarou, *Concealed Under Petticoats: Married Women's Property and the Law of Texas, 1840–1913* (New York, 1986); and Joan Hoff, *Law, Gender, and Injustice: A Legal History of U.S. Women* (New York, 1991). On Eugenics see Steven Noll, "'A Far Greater Menace': Feebleminded Females in the South, 1900–1940," in Virginia Bernhard, et. al., *Hidden Histories of Women in the New South* (Columbia, MO, 1994), 31–51.

Chapter Five

On the woman suffrage movement in the South see Marjorie Spruill Wheeler, *New Women of the New South: The Leaders of the Woman Suffrage Movement in the Southern States* (New York, 1993); Marjorie Spruill Wheeler, ed., *Votes for Women! The Woman Suffrage Movement in Tennessee, the South, and the Nation* (Knoxville, TN, 1995); Roslyn Terborg-Penn, *African American Women in the Struggle for the Vote, 1850–1920* (Bloomington, IN,1998); Elna C. Green, *Southern Strategies: Southern Women and the Woman Suffrage Question* (Chapel Hill, NC, 1997); Aileen S. Kraditor, *The Ideas of the Woman Suffrage Movement, 1890–1920* (New York, 1965); Suzanne Lebsock, "Woman Suffrage and White Supremacy: A Virginia Case Study," in Nancy A. Hewitt and Suzanne Lebsock, eds., *Visible Women: New Essays on American Activism* (Urbana, IL, 1993), 62–100; and A. Elizabeth Taylor, *The Woman Suffrage Movement in Tennessee* (New York, 1957). On voting women and politics see Lorraine Gates Schuyler, *"The Weight of Their Votes": Southern Women, Civic Culture, and Political Leverage* (Chapel Hill, NC, 2007); Pamela Tyler, *Silk Stockings and Ballot Boxes: Women and Politics in New Orleans, 1920–1963* (Athens, GA, 1996); David Fort Godshalk, *Veiled Visions: The 1906 Atlanta Race Riot and the Reshaping of American Race Relations* (Chapel Hill, NC, 2005); Kristi Andersen, *After Suffrage: Women in Partisan and Electoral Politics before the*

New Deal (Chicago, 1996); and Anita Goodstein, "A Rare Alliance: African American and White Women in the Tennessee Elections of 1919 and 1920," *Journal of Southern History* 64 (May 1998), 219–46. See also Judith N. McArthur and Harold L. Smith, *Minnie Fisher Cunningham: A Suffragist's Life in Politics* (New York, 2003). Although Tampa, Florida, is not discussed at length in this text, Nancy Hewitt's *Southern Discomfort: Women's Activism in Tampa, Florida, 1880s–1920s* (Urbana, IL, 2001) creates a picture of constant movement, of competing and sometimes opposing dynamics among Anglo, Cuban, black, and Italian women with multiple meanings to the term "women's activism."

Chapter Six

For overview discussions of the South and women and gender in the 1920s see Anne Firor Scott, *The Southern Lady from Pedestal to Politics, 1830–1930* (Chicago, 1970 and 1995). An older but still useful analysis of changing historical interpretations of women in the 1920s is Estelle Freedman, "The New Woman: Changing Views of Women in the 1920s," *Journal of American History* 61 (September 1974): 372–93. On popular culture in the 1920s see Paula S. Fass, *The Damned and the Beautiful: American Youth in the 1920's* (New York, 1977); and Ted Ownby, *Subduing Satan: Religion, Recreation, and Manhood in the Rural South, 1865–1920* (Chapel Hill, NC, 1990).

Useful studies of women in the 1920s and in later decades include William H. Chafe, *The American Woman: Her Changing Social, Economic, and Political Role, 1920–1970* (New York, 1972); Chafe, *Women and Equality: Changing Patterns in American Culture* (New York, 1977); and Amy Thompson McCandless, *The Past in the Present: Women's Higher Education in the Twentieth-Century American South* (Tuscaloosa, AL, 1999).

On Atlanta's night life see Tera Hunter, *To 'Joy My Freedom: Southern Black Women's Lives and Labors after the Civil War* (Cambridge, MA, 1997); Georgina Hickey, *Hope and Dan-*

ger in the New South City: Working-Class Women and Urban Development in Atlanta, 1890–1940 (Athens, GA, 2003). For studies of the blues see Jeffrey Carroll, *When Your Way Gets Dark: A Rhetoric of the Blues* (West Lafayette, IN, 2005); Hazel V. Carby, " 'It Jus Be's Dat Way Sometime': The Sexual Politics of Women's Blues," *Radical America* 20 (No. 4, 1986): 9–22.

On the Southern Renaissance an older but reliable source is George Brown Tindall, *The Emergence of the New South, 1913–1945* (Baton Rouge, LA, 1967); see also Daniel Joseph Singal, *The War Within: From Victorian to Modernist Thought in the South, 1919–1945* (Chapel Hill, NC, 1982); and James C. Cobb, *Away Down South: A History of Southern Identity* (New York, 2005) which has an especially insightful chapter on southern writers. See also Henry Louis Gates and Gene Andrew Jarrett, eds., *The New Negro: Readings on Race, Representation, and African American Culture, 1892–1938* (Princeton, 2007).

For sources specific to southern women writers see Anne Goodwyn Jones, *Tomorrow is Another Day: The Woman Writer in the South, 1859–1936* (Baton Rouge, LA, 1981); Anne Goodwyn Jones and Susan V. Donaldson, eds., *Haunted Bodies: Gender and Southern Texts* (Charlottesville, VA, 1997); and Carolyn Perry and Mary Louise Weaks, eds., *The History of Southern Women's Literature* (Baton Rouge, LA, 2002).

On Zora Neale Hurston see *Their Eyes Were Watching God* (Philadelphia, 1937); Lucy Anne Hurston, *Speak, So You Can Speak Again: The Life of Zora Neale Hurston* (New York, 2004); and Hazel V. Carby, *Reconstructing Womanhood: The Emergence of the Afro-American Woman Novelist* (New York, 1987). On Katharine Du Pre Lumpkin see *The Making of a Southerner* (New York, 1946); Jacquelyn Dowd Hall, "'You Must Remember This': Autobiography as Social Critique," *Journal of American History* 85 (September 1998): 439–46; and Darlene O'Dell, *Sites of Southern Memory: The Autobiographies of Katharine Du Pre Lumpkin, Lillian Smith, and Pauli Murray* (Charlottesville, VA, 2001). On Lillian Smith see *Strange Fruit* (New York, 1944); Smith, *Killers of the Dream* (New York, 1949); and Anne C. Loveland, *Lillian Smith: A Southerner Confronting the*

South, A Biography (Baton Rouge, LA, 1986). Letters from Lillian Smith can be found in *How am I to be Heard: Letters of Lillian Smith*, edited by Margaret Rose Gladney (Chapel Hill, NC, 1993). On *Gone with the Wind*, see Margaret Mitchell, *Gone with the Wind* (New York, 1936); Catherine Clinton, "Gone with the Wind," in Ted Mico, John Miller-Monzon, and David Rubel, eds., *Past Imperfect: History According to the Movies* (New York, 1995), 132–35; Catherine Clinton, *Tara Revisited: Women, War, and the Plantation Legend* (New York, 1995); Richard Harwell, ed., *Gone with the Wind as Book and Film* (Columbia, SC, 1983); Darden A. Pyron, ed., *Recasting: Gone with the Wind in American Culture* (Gainesville, FL, 1983); and Grace Elizabeth Hale, *Making Whiteness: The Culture of Segregation in the South, 1890–1940* (New York, 1998).

For a discussion of the events leading up to the Atlanta race riot of 1906 and its consequences see David Fort Godshalk, *Veiled Visions: The 1906 Atlanta Race Riot and the Reshaping of American Race Relations* (Chapel Hill, NC, 2005); Nancy Maclean, "The Leo Frank Case Reconsidered: Gender and Sexual Politics in the Making of Reactionary Populism," *Journal of American History* 78 (December 1991): 917–48; and Leonard Dinnerstein, *The Leo Frank Case* (New York, 1968).

On *The Birth of a Nation* see Jack Temple Kirby, *Media Made Dixie: The South in the American Imagination* (Baton Rouge, LA, 1978); Leon F. Litwack, "The Birth of a Nation," in Ted Mico, John Miller-Monzon, and David Rubel, eds., *Past Imperfect: History According to the Movies* (New York, 1995), 136–41. For *Within Our Gates* see J. Ronald Green, *Straight Lick: The Cinema Of Oscar Micheaux* (Bloomington, IN, 2000); Green, *With a Crooked Stick—The Films of Oscar Micheaux* (Bloomington, IN, 2004); and Patrick McGilligan, *Oscar Micheaux, The Great and Only: The Life of America's First Black Filmmaker* (New York, 2007). For a nuanced view of the complexities of black on white rape see Lisa Lindquist Dorr, *White Women, Rape, and the Power of Race in Virginia, 1900–1960* (Chapel Hill, NC, 2004).

On the CIC and the Association of Southern Women for the Prevention of Lynching see Morton Sosna, *In Search of the Silent South: Southern Liberals and the Race Issue* (New York, 1977); Henry E. Barber, "The Association of Southern Women for the Prevention of Lynching," *Phylon* 34 (December 1973): 378–89; Jacquelyn Dowd Hall, *Revolt Against Chivalry: Jessie Daniel Ames and the Women's Campaign Against Lynching* (New York, 1979); and Lewis Nordyke, "The Ladies and the Lynchers," *Reader's Digest* (November 1939).

Chapter Seven

For overviews of the Great Depression and the New Deal among many excellent histories, start with Michael E. Parrish, *Anxious Decades: America in Prosperity and Depression, 1920–1941*(New York, 1992); William E. Leuchtenburg, *Franklin D. Roosevelt and the New Deal* (New York, 1963); Frank Freidel, *FDR and the South* (Baton Rouge, LA, 1965); Roger Biles, *The South and the New Deal* (Lexington, KY, 1994); Biles, "The Urban South in the Great Depression," *Journal of Southern History* 56 (February 1990): 71–100; J. Wayne Flynt, *Dixie's Forgotten People: The South's Poor Whites* (Bloomington, IN, 1979); Raymond Wolters, *Negroes and the Great Depression: The Problem of Economic Recovery* (Westport, CT, 1970); and Pete Daniel, *The Shadow of Slavery: Peonage in the South, 1901–1969* (Urbana, IL, 1972). Instructive interpretations of federal policies toward the South can be found in James C. Cobb, "'Somebody Done Nailed Us on the Cross': Federal Farm and Welfare Policy and the Civil Rights Movement in the Mississippi Delta," *Journal of American History* 77 (December 1990): 912–36; and Jacqueline Jones, "Federal Power, Southern Power: A Long View, 1860–1940," *Journal of American History* 87 (March 2001): 1392–96.

On farming women, the economic downturn of the 1920s, and the Great Depression see Melissa Walker, *All We Knew Was to Farm; Rural Women in the Upcountry South, 1919–1941* (Baltimore, 2000); Rebecca Sharpless, *Fertile Ground, Narrow*

Choices: Women on Texas Cotton Farms, 1900–1940 (Chapel Hill, NC, 1999); Sharpless, "Southern Women and the Land," *Agricultural History* 67 (Spring 1993), 30–42; and Lu Ann Jones, *Mama Learned Us to Work: Farm Women in the New South* (Chapel Hill, NC, 2002). Margaret Jarman Hagood, *Mothers of the South: Portraiture of the White Tenant Farm Woman* (New York, 1977, 1939) remains a classic; and journalist Robert A. Caro, *The Years of Lyndon Johnson: The Path to Power* (New York, 1983) has written perhaps the most controversial biography of Johnson to date, but his chapter, "Sad Irons" provides a graphic picture of Texas Hill Country farm life. Neil Foley's account of women's roles on Texas farms is especially valuable for understanding the centrality of their mostly unpaid work. Foley, *The White Scourge: Mexicans, Blacks, and Poor Whites in Texas Cotton Culture* (Berkeley, CA, 1997).

On women's lives in the South during the Depression see Jacqueline Jones, *Labor of Love, Labor of Sorrow: Black Women, Work, and the Family from Slavery to the Present* (New York, 1985); Julia Kirk Blackwelder, *Women of the Depression: Caste and Culture in San Antonio, 1929–1939* (College Station, TX, 1984); and Blackwelder, *Now Hiring: The Feminization of Work in the United States, 1900–1995* (College Station, TX, 1997). On race in the 1930s see Patricia Sullivan, *Days of Hope: Race and Democracy in the New Deal Era* (Chapel Hill, NC, 1996).

For a history of textile mill workers and labor organizing see Jacquelyn Dowd Hall, et al., *Like a Family: The Making of a Southern Cotton Mill World* (Chapel Hill, NC, 1987); Hall, "Disorderly Women: Gender and Labor Militancy in the Appalachian South," *Journal of American History* 73 (1986), 354–82; and Victoria Byerly, ed., *Hard Times Cotton Mill Girls: Personal Histories of Womanhood and Poverty in the South* (New York, 1986). For sheer readability and intriguing analysis refer to journalist John Egerton's *Speak Now against the Day: The Generation before the Civil Rights Movement in the South* (Chapel Hill, NC, 1994). Important studies of southern radical labor movements and women workers are Robin D. G. Kelley, *Hammer and*

Hoe: Alabama Communists During the Great Depression (Chapel Hill, NC, 1990); Glenda Elizabeth Gilmore, *Defying Dixie: The Radical Roots of Civil Rights, 1919–1950* (New York, 2008); Zaragosa Vargas, "Tejana Radical: Emma Tenayuca and the San Antonio Labor Movement during the Great Depression," *Pacific Historical Review* 66 (November, 1997), 553–80; and Johnetta Gladys Richards, "The Southern Negro Youth Congress; A History, 1937–1949" (Ph.D. dissertation, University of Cincinnati, 1987). On the Scottsboro Boys see Dan T. Carter, *Scottsboro: A Tragedy of the American South* (Baton Rouge, LA, 1969, 2007).

On New Deal programs in the South see an older but helpful study of the CCC by John A. Salmond, "The Civilian Conservation Corps and the Negro," *Journal of American History* 52 (June 1965): 75–88. On the Farm Security Administration an intriguing and helpful study is Nicholas Natanson, *The Black Image in the New Deal: The Politics of FSA Photography* (Knoxville, TN, 1992). For studies of women in New Deal agencies such as the FERA or the WPA see Martha H. Swain, *Ellen S. Woodward: New Deal Advocate for Women* (Jackson, MS, 1995); Swain, "A New Deal for Southern Women: Gender and Race in Women's Work Relief," in Christie Anne Farnham, ed., *Women of the American South: A Multicultural Reader* (New York, 1997), 241– 57; Landon R. Y. Storrs, "Gender and Sectionalism in New Deal Politics: Southern White Women's Campaign for Labor Reform," in Thomas H. Appleton Jr., and Angela Boswell, eds., *Searching for Their Places: Women in the South Across Four Centuries* (Columbia, MO, 2003), 218–37; Storrs, *Civilizing Capitalism: The National Consumers' League, Women's Activism, and Labor Standards in the New Deal* (Chapel Hill, NC, 2000); Lucy R. Mason, *Standards for Workers in Southern Industry* (New York, 1931); Mason, *To Win These Rights: A Personal Story of the CIO in the South* (New York, 1952); John A. Salmond, *Miss Lucy of the CIO: The Life and Times of Lucy Randolph Mason, 1882–1959* (Athens, GA, 1988); and Suzanne Mettler, *Dividing Citizens: Gender and Federalism in New Deal Public Pol*icy (Ithaca, NY, 1998).

Epilogue

For studies of the South during and after World War II see David R. Goldfield, *Promised Land: The South Since 1945* (Arlington Heights, IL, 1987); and for an interpretive and readable account of the South with an eye to the present see Goldfield, *Still Fighting the Civil War: The American South and Southern History* (Baton Rouge, LA, 2002). To find those who envisioned a more progressive South in the postwar period look to Morton Sosna, *In Search of the Silent South: Southern Liberals and the Race Issue* (New York, 1977); John Egerton, *Speak Now Against the Day: The Generation Before the Civil Rights Movement in the South* (New York, 1994); and Pete Daniel, *Lost Revolutions: The South in the 1950s* (Chapel Hill, NC, 2000).

For studies of women in World War II and the South see Mary Martha Thomas, *Riveting and Rationing in Dixie: Alabama Women and the Second World War* (Tuscaloosa, AL, 1987); Karen Tucker Anderson, "Last Hired, First Fired: Black Women Workers during World War II," *Journal of American History* 69 (June 1982): 82–97; Judy Barrett Litoff, "Southern Women in a World at War," in Neil R. McMillen, ed., *Remaking Dixie: The Impact of World War II on the American South* (Jackson, MS, 1997), 56–69; Darlene Clark Hine, *Black Nurses in White: Racial Conflict and Cooperation in the Nursing Profession, 1890–1950* (Bloomington, IN, 1989); Lorraine Nelson Spritzer and Jean B. Bergmark, *Grace Towns Hamilton and the Politics of Southern Change* (Athens, GA, 1997); and John D. Chamberlain, *Victory at Home: Manpower and Race in the American South during World War II* (Athens, GA, 2003).

On women writers during and after World War II see, Anne C. Loveland, *Lillian Smith: A Southerner Confronting the South* (Baton Rouge, LA, 1986); Margaret Rose Gladney, ed., *How Am I to Be Heard? Letters of Lillian Smith* (Chapel Hill, NC, 1993); Darlene O'Dell, *Sites of Southern Memory: The Autobiographies of Katharine Du Pre Lumpkin, Lillian Smith, and Pauli Murray* (Charlottesville, VA, 2001); Sarah Patton Boyle, *The Desegregated Heart: A Virginian's Stand in Time of Transi-*

tion (Charlottesville, VA, 1962); Joanna Bowen Gillespie, "Sarah Patton Boyle's Desegregated Heart," in Janet Coryell, et al., eds., *Beyond Image and Convention: Explorations in Southern Women's History* (Columbia, MO,1998), 158–83. On civil rights activists refer to Vicki L. Crawford, Jacqueline Anne Rouse, and Barbara Woods, eds., *Women in the Civil Rights Movement: Trailblazers and Torchbearers, 1941*–1965 (Brooklyn, NY, 1990); Belinda Robnett, *How long? How long?: African-American Women in the Struggle for Civil Rights* (New York, 1997); Barbara Ransby, *Ella Baker and the Black Freedom Movement: A Radical Democratic Vision* (Chapel Hill, NC, 2003); and Virginia Foster Durr, *Outside the Magic Circle: The Autobiography of Virginia Foster Durr* (Tuscaloosa, AL, 1985); and Durr, *Freedom Writer: Virginia Foster Durr, Letters from the Civil Rights Years,* edited by Patricia Sullivan (New York, 2003).

Anthologies worth noting include the series from the Southern Association for Women Historians. Virginia Bernhard, et al., eds., *Southern Women: Histories and Identities* (Columbia, MO, 1992); Virginia Bernhard, et al., eds., *Hidden Histories of Women in the New South* (Columbia, MO, 1994); Janet Coryell, et al., eds., *Beyond Image and Convention: Explorations in Southern Women's History* (Columbia, MO, 1998); Janet L. Coryell, et al., eds., *Negotiating Boundaries of Southern Womanhood: Dealing with the Powers That Be* (Columbia, MO, 2000); Thomas H. Appleton, Jr., and Angela Boswell, eds., *Searching for Their Places: Women in the South Across Four Centuries* (Columbia, MO, 2003); and Angela Boswell and Judith N. McArthur, eds., *Women Shaping the South: Creating and Confronting Change* (Columbia, MO, 2006). Also see Nancy A. Hewitt and Suzanne Lebsock, eds., *Visible Women: New Essays on American Activism* (Urbana, IL, 1993); Melissa Walker, et al., eds., *Southern Women at the Millennium: A Historical Perspective* (Columbia, MO, 2003); Martha H. Swain, et al., eds., *Mississippi Women: Their Histories, Their Lives* (Athens, GA, 2003); and Bruce A. Glasrud and Merline Pitre, eds., *Black Women in Texas History* (College Station, TX, 2008).

For general overviews of the history of the New South there are several useful texts. John B. Boles, *The South Through Time: A History of an American Region*, Vol. II (Upper Saddle River, NJ, 2004); Tom E. Terrill and William J. Cooper, Jr., *The American South: A History*, Vol. II (Boston, 2002); Jeanette Keith, *The South: A Concise History*, Vol. II. (Upper Saddle River, N.J., 2002); and Paul D. Escott, David R. Goldfield, Sally G. McMillen, and Elizabeth Hayes Turner, eds., *Major Problems in the History of the American South*, Vol. II. *The New South* (Boston, 1999).

INDEX

Women and Gender in the New South, 1865–1945
Developmental Editor: Andrew J. Davidson
Copy Editors: Lucy Herz and Andrew J. Davidson
Production Editors: Lucy Herz and Linda Gaio
Typesetter: Bruce Leckie
Proofreader: Claudia Siler
Indexer: Pat Rimmer
Printer: Versa Press